GREEN, PINK & SILVER?

GREEN, PINK & SILVER?

THE FUTURE OF LABOUR IN EUROPE

VOL. 2

EDITORS

MIROSLAV BEBLAVÝ
ILARIA MASELLI
MARCELA VESELKOVÁ

CONTRIBUTORS

ATTILA BARTHA
MIROSLAV BEBLAVÝ
IAIN BEGG
ARNO BEHRENS
SERGIO CARRERA
BERT COLIJN
KEES DOL
JOHN DOLING
KATHARINA EISELE
MARJA ELSINGA
OLENA FEDYUK
MARINA FISCHER-KOWALSKI
RODRIC FREDERIX
JOHANNES GEYER
BENT GREVE
MICHAELA GSTREIN
ELSPETH GUILD
WILLI HAAS
CHRISTOPHE HEYNDRICKX
NICHOLAS HORSEWOOD
SILVIA HUDÁČKOVÁ
AGNIESZKA KAMIŃSKA
IGA MAGDA
FRITS MEIJER
VERA MESSING
JOKO PURWANTO
MAREK RADVANSKÝ
ANNA RUZIK-SIERDZIŇSKA
TOMÁŠ SIROVÁTKA
ERIKA SCHULZ
HENK VISSCHER
DOMINIK WIEDENHOFER
VIOLETTA ZENTAI

CENTRE FOR EUROPEAN POLICY STUDIES (CEPS)
BRUSSELS

The Centre for European Policy Studies (CEPS) is an independent policy research institute in Brussels. Its mission is to produce sound policy research leading to constructive solutions to the challenges facing Europe. The views expressed in this book are entirely those of the authors and should not be attributed to CEPS, the European Union or to any other institution with which they are associated.

ISBN 978-94-6138-444-7

Centre for European Policy Studies
Place du Congrès 1, B-1000 Brussels
Tel: (32.2) 229.39.11 Fax: (32.2) 219.41.51
E-mail: info@ceps.eu
Internet: www.ceps.eu

TABLE OF CONTENTS (OVERVIEW)

TABLE OF CONTENTS (IN DETAIL)

List of Figures

List of Tables

PREFACE

Over the last four years, the Centre for European Policy Studies has been deeply engaged as the coordinator of a major research project funded by the European Commission called NEUJOBS. Our objective has been to analyse possible future developments in European labour market(s) under the main assumption that European societies are now facing or preparing to face profound transitions, or what we call 'megatrends', that will have a major impact on employment. These natural and societal megatrends will reshape the global conditions for Europe, posing numerous challenges to societies and policy-makers in the area of labour.

A first volume of papers, produced in the first half of the project, attempted to explain what the findings from various social sciences mean for the future of labour in Europe. This second volume concentrates on employment in specific sectors, such as transport, energy and housing, and for specific groups in the labour force, notably women, elderly and migrants. Our findings are addressed not only to policy-makers, business persons, fellow academics and journalists, but to any concerned individual who is interested in the shape, size and character of the labour markets of tomorrow and beyond.

The editors would like to thank the entire network of the NEUJOBS project for the strong commitment shown throughout the project as well as in the preparation of this book. They are particularly grateful to Elisa Martellucci for the enormous assistance in the dissemination of this volume and the project in general. They would also like to thank Anil Shamdasani and Anne Harrington for patiently improving the text and Els Van den Broeck and John Hate for improving its appearance. In his capacity as the project's Scientific Officer, Marc Goffart provided invaluable support to both the project as a whole, and also to this book.

Miroslav Beblavý, Ilaria Maselli & Marcela Veselková
Brussels, February 2015

1. GREEN, PINK & SILVER? THE FUTURE OF LABOUR IN EUROPE

MIROSLAV BEBLAVÝ, SILVIA HUDÁČKOVÁ, DOMINIK WIEDENHOFER, WILLI HAAS AND MARINA FISCHER-KOWALSKI[*]

European societies face profound global changes over the coming decades that will alter the nature of work and employment and require pro-active and anticipatory policy responses. These global changes are driven by the socio-ecological transition (SET), described and analysed in detail in Volume 1. In this second volume, we map the impact of these changes on specific sectors of the European economy that are most sensitive to this transition and on groups, such as women, elderly, migrants and Roma, that form the key labour market reservoir of the future. In that sense, we ask whether the future of labour is indeed not just green, but also driven by colours pink (women) and silver (elderly).

The socio-ecological transition consists of complex non-linear processes whose exact unfolding is difficult to foresee. The drivers of these transitions for Europe have been described as 'global megatrends' that will have substantial and potentially adverse impacts on European societies and labour and will invoke European policy responses to both limit these adverse effects and make use of opportunities.

---

[*] Miroslav Beblavý: Senior Research Fellow at CEPS and Member of the Slovak Parliament; Silvia Hudáčkováis: Slovak Governance Institute; Dominik Wiedenhofer: Researcher at the Institute of Social Ecology, Alpen Adria University, Klagenfurt; Willi Haas: Senior Researcher and Lecturer at the Institute of Social Ecology, Alpen Adria University, Klagenfurt; and Marina Fischer-Kowalski: Founder and long-term director of the Institute of Social Ecology, Alpen Adria University, Klagenfurt.

'Societal megatrends' include demographic dynamics, ongoing shifts of the global economic and political centres of gravity and the growing use of information and communication technologies, which facilitate new forms of knowledge-sharing. 'Natural megatrends' are the onset of climate change and frequently more extreme weather events, increasing pressure on fossil fuels from rising global demand and stagnating to declining supply, and rising challenges to resource security, in particular due to increasing volatility of supply and prices. These six megatrends can be expected to have far-reaching implications for production and consumption patterns, and therefore also employment, in European societies.

To take into account the uncertainty concerning the severity and speed of these changes, we distinguish between equally likely 'friendly' and 'tough' variants of each megatrend for two distinct time frames: by 2025 and by 2050. The combined outcomes of each global future for Europe are then modelled to understand the consequences of these trends. In the previous volume, we sketched out two potential strategies for European policy-makers to cope with changing global conditions and to actively shape the future of labour in Europe. Beyond a 'business-as-usual' approach, more pro-active strategies of 'ecological modernisation' and an even more ambitious 'sustainability transformation' were explored. While the specifics of how the global megatrends actually materialise in the future are important, future jobs and therefore prosperity and welfare in Europe rely on the success of these strategies in pro-actively seeking appropriate policies to achieve desired outcomes.

Most European countries will see their working-age population shrink due to ageing and reduced fertility. Even under the assumptions of the 'friendly' scenario (higher fertility, extended life expectancy and increased immigration), most EU countries cannot escape the prospect of a declining working-age population, while improvements in life expectancy will have only a minor impact. Even though migration can bring about immediate changes in European population growth, it is unlikely to fully compensate for the decline in the working-age population, although opportunities to increase the labour supply differ from one country to another.

The decrease in labour supply, combined with the gradual upgrading of skills (or 'upskilling') of the population, should lead to wage increases for the highly skilled, while the ongoing polarisation of the labour market could negatively affect low- and medium-skilled jobs. Projections of trends under both the 'friendly' and the 'tough' global scenarios suggest that higher wages will provide relief for public finances and partially compensate for the increase in pension and healthcare bills. However, research from this project also suggests potentially strong divergences and polarisation of skill levels in the labour-supply projections for Europe. The supply of low-skilled labour is similar in both scenarios, and the main differences arise from the supply of high-skilled labour. The potential quantity of high-skilled workers reaches almost 105 million in 2030 in the 'friendly' scenario, and only 83 million in the 'tough' scenario (20% lower). This decrease of the labour force in terms of both quantity and in the 'tough' scenario, also in terms of skills, reduces long-term potential economic growth, makes rebalancing European public finances more difficult, and impedes Europe's adaptation to a fundamentally changing world.

Overall demand for employees will also be determined by macroeconomic conditions, structural change and the potential for job creation even with low economic growth. Net job creation varies from no rise in employment in the 'tough' global scenario to an annual creation of 1.5 million jobs in the 'friendly' future. High-skilled employment in the non-tradable sectors is growing fast and is the major contributor to employment creation in both scenarios. At the same time, a lasting destruction of low-skilled employment in the tradable sectors can be expected. In the non-tradable sectors, low-skilled employment is better protected, but the projections are still pessimistic compared to past trends.

In the 'friendly' global scenario, employment growth in Europe is mainly driven by the creation of an additional 15 million jobs in the private-services sector between 2010 and 2030. The construction sector also exhibits non-negligible job creation, with 3.9 million additional jobs over the same period. In the 'tough' scenario, the fall in employment is large in the non-market services, with 3.1 million fewer jobs in 2030 compared to 2010. In the private-services sector, employment creation of only 3.5 million jobs is estimated, which is much lower than in the more optimistic scenario. In both scenarios, most jobs are destroyed in agriculture and industry sectors.

From a European perspective, the specific potential for policy interventions to alleviate the negative impacts and enhance the positive developments for Europe and the labour market is therefore of paramount interest. The NEUJOBS project aimed to offer qualified answers, which will be explored below and in the following chapters.

1.1 Limits of power: Energy, growth and employment

The energy system is at the heart of the SET away from fossil fuels. The current EU energy mix is still dominated by fossil fuels, with more than three-quarters of EU energy consumption being based on oil, gas or coal, which the energy sector transforms into useful energy such as fuel, electricity or heating and then delivers to industry, households and transport. Therefore, the energy sector is highly relevant for greenhouse gas (GHG) emissions. Its importance for employment is much smaller: the total number of direct jobs provided by the EU energy supply sector in 2011 is estimated at between 1.5 million and 2.2 million, representing a share of 0.7-1% of the total employed workforce in that year.

As shown in Chapter 2, renewable resources are playing a growing role in the European economy, having reached a share of 14% of final energy consumption and 23.5% of electricity produced. The production of renewable energy in the EU28 has increased by over 80% since 2000, albeit from a low base, and the share of renewables in final energy consumption is continuing to rise in almost all EU member states. Energy efficiency is also improving in energy-intensive manufacturing industries and in service sectors.

Even though energy is at the centre of the socio-ecological transition, net employment changes in the electricity generation sector are likely to be small because of the small share of this sector in overall employment, which is not expected to change dramatically. Employment in this sector usually moves together with the economy in the long run, but the SET may result in large shifts in labour productivity due to changes in the types of employment that are needed to support the economy. The sector could become significantly more labour intensive if there is a change in the composition of the energy mix. For example, employment in the energy sector could increase by more than 3 million in 2050 if a rapid shift to renewable energy sources were to occur. If the RES share were to increase at a slower pace, there would still be more than one million extra jobs created in the sector.

The renewables sector is subject to rapid technological progress and cost reductions. When looking at the jobs that can currently be classified as 'green' in the European economy, we see that most of the dark green jobs are in the research and development of solar and wind technologies. More technological developments in the renewables sector will likely result in even more cost-efficient production, also spurring green employment.

1.2 Biking to work? Transport policy, sustainability and employment

The transport sector directly employed more than 10 million people in 2009, accounting for 4.5% of total employment in the European Union. Around 55% of these people worked in land transport, 2% in sea transport, 4% in air transport, 22% in warehousing and supporting transport activities (cargo handling, storage and warehousing), and the remaining 17% in postal and courier activities. Transportation was responsible for 29% of all EU28 GHG emissions in 2010 and while the slight decline observed recently is partly attributable to the crisis, much more substantial reductions are required to achieve EU climate goals.

We distinguish two broad paths for structural change in the transport sector. The first is to make significant changes to the propulsion technology used and the relative carbon intensity of transport (through the electrification of road transport, biomassification using 2nd or 3rd generation biofuels, or an efficiency revolution that would involve lightweight solutions for vehicles and/or downsizing to vehicles such as 1- or 2-litre engine cars). A second path for structural change is to focus on behavioural change. Many of the technological options presented above tend to increase the cost of acquiring a car, but reduce the actual cost of driving. Without any correction to the demand for transport services, technological options will therefore not be sufficient to reduce overall transport emissions. Adjusting the tax system to better reflect the damage that transport inflicts on the environment and on public health (i.e. the internalisation of external cost), stimulating the use of public (collective) transport and reducing the need for 'physical interaction' (by use of information technology) are essential steps to achieve structural change.

In Chapter 3, we try to discover whether there are policies that can reduce our carbon emissions and at the same time create jobs. We identify six key factors that are expected to shape the sector and project them in *friendly* and *tough* scenarios. Changes in transport policy are collapsed into 'status quo', 'modernisation' and 'sustainability' scenarios. We find that a combination of the latter two approaches to policy can reduce structural emissions of greenhouse gases and related pollutants by 1-8% compared with the status quo, with small net benefits in terms of employment. The impact of each policy is similar under different background conditions (tough or friendly), even when the impacts of the tough and friendly scenarios on the EU economy overall are substantially different.

No single transport-related policy could match the effectiveness of a general improvement in energy-efficiency standards while stimulating the labour market. For instance, the introduction of electric vehicles leads to environmental benefits, but has only a modest impact on job creation. Fuel-efficiency standards give a small boost to the labour market in some countries, but we did not find universal evidence of a labour market stimulus.

Policies oriented to behavioural changes, such as changing the tax base to discourage private motor vehicle use, lead to slightly positive labour market outcomes because they lead to greater employment in the public-transport sector. Improvements in transport efficiency lead to more positive labour market outcomes, but have less impact on pollution and emissions. These savings lead to an important net increase in economy-wide employment.

To allow cities more control over urban traffic, we advise the establishment of road-charging zones, or alternatively Low Emission Zones. The policies that are most likely to contribute to sustainability, while at the same time stimulating employment, are those that boost cycling, encourage use of public transit and promote energy efficiency. Investments in public infrastructure, increased transport efficiency and improvements in energy efficiency have the largest impact on employment per million euros spent, especially in eastern and southern European countries.

1.3 Demand and supply of labour in the housing sector

There are currently around 230 million dwellings in the European Union and, in terms of floor space, they account for 75% of the total building stock. Homes constitute the largest single land use in the built environment and were responsible for some 40% of direct energy usage and 25% of CO_2 emissions in 2010. Homes are generally the largest single item of expenditure in household budgets, and the largest form of household wealth for the majority of the working population. Therefore, housing can be expected to have an impact on employment in the context of the socio-ecological transition.

Chapter 4 focuses on three specific linkages of the housing sector with employment: energy renovation of housing stock, direct employment on mortgage markets, and the extent to which the tenure structure of member states influences the willingness and ability of households to be active in labour markets, as well as the nature of their activity.

The building stock is important for energy-efficiency targets. Across the member states there are many existing programmes to bring existing dwellings up to acceptable energy standards. Looking to 2020, estimates of the total number of jobs created by energy renovations vary from 0.28 million to 1.40 million. Policy-makers should act to ascertain that efforts to reach the targets are intensified in the coming years. This will require increased levels of investment, which will depend on the financial capacity of private owners; access to appropriate forms of loan finance will need to be developed. One way in which this could be achieved is through the use of housing finance markets, which would effectively allow owners to use existing housing equity either directly or as collateral.

The emphasis of mortgage markets is being switched from growth in new lending to stability and safety. This will mean more information, verification and monitoring, and these functions offer considerable capacity for further growth of employment in the field of mortgage markets affected by the crisis.

To create a flexible market that allows households to invest in housing, policy should support forward mortgages and also put an emphasis on reverse mortgages that allow households to dis-invest when needed. Another direction of expansion for housing finance markets is in supporting energy-reduction activity, i.e. expanding the opportunities for households to do this by taking out loans against the collateral of their homes.

The potential impacts of housing tenure on labour supply are complex. The size of the home-ownership sectors, rates of house price inflation and levels of housing debt are all important. A widely held view is that labour mobility is lower for homeowners due to the higher transaction costs leading to a disincentive to relocate for a new job. As a consequence, the housing market could be responsible for a mismatch between vacancies and the unemployed within a country, and also between nations. Our investigations indicate that although there is some evidence of this, the main influence of the housing market appears to relate to the stock of outstanding mortgages. Homeowners with mortgages may be less able to respond to changing employment circumstances.

1.4 Ageing and job growth in healthcare and long-term care services

Health and social work are important and highly dynamic sectors of the economy; in all European countries the healthcare workforce even increased during the economic crisis. In Chapter 5 we examine how population ageing and societal change will affect the health and long-term care workforce. The numbers regarding healthcare workers differ across the countries studied, but a common feature is that the health and social work workforce is characterised by high shares of women, the elderly and those in part-time employment. Taking into account health workers aged 50-54 years (3.2 million workers), it can be expected that more than 6 million employees will exit the health and social care market by 2025. The high share of the elderly in the health workforce is a challenge in all countries studied.

We identify the following influences on the demand of health workforce: changes in morbidity, medical technological innovations, changes in treatment methods and changes in the organisation of care services. Our data show that population size and population ageing have a significant influence on the demand for health services, and an increase in demand for hospital activities and ambulatory health care services can be expected. However, we observe considerable variation across treatments. A strong age-demand relationship can be observed for hospital treatments, while the increase in the ambulatory healthcare workforce is lower. In the tough scenario a decline in the ambulatory health workforce is even estimated in Germany and Poland due to the shrinking population. For primary care, mostly provided by general practitioners, the relationship is not as strong as for hospital care. The results of the tough scenario indicate that the demand for health services will exceed the health workforce supply in all countries except for Poland.

The gap in the formal long-term care market is expected to widen until 2025. In the tough scenario, the number of residents in nursing homes and recipients of home-care services will increase, and in the friendly scenario (which assumes higher economic growth, higher employment, higher shares of highly educated people and higher population growth compared to the tough scenario) the increase in the number of formal-care recipients is even higher, both in institutional care and in home care.

What can be done to reduce the gap? We discuss three measures aimed at meeting the future care demand. The first is for governments to adopt measures to increase the informal care potential, for example, care leave, financial support to family carers, training, counselling, flexible working-time arrangements for carers, ICT to reduce the caregiving burden, and support from professional caregivers. The second option is to recruit long-term care workers from abroad, whose relative merits we discuss in detail in Chapter 12. Finally, the domestic long-term care workforce can be supported by more favourable working conditions. Relevant measures include an increase in wages, an increase in flexible working-time arrangements, an increase in the standing of the nursing and caring professions, changes in the amount of vocational training required, an increase in competences, a reorganisation of caring tasks and a reduction in formal documentation tasks.

The long-term care workforce also consists of informal caregivers, and their future numbers will be influenced by two trends: i) changes in living arrangements, with more people in the middle-age groups living alone, and ii) an increase in the very oldest living together due to the increase in life expectancy. At the same time, the increase in female labour-force participation is reducing the capacity to provide intensive informal care to elderly relatives, while the number of informal caregivers aged over 50 increases significantly in both demographic scenarios in all countries studied.

1.5 Two faces of ageing: Older workers and older consumers

Population ageing in European countries is an inevitable process. Eurostat demographic projections show that the number of people between the ages of 50 and 74 as a share of the population aged 20-74 will increase in the EU27 countries from the current 40% to 47% by 2050. As a result, older people represent an increasing share of the employed.

In Chapter 6, we show that particular circumstances and policies anticipating this process could actually boost employment and innovation within EU member states. The first part of the chapter is dedicated to the possibilities for labour market adaptation to the ageing process, especially the possibilities for workers to stay economically active and productive for longer. Recent public system pension reforms have increased retirement ages, but this approach requires more than just a simple adjustment of social security schemes related to older workers and retirees.

What efficient policy measures could discourage people from taking retirement too early, thereby decreasing the costs of the pension system and the risk of poverty at old age? Preventing skill obsolescence at older ages requires more investment in lifelong learning. Attitudes of employers are usually an important determinant for the demand for older workers, and safety-at-work measures and support for families with care duties can influence the activity of certain groups of employees. Research also indicated that flexible working time would be an advantage. As health status and disability are important in all countries, public support should be used to address the social and physical health issues of older persons and promote preventative healthcare and healthy lifestyles at younger ages.

Keeping the elderly in the labour market not only has a positive effect in decreasing the burden on the pension systems, in countries where the employment rate of older ages is high, the level of engagement in social life of older people is also higher. Moreover, higher economic activity is found in countries where people claim to be happiest.

Working in a typical 'green' job, which is often physically demanding, decreases the likelihood of wanting to stay employed longer in countries that have high employment rates at older ages but short average professional careers. In more intellectually demanding occupations (ISCO 1-4), wages increase until retirement, while in more manual occupations (ISCO 5-9) they start decreasing even as early as at the age of 46. This creates an incentive for people engaged in non-manual tasks to work for longer. Moving from physically demanding to intellectually demanding work environments could lead people to remain active in the labour market for longer periods of time in the future.

The second part of Chapter 6 is dedicated to the influence of ageing on the structure of consumption and its effect on employment in particular economic sectors. Changes in the level of household consumption and in the structure of consumption should both be the driving forces of what is often referred to as the 'silver economy'. This refers to the set of economic activities linked to the production of goods and services targeting the elderly, and the segment is expected to grow significantly. Ageing therefore provides an opportunity to enhance the competitiveness of the European economy.

The complexity of the 'silver economy' lies in the fact that the elderly in the various member states in Europe do not have identical consumption habits. There are many economic, social and cultural factors that influence consumption patterns. Aggregate demand of households divided by age groups is determined by several factors, and most important is the number of households and their wealth. Therefore, silver demand is rather strictly divided between western and central and eastern Europe. The number of households with a head of household aged over 60 in 2030 will significantly increase in both scenarios. According to the results of estimations, we can expect an increased share of 'silver demand' in future.

The sectors with the highest growth potential are those producing or providing food and beverages, housing and utilities, restaurants and hotel services, privately financed health, and social and long-term care. In both scenarios, the highest increase in total private demand is expected to target healthcare services for two reasons. The first is the fact that there will be more elderly citizens demanding care services, and the second is the fact that there will also be a large group of aware younger-age cohorts demanding preventive healthcare. The net effect of the 'silver economy' will be a loss of 1.9 million jobs in the tough scenario and a gain of 3.9 million jobs in the friendly scenario.

1.6 Women as workers – in the middle of a marathon

The previous two decades were a period of further important changes in the position of women in European labour markets. Women constitute an increasingly large share of the total workforce, and this trend will continue. Women in the older age groups (45-64 years) experienced the most notable employment improvements, but significant positive employment changes were also observed among prime-aged women. Conversely, employment rates among younger women (under 25 years of age) decreased in most EU countries, mainly due to increasing female enrolment in tertiary education. However, despite a considerable improvement, the labour potential of women is far from being fully utilised. Chapter 7 summarises the main components of the necessary policy mix, describing the challenges and the potentially best solutions in the fields of education, maternity, retirement, lifelong learning, care choices, flexible employment contracts and wages.

Most of the policy recommendations proposed and discussed are not new, and are already at the top of the agenda in EU countries. However, what is required is constant revision of the policy solutions to take account of changing needs and labour market settings. No one-size-fits-all set of policies is possible, and not just because of diversity in the labour market institutions across EU countries – the structure of the labour demand also matters.

The most important recommendation for the components of the policy mix relates to the institutional setting helping to reconcile jobs with family life. Here, flexible employment arrangements and improved access to childcare facilities are crucial – such facilities should be widely accessible and also affordable. Greater involvement of men in family life would be of considerable importance to increasing female employment, and this should be supported by legal changes, such as more parental leave targeted at fathers.

Another set of policies affecting female employment concerns the redesigning of pension systems in order to lower disincentives to withdraw from the labour market – at an older age, but also during child-related career breaks – without penalising people for taking maternity leave.

Well-educated women have higher employment rates, so the increasing share of women graduating from tertiary education positively stimulates total employment rates. Finding a first job is harder for women despite the fact that they are, on average, more educated than men. School-to-work transitions are easier in countries where studying is frequently combined with work; hence this educational model should be supported by public policies (for example, by the introduction of apprenticeship programmes).

Even though lifelong learning improves employability, women are less likely to participate in formal further education. However, they outnumber men in non-formal training. Women might therefore benefit from the recognition of informal learning (for example, their care competences could be formally recognised). Flexible job provisions would be helpful for women who wish to increase or update their qualifications, and would also help parents to cope with childcare. However, flexible employment forms appear to be a mixed blessing from a wage perspective.

Gender pay gaps remain a challenge, in particular among older workers. The ongoing demographic changes, in particular the increasing share of women employed aged 50 and over, will probably lead to a deepening of the gender pay gaps, especially in those countries where the female labour participation rates are low at the moment.

1.7 A common labour immigration policy for the EU? Rethinking 'attractiveness' and socio-economic inclusion

In 2012, an estimated 1.7 million immigrants came to the EU from countries outside, and an additional 1.7 million people previously residing in one EU member state migrated to another member state. While migration can bring about immediate changes in population growth, it is unlikely to be able to fully compensate for the decline in the working-age population. And yet, labour immigration policies have been high on the agenda of policy-makers, who have attempted to develop an 'attractive' labour immigration policy with the objective of encouraging foreign highly skilled workers to come to the EU.

Chapter 8 analyses the determinants of and challenges for EU labour immigration policy. For this purpose, the chapter sketches the current EU framework for immigration law and policy and then highlights specific key aspects and debates surrounding the attractiveness and selectiveness of labour migration policies.

There are a number of dilemmas and challenges associated with labour migration policies. First, to whom should the policies be attractive? It must be borne in mind that 'attractiveness' of migration policies is in the eye of the beholder. One might think that for migrant workers, 'attractiveness' may well concern issues related to security of residence, non-discrimination, access to fundamental social rights and the compliance with international labour standards. This aspect is closely connected to the next point.

How can an immigration policy be made 'attractive'? Among the factors that make a particular immigration policy attractive, reference is often made to an improved set of rights and benefits conferred on foreign workers (the ease of the administrative procedures, unrestricted access to the labour market, provision of information/employer sponsorship, and so on).

What kind of foreign worker is to be 'attracted' by an immigration policy? The paradigm of attractiveness often refers to a selection logic focusing on those individuals considered to be 'the brightest' as the ideal type of migrant workers to be recruited. But what criteria are used to categorise a worker as belonging to a specific skill group? Chapter 8 challenges the assumption that exact methodologies exist to identify and locate preferable 'skills' and 'needs', and highlights that the underlying problem in any trade-off framework is legitimising inequality of treatment on the basis of dubious grounds related to 'quotas', 'skills' or 'needs', which are often hugely politicised and centred around short-term concerns.

EU immigration policy is affected by fragmentation and dispersion dynamics, which leads to legal complexity and uncertainty. For the next generation of EU labour immigration policy, action must be taken to overcome fragmentation, legal uncertainty, discrimination and competing multi-layered migratory statuses. Another priority should be overcoming current formal and informal obstacles to the recognition of qualifications and diplomas, as they constitute barriers to international mobility. Better enforcement of current EU standards should also be a priority. Enhancing and consolidating the dialogue with and inputs from social partners and civil society organisations are equally important. Finally, strategic partnerships with relevant actors, such as the Council of Europe, the UN and ILO, could be useful in this area.

1.8 Policy puzzles with the employment of Roma

There are several reasons why we devote a special chapter (Chapter 9) to the employment of the Roma population in this volume. The Roma population represents the *EU's* largest ethnic *minority* group, estimated at 6 million EU citizens. Not only is it a transnational issue that needs to be looked at from a supranational perspective, but Roma also experience enduring and severe exclusion from the primary labour market, which forms an important constraint on some European societies in meeting the Europe 2020 target of an employment rate of 75%. According to a UNDP 2012 survey that examined 11 EU member states, only one in three Roma aged 20-64 surveyed was in paid employment. Roma are a young population with relatively high fertility rates, and can be regarded as an important resource in ageing European societies.

The intersection of several sectors must address the social and labour market exclusion of Roma. We focus on the policy implications with regard to labour market policies. Direct job creation is a key programme type in most countries. Such programmes have great potential, but they do not intervene in the roots of long-term unemployment. In Hungary, Slovakia and Bulgaria, public work schemes trap beneficiaries in a cycle of welfare support and public work. Inefficiency is also caused by additional labour market services not being offered.

How should governments target active labour market policies in such a way that they reach out to vulnerable Roma? The dominant mode of targeting is mainstreaming, that is, defining characteristics of vulnerability and addressing these, irrespective of the ethnicity of the recipient. We believe that this approach necessarily leads to Roma being overlooked by these policies. Instead, we argue for the positive impact of affirmative action. Governments should apply measures such as employing Roma in public offices in charge of designing and implementing active labour market policies, giving preference to Roma applicants for jobs in public offices and promoting the active participation of Roma NGOs in the design and monitoring of the implementation of those policies that target the disadvantaged long-term unemployed. The high level of informal employment among Roma is also due in great part to high wage costs, especially in Hungary and Slovakia. Wage subsidies have the potential to increase formal employment of the low skilled.

An important prerequisite for improving the labour market inclusion of Roma is the services of employment offices (EOs). These need to provide high-quality, tailored services. Unemployed Roma view EOs as purely administrative units that do not provide meaningful support; this needs to change. Moreover, Roma unemployed describe experiences of open discrimination by EO staff in Romania and Bulgaria. This problem could be addressed by implementing awareness-raising and sensitivity-training for EO servants. To achieve better outreach to and understanding of marginalised Roma communities, the employment of staff from the Roma community in EOs is desirable. An additional barrier is the geographical distance of EOs. A suitable solution for bridging geographical distances was found in one Hungarian settlement, where the EO operated a mobile office.

1.9 Social services as an option for sustainable employment growth

The number of health and social services workers aged between 15 and 64 was 22.8 million in 2013, which accounts for 10.7% of the total employment in the EU. Unlike in the overall economy, the number of workers in this sector has been steadily growing, with a net creation of 1.3 million jobs between 2009 and 2013.

The high levels of unemployment in the overall economy may be partially corrected by the growth of employment in social services, since there are convincing arguments for further employment growth in this sector in the future. Chapter 10 focuses on health and social services, which is where the welfare state has the possibility to create jobs as part of a social investment strategy. We analyse the developments in this sector and identify key policies that would maximise the growth of employment. How much will the low-skilled groups affected by unemployment risks profit from this growth? In countries where social services are more developed, growing employment in health and social services brings not only jobs for high-skilled professionals, but also many jobs in cleaning and other similar tasks.

We look at the drivers of demand and supply that influence employment in this sector and consider possible future developments. On the demand side, employment growth in social services will be driven primarily by the changing roles of women - their growing labour market participation leads to increasing demand for care services. Surprisingly, the ageing of society did not prove to be significantly correlated with social-service employment. Welfare state models and family models may imply alternative or informal caring options when public social services are insufficient.

On the supply side, politics matters - a deliberate strategy to foster public sector employment with an emphasis on social services is important. Fiscal policies have been the most important factor in supporting the growth of the sector. However, it is hard to foresee increased public investment in social services in countries where this expenditure used to be low and that are facing increasing public deficits. In the long term, fiscal sustainability is the first prerequisite for expanding employment in social services.

In most countries, mixing public and private sources will be necessary for sustainable public finance. This strategy may bring important employment gains if and when governance frameworks provide effective regulation of the use of the available resources: setting quality and professional standards and control systems; maximising choice of services for users (the state as direct service provider is diminishing its role, while the market and NGOs are becoming more important); and combining universal accessibility of services with targeted support to the users.

In countries where the economic realities are less favourable for financing social services, an important issue is the ability of policy-makers to modernise the welfare state by redirecting expenditure from benefits towards social services. Innovations in welfare technologies can bring increases in employment and improvements in job quality, but they can also make (unskilled) work such as cleaning and other home help tasks redundant.

1.10 Employment trends in childcare and social inclusion services

Childcare and social inclusion services accounted for 6.1% of total EU27 employment in 2011 (each accounting for 2.6% and 3.5%, respectively). In total, the sectors provided employment for more than 13 million people.

Women strongly dominate both sectors across the EU, making up 88.3% of those employed in childcare and 82.4% of those in social inclusion services.

In Chapter 11, we aim to shed more light on employment patterns, development paths, changes in skills and employment conditions, but also to determine if this sector could offer new employment perspectives, especially for older workers.

Despite the crisis-related budget cuts, the health and social work sector has been growing over the last ten years in the EU. The same is true for the childcare and social services sub-sector, which is a small but important part of this sector. Longer lifespans and the increasing autonomy of the elderly, as well as expected support for a work-life balance throughout life, result in increasing demand for such services. It appears that the numbers presented above will grow even further.

Gender segregation is a general phenomenon of work in this sector and persists throughout Europe. Women dominate, with 5.6 women for every man employed in the sector in 2011. Investigating the age structure over time, we see that those employed in childcare and social inclusion services tend to be young or middle-aged workers. However, new positions currently seem to be mostly taken up by older women. Explanations might include the ageing of the (female) workforce, lower sectoral pay or low job stability, but also the possession of required skills, easy re-entry or the availability of (often flexible) part-time work in the sector. The sector seems to offer interesting opportunities for job-searchers with various skills and employment requests.

We also observe generally increasing skill levels. Many employees in childcare and social inclusion services work part-time, but the direction of the causality remains unclear. Does the sector require more part-time work than other sectors, and women being willing to provide this leads to the sector becoming 'female'? Or does the sector attract more women, who often prefer part-time contracts and thus increase the share of part-time work in the sector?

While the share of female workers is high in all countries, the extent of part-time work varies. Although one would expect large gender income gaps in this labour market sector, the gaps are actually smaller than in the overall economy, although they have grown slightly over time.

Despite initial fears that growth might be in low-skilled jobs only and thus result in a decrease in job quality or working conditions, this was not the case. Countries follow different development paths depending on their initial situation in terms of sectoral size, age structure and welfare regime orientation. Nevertheless, the overall trend is towards skill increases, an increase of part-time jobs and an even stronger feminisation of the sector. Families that use such services should expect a growing share of older but well-educated service providers.

1.11 Low-skilled migration: Immigrant workers in European domestic care

According to the ILO, domestic work was a source of employment for at least 2.5 million workers in Europe in 2013, most of who were female migrants. Concerning future prospects, we forecast a significant increase in care demand by 2025 in EU member countries of 15-22% in the tough scenario and 28-39% in the friendly scenario. The care workforce supply, however, will not be able to meet the growing care demand without significant migrant labour inflows. These trends raise a number of policy-related questions in the areas of migration, care and employment, which we address in Chapter 12.

Why have certain countries proved to be particularly attractive to immigrant care workers? The role of migrants in the provision of care is fairly uneven across Europe. Several factors matter in this respect, which result from the specific features of national welfare and care regimes: institutional provision of care (kindergartens, social workers, retirement homes, etc.), policies on work-life balance and monetary subsidies for care provision (e.g. welfare payments or tax relief). By imposing certain migration regimes or occupational quotas for domestic workers, states can create indirect incentives for a rising market of private-care workers of immigrant origin. Concerning the inclusion of immigrant populations, at least two dimensions matter: i) legal, formal access to citizenship and ii) the multicultural policy framework shaping the socio-political inclusion of immigrant populations.

How do the different European welfare and care regimes, and state and market policy mixes, shape the inflow of low-skilled migrants into the care sector? Family-centred care policy patterns provide incentives for informal care use not only in several Mediterranean countries, but also in post-socialist countries.

The demand for migrant care workers is typically a demand for work under substandard conditions. Without permission to work, immigrants with irregular status become particularly vulnerable to abusive working conditions. Decent employment of migrant and native domestic-care workers requires strong state regulatory and monitoring capacities and an advanced gender-equality policy. The issue of immigrant care labour should be addressed in a complex way. Cross-national welfare and social security provisions should be a priority in establishing legal and fair working conditions for both native and immigrant care workers.

If informality dominates labour transactions in the care sector and the state regulatory and monitoring capacities are weak while the structural pull factors of immigration remain, strict migration regimes in themselves will not block irregular migration into the domestic-care sector. On the contrary, they will reinforce the vulnerability of migrant care workers.

The under-development of formal institutional care in central and east European countries implies that informal care is becoming the dominant option. This provides another incentive for the recruitment of migrant domestic-care workers. CEE countries function both as sending and receiving entities of low-skilled care workers, and thus are themselves in the process of building migration-policy regimes. In addition, in the predominantly sending countries, the massive outflow of female care workers aggravates welfare, care and family-policy tensions, in particular due to the particularly low level of fertility and the general withdrawal of publicly provided welfare and care services over the last two decades.

1.12 The future of labour in Europe: Key messages for policy-makers

Chapter 13 summarises the key implications and messages for both EU and national policy-makers and elaborates on the findings presented in the previous chapters.

One of the key current European employment issues is insufficient demand for labour. It is clear that the policy choices and the availability of funding will have a pronounced impact on a number of key sectors and that there will be multiple channels through which policy decisions influence the net creation of new jobs. Jobs in health and long-term care, the demand from older consumers and the outlook for demand for labour derived from energy policies are considered here.

The second policy theme focuses on the shrinking labour supply due to ageing. Two principal solutions to ensure a sufficient labour supply in an ageing society are discussed: activating a higher proportion of the population (including those outside standard working-age groups) and boosting the labour supply with immigrants.

The concluding section challenges the orientation and governance of EU policies. Europe today is different from the Europe of the pre-crisis years in many respects. Attention to sustainability is likely to be renewed as a (or even ***the***) defining norm for the European policy responses to the socio-ecological transition, which would highlight the importance of the knowledge generated within the NEUJOBS project. The section offers some novel perspectives to the reader by widening the scope for new thinking on some of the principal mechanisms through which EU-level action can be influential.

The NEUJOBS project's mission was to map the future of employment in Europe under the new conditions of the socio-ecological transition. Together, the two volumes of *The Future of Labour in Europe* offer a concise version of the very detailed cartographic documents produced in more than 100 research papers.

Although no one can foresee the future with any certainty, estimates based on evidence are highly relevant politically. As Harry Truman once said, "[y]ou can always amend a big plan, but you can never expand a little one. I don't believe in little plans. I believe in plans big enough to meet a situation which we can't possibly foresee now." This is the motto to which the NEUJOBS project adhered and on which we urge policy-makers to reflect in the current environment.

2. LIMITS OF POWER: ENERGY, GROWTH AND EMPLOYMENT

*BERT COLIJN AND ARNO BEHRENS**

Energy use is a vital part of our economic system. The impact of energy on economic growth has increased dramatically since the 1800s, but concerns about depletion and pollution of the environment have emerged during the last 50 years. Even though it often seems that a turnaround is far away, there are signs that the shift towards a decarbonised and resource-neutral economy has already started. Particularly in Europe, renewable resources are playing a growing role in the economy, having reached a share of 14% of final energy consumption and 23.5% of electricity produced, with positive effects on greenhouse gas emissions. These are first signs of a socio-ecological transition (SET), which we define as "a transition between two different societal energy regimes (sources and dominant conversion technologies of energy)".[1]

In this chapter, the broad relationship between energy, economic growth and employment is examined. We start from the assumption that economic growth is the product of the increase in jobs and the rise in the productivity of those jobs. Energy has been an important catalyst of economic growth by increasing productivity through the use of machinery and equipment powered by fossil fuels. While mechanisation has sometimes been seen as a job-killer, in the longer term there is overwhelming evidence that productivity growth and job creation go hand in hand.

We begin our discussion with a review of how the current trends fit in with the concept of the SET through increased energy efficiency and the

---

* Bert Colijn: Senior Economist at The Conference Board; Arno Behrens: Research Fellow and Head of the Energy unit at CEPS.

shift towards renewables. We then focus on how energy regimes have changed and what impact this has had on economic growth and productivity. Finally, we examine the impact of all these developments on employment, with a focus on the energy sector.

2.1 The energy system lies at the heart of the socio-ecological transition

Sieferle et al. (2006) describe two great socio-economic regime changes in human history. The first was the Neolithic Revolution some 4,500-10,500 years ago, which transformed hunter-gatherers into agrarian societies.[2] The second was the Industrial Revolution, which led to the transition of agrarian societies into industrial societies with a strong dependence on fossil fuels. While in many parts of the world this transition *into* fossil fuels is ongoing, the EU is dedicated to substantial greenhouse gas (GHG) emissions reductions in the long term, and therefore also to a new transition *away* from fossil fuels. This chapter is thus concerned with an SET "away from fossil fuels, towards solar and other low-carbon energy sources".[3] If the EU is to meet its long-term objective of reducing GHG emissions by at least 80% compared with 1990 levels by 2050, the share of fossil fuels in the energy mix will need to decrease from over 75% in 2011 to around 70% by 2020, and to 40-50% by 2050.

The energy system lies at the heart of the SET away from fossil fuels. However, the current EU energy mix is still dominated by fossil fuels, with more than three-quarters of EU energy consumption being based on oil, gas and coal.[4] It is thus evident that the new transition will require substantial technological and political efforts in the EU in order for its energy sector to radically change in favour of low-carbon technologies. However, as with previous transitions, the availability of new technologies will not be sufficient to start the transformation process. Fundamental change will take place only if technology is able to achieve positive feedback with complementing technical, cultural, economic and social developments.[5]

Not all parts of the energy system will be decarbonised to the same extent, owing to large differences between sectors. Whereas many scenarios exist under which power generation can be largely carbon-free by 2050, there may still be significant GHG emissions far beyond this date. Transport currently relies almost exclusively on oil and other fossil fuels, while carbon-free generation capacity in the power sector already exists (renewables and nuclear). The energy transition(s) are also likely to differ considerably across European regions, inter alia because the potential for renewables varies, but also because of differences in GDP per capita, which affects ability and willingness to pay. It is clear that the energy transition will have an impact on the EU labour market. While the number of 'green jobs' will expand in conjunction with a growing number of jobs in low-carbon technologies, other sectors, such as the oil and refining industries, will see decreasing employment. The net effect of these two developments is of relevance in assessing the employment impact of the decarbonisation in the energy sector.

While the number of 'green jobs' in low-carbon technologies will expand, other sectors, such as the oil and refining industries, will see decreasing employment.

2.2 The importance of energy for economic growth is limited

Over the past centuries, energy use has increased dramatically, which has resulted in rapid resource depletion and pollution of our environment.[6] From the point of view of the socio-ecological transition, it is important to understand the relationship between energy use and economic growth, as this determines whether we are able to sustain higher wealth levels per energy input over time. Energy is one of the key inputs for economic output, and lower energy inputs could therefore also result in lower production. If, *ceteris paribus*, less energy is used, that means there is less output being produced. Because of this, energy input reductions have a negative effect on economic growth. To understand the impact of energy-input reductions on economic growth, we have decomposed growth in economic output into the five largest input categories - labour, capital, energy, material and services - and have looked at which factors make the largest contributions to economic growth.

For this purpose, the EUKLEMS database[7] has been extended and updated with energy inputs for the six countries examined.[8] In Figure 2.1, the contributions to economic growth from the various inputs over time can be seen for the EU6. The impact of energy on growth is limited compared to the other inputs, as changes in energy input only resulted in a change of just over 0.25% in economic growth. In fact, only labour composition contributes less to growth than energy, and when

The impact of energy on growth is limited compared to other inputs, as changes in energy input only resulted in a change of just over 0.25% in economic growth.

the contributions of the labour components are taken together, it shows that out of all the inputs, energy makes the smallest contribution to growth.

Figure 2.1 Absolute contribution of various inputs to gross economic output for EU6, 1995-2009*

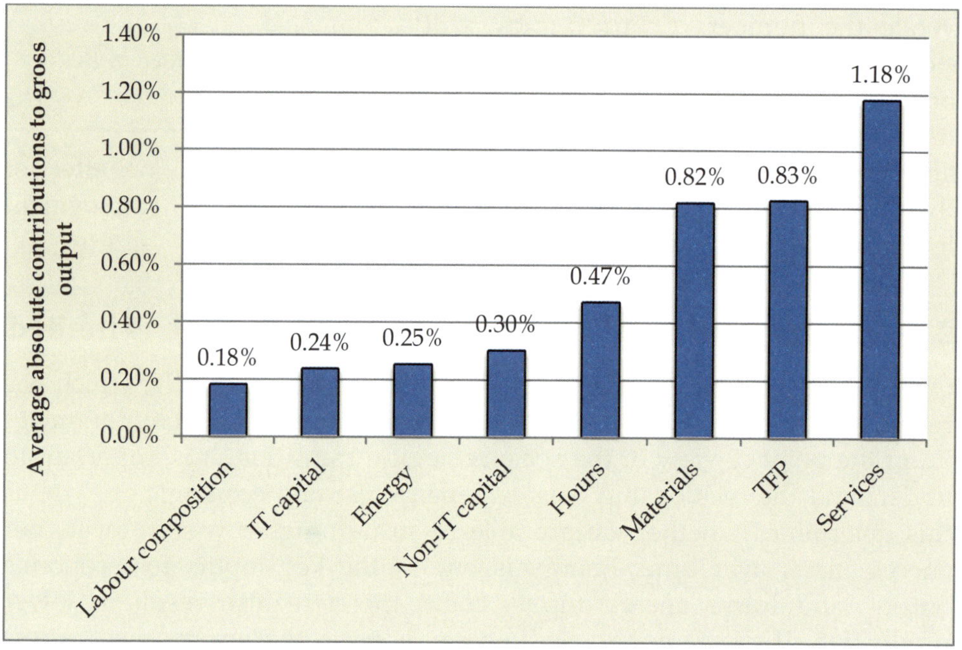

* EU6 = Finland, Germany, Italy, the Netherlands, Spain and the UK.

Note: IT stands for information technology and TFP for total factor productivity.

Source: Colijn and Van Ark (2014).

Across countries, however, there are large differences in the growth contributions from energy. Spain has seen large contributions of energy to economic growth, but the country was also experiencing a construction boom in the time period that we have studied, which can explain some of this high impact. Germany and the UK saw negative contributions from energy to economic growth of -0.02% and -0.01%, respectively, between 1995 and 2009. This shows that the direct impact of decarbonisation on economic growth is negative, but marginal compared to the impact of other inputs.

It is important to note that there is a difference between energy and materials. As can be seen in Figure 2.1, the input of materials is much more important to economic growth than that of energy (in the range of 0.8% compared to 0.2%). In Spain, the annual contribution to economic growth from materials was 1 percentage point, which accounts for roughly a third of total economic growth. Of course, the Spanish construction bubble had an important impact on this, but Germany and Finland also saw sizable contributions from materials to economic growth. This shows that reducing material input into production will likely have more negative consequences for economic growth than decarbonising. From the perspective of the socio-ecological transition, it is just as important to reduce the amount of finite materials used as it is to reduce the amount of energy, so this is something that clearly poses a concern moving forward.

Figure 2.1 indicates that the reduction in economic growth due to the direct effect of decarbonisation is limited, as can be seen from the small impact of energy inputs, but it is still a reduction. There are also indirect effects that are important in assessing the impact of energy on the economy. Energy is usually necessary for machinery to operate, which means that capital is influenced by energy inputs. This is also the case for materials, as they usually require energy to be extracted or to be used as an input for production. Among the indirect effects, one should count technological progress, which is at the same time one of the less tangible but also one of the most important factors for future economic growth, as production systems move towards clean sources.

We used a random effects generalised least squares model to analyse the effects of energy on other inputs in the production process,[9] and found that energy has a significant impact on the input of capital and materials. We did not find a significant effect of energy on services, which is likely due to the lower dependence of services on energy inputs than the other two. The lagged impact of energy (we used a lag of one year) was not significant for any of the other economic inputs, so the causal effect of a reduction in energy on production a year later seems to be rather marginal.

To assess the technology component, we also added R&D investments to the model to see how this interacts with economic inputs as it correlates negatively with energy intensity.[10] Here we find significant relationships with all variables, and the lagged effect on capital stock is also significant. The significant relationship between energy and R&D intensity suggests that there is a positive spillover effect of energy on economic growth through total factor productivity (TFP). Total factor productivity is the improvement in

Efficiency gains in energy and technological change are positively related. This emphasises the (indirect) importance of innovation in energy for economic growth in the years ahead.

output that is not attributable to increases in any of the inputs, and is often used as a proxy for technological progress. When adding TFP to our model, we do indeed find a negative relationship between energy use and TFP growth, meaning that a decline in energy use in one year leads to an increase in TFP in the year after. This confirms the notion that efficiency gains in energy and technological change are positively related, and emphasises the importance of innovation in energy for economic growth in the years ahead.

Overall, the effects of decarbonisation on economic growth are ambiguous and minor. The direct effects from reducing energy inputs have a negative impact on growth, albeit minor (the smallest impact out of all the economic inputs). It has to be noted here, however, that the direct impact alone is not the most important and that a shock in energy supply can have far-reaching negative implications for the economy; think of the oil crises of the 1970s and 1980s, when many advanced economies contracted due to energy input shocks. This follows from the cost-share theorem, which argues that the price effects from one factor of production will have negative effects on other inputs, thus increasing the effect on economic growth.[11]

The impact of energy reductions on technological change is positive, and this in turn has a positive impact on economic growth. Once again, the impact is not large, but it is encouraging to see an established positive indirect link between energy input reductions and economic growth through technological progress. It therefore seems clear that innovation that spills over from better energy use will help maintain economic growth while transitioning to a more sustainable economy.

The production process has become significantly more energy efficient over time.

When looking at the behaviour of energy inputs and economic output, we find that energy efficiency increased in four out of the six countries over the period 1995-2009: Germany, the UK, Finland and the Netherlands.[12] Only Spain and Italy saw declines of overall energy efficiency over the period, which is in line with the slow labour productivity growth that these countries experienced. Overall, efficiency gains were made, which is a sign that the socio-ecological transition is occurring, as less energy input (in monetary terms) is used to create economic output. The question is whether this is because of less energy actually being used, or other factors that are at play. Stern explains the four factors that can influence the relationship between energy inputs and output: substitution with other inputs (such as materials or labour), technological change, changes in the composition of energy inputs and changes in the composition of outputs.[13]

Some of the above-mentioned factors may not actually indicate that a transition towards a more sustainable economy is taking place. It could be that a change in the composition of energy inputs from expensive, but clean, fuel to cheaper fossils - for example, from renewable energy sources (RES) to coal - is taking place. Similarly, if the nature of output were to change towards less energy-intensive production - of services, for example, as we see across advanced economies - then declines in energy inputs may be the result of this phenomenon rather than due to more sustainable manufacturing production. To address these effects, we looked at the breakdown of the total economy between services and manufacturing and found that, even though economic output has increasingly moved towards services over time, in both sectors there have been improvements in energy efficiency. To see whether the greater efficiency is due to less energy used, rather than to changes in input composition from expensive and cleaner to cheaper fossil-fuel sources, we also investigated 'emissions productivity', i.e. the amount of output produced in euros per tonne of CO_2 emitted. Here we also confirm that production is becoming cleaner, especially in manufacturing - economic output per tonne of CO_2 emitted increased over the period 1995-2009.

Production is becoming cleaner, especially in manufacturing – economic output per tonne of CO_2 emitted increased over the period 1995-2009.

Cleveland et al. argue that most emissions reductions come from a change in the fuel mix, as more energy production is becoming renewable in Europe.[14] The shift towards renewable energy partly explains the decline in CO_2 emissions per unit of output produced. Improvements in the efficiency of energy use are also identified in previous studies. Mulder and De Groot, for example, find improvements in energy efficiency and also convergence between European countries,[15] i.e. a catch-up is happening between countries in terms of efficient use of energy, which makes sense as technological advancements will at some point become more widely accessible. They also find that the price element is important in this regard. Energy-efficiency gains are positively correlated with price increases. This means that businesses invest more in energy efficiency when prices are higher to reduce the burden of the higher costs.

It has to be noted that over this same period, a lot of manufacturing activity was outsourced to other parts of the world, most notably to the Asia-Pacific region. This is a global composition effect that could favourably impact the European results, as more energy-intensive production shifts elsewhere. Even though this is definitely a factor in the decline in energy intensity of production in Europe, Weisz suggests that the effects of outsourcing on energy-efficiency improvements have been relatively small and that actual improvements in industries are the main cause of the declines.[16]

2.3 Decarbonisation of the EU economy is possible

Having established the relationship between energy and economic growth by looking at the previous decades, it is also interesting to see how decarbonisation through energy efficiency and changes in the energy mix could continue in the future. We take into account a broad range of scenarios – from international institutions (European Commission, International Energy Agency, International Institute for Applied Systems Analysis), European research projects (AMPERE, SECURE), NGOs (European Climate Foundation, Greenpeace) and industry (Eurelectric) – all of which depict a decarbonisation of the EU energy sector in line with the projected EU contribution to limiting global warming to 2°C above pre-industrial levels.

Behrens et al. conclude that decarbonisation of the EU economy is possible using currently known technologies.[17] Regarding energy demand, the authors show that demand would need to decrease by some 2-6% by 2020, and by 20-30% by 2050 (compared with 2010). It is worth noting that these reductions in demand will need to be achieved within the context of a growing EU economy, thus requiring an absolute decoupling of economic growth from energy demand.[18] Energy efficiency plays a crucial role in achieving demand reductions, and high energy-efficiency assumptions lead to higher reductions in energy demand. The share of RES (renewable energy sources) increases from around 10% in 2011 to around 20% in 2020, and to somewhat above 40% by 2050. Fossil fuels will continue to play an important role, but their share in the energy mix may decrease from more than three-quarters in 2011 to around 70% in 2020, and to 40-50% in 2050.

Decarbonisation of the EU economy is possible using currently known technologies.

The power sector is likely to be the main enabler of decarbonisation, and many scenarios assume a decarbonisation in the sector of up to 95% by 2050 (compared with 1990). These savings will need to be achieved in the face of growing electricity demand. In fact, all decarbonisation scenarios project growing electricity generation, mainly driven by increasing demand in transport and heating/cooling. By 2020, electricity demand could grow by about 5-10%, and the increase may be in the range of 30-50% by 2050 (both compared with 2010). Energy efficiency and the upscaling of RES are the two key strategies to decarbonise the power sector. Regarding RES, their share in power generation is generally projected to increase from about 20% in 2010 to 35% by 2020 and to 60-85% by 2050. Wind and hydro will be the most important RES in power generation in 2020. By 2050, biomass and solar PV (photovoltaic) will also contribute significantly to the electricity mix. There is a large degree of uncertainty about the future importance of nuclear and carbon capture and storage (CCS) in power generation.

It is important to note that the rising share of variable RES, such as wind and solar PV, will require an increase in installed electric capacity that is larger than the increase in power output. In order to have sufficient levels of back-up capacity (and provided that there is no change in power market design), electrical capacity is projected to increase by about 20-30% by 2020, and by 80-100% by 2050 (both compared with 2010). This is due to lower capacity factors – i.e. a lower ratio of actual full load hours to total number of hours per year (8,760) – associated with intermittent RES. In fact, the average capacity factor over the whole European electricity system is projected to decrease from roughly 42-45% in 2010 to 37-40% in 2020 and to 25-33% in 2050, depending on the scenario. However, the flexibility of the electricity system needed to maintain the supply-demand balance with high levels of renewable generation will not only be achieved through additional generation capacity, but also through better interconnection of transmission lines, more flexible distribution, demand-side response and management, and storage.

> *The rising share of variable RES, such as wind and solar PV, will require an increase in installed electricity capacity that is larger than the increase in power output. This will require significantly more manpower than traditional energy production.*

The expansion of renewables will require significantly more manpower than traditional energy production. This means that the productivity of the energy sector is likely to decrease as the socio-ecological transition unfolds, which could be an issue from an economic competitiveness perspective. The costs for European businesses to use energy would likely increase, making the decision to import less clean energy from outside or to move production to other parts of the world more attractive. This scenario shows the importance of improving labour productivity in these sectors.

2.4 The macro effects of energy efficiency improvements on the labour market seem to be ambiguous

The next question is what effect the decarbonisation of the economy will have on employment in Europe. We have seen in the previous part of this chapter that the economy is indeed using energy more productively, reducing both costs and greenhouse gas emissions. Besides that, we also see that the effect on economic growth is relatively small. We will now look at the effects of the socio-ecological transition on employment. First we will look at the macroeconomic effects, and then zoom in on the employment effects in the energy sector itself.

When looking at the macro economy, complementarity between energy use and the growth of labour, both skilled and unskilled, exists.[19] This means that reductions in energy use are usually met by reductions in employment, making the direct effect of declines in energy demand on employment negative. This is partly because of labour-capital substitution, but also because both are positively related to overall economic output. From a labour market perspective, this means that the socio-ecological transition may have a negative impact on the availability of jobs in Europe, which is an observation that raises concern given the current employment situation and the sluggish job-market outlook for the years ahead.

In terms of the impact of innovation on the distribution of jobs, recent work by Maselli and Massari et al. describes the impact of information and communications technology (ICT) on polarisation in the labour market.[20] They find that ICT has resulted in a 'hollowing out' of jobs in the middle range of the skill spectrum. This is because of the demand for service tasks that can be found in the lower tail of the wage distribution and the demand for abstract tasks found at the higher end of the spectrum. Offshoring of middle-skilled tasks is one of the reasons why the share of income of the middle classes in advanced societies has declined. Ketteni et al. come to a parallel conclusion that the mismatch between skill demand and skill supply can be attributed to the adoption of ICT capital, as it is a substitute for unskilled labour and a complement to high-skilled labour.[21] Trends in ICT adoption are therefore important in order to gauge the trend in skill demand on a macro level in the European economy.

As the long-term effects of the SET on macroeconomic growth are ambiguous, this is also the case for employment. In the long run, employment and economic growth are strongly correlated and this means that unless drastic productivity changes occur due to the socio-ecological transition, no large changes in labour demand can be expected. This last point is important, as the labour productivity of certain types of energy production can be dramatically different from others. Current fossil energy sources, in particular, require low amounts of labour, as they use mostly capital to produce. Renewable energy sources are different in this regard, as they still require a lot of human input (the second part of this chapter will offer more detailed insights into this). This can result in more significant employment improvements, but also in losses of global competitiveness as productivity declines. Whether this will be the case or not is discussed in greater detail below.

2.5 Fewer than 1 in 100 employees in Europe work in the energy sector

When zooming in on the specific changes in employment in the energy sector, we will first look at the employment level, employment structure and labour intensity of today's energy sector.[22] As earlier in the chapter, we focus exclusively on energy supply, and in particular on activities linked to primary (fossil) energy carriers as well as on the power sector.[23]

The total number of direct jobs provided by the EU energy supply sector in 2011 is estimated at between 1.5 million (European Commission DG Energy) and 2.2 million (Eurostat Labour Force Survey), representing a share of 0.7-1% of the total employed workforce in that year. To put this into perspective, the energy sector employs fewer people than, for example, the agriculture, forestry and fishing sector (5.2%) or the information and communications sector (2.8%) (Eurostat, 2013c). DG Energy estimates and Labour Force Survey (LFS) data provide the low and high ends of the range, respectively, of employment levels summarised in Table 2.1. DG Energy and LFS data are roughly confirmed by estimates of

The total number of direct jobs provided by the EU energy supply sector in 2011 is estimated at between 1.5 million and 2.2 million.

industry associations. Table 2.1 shows that electric power generation, transmission and distribution (summarised in the category "electricity") is by far the largest employer, providing roughly 55-60% of all direct jobs in the energy sector. The extraction of primary fossil fuels employs less than a quarter of all direct jobs, while other oil and gas activities (including oil refining, manufacture and distribution of gas) provide less than 20%.

Table 2.1 Direct employment in the energy sector, 2011

Activity	Range	DG Energy	LFS	Industry
Mining of coal and lignite	229,000 - 345,000	229,401	345,000	238,200[24]
Oil and gas extraction[25]	113,000 - 187,000	113,171	186,939	91,765[26]
Oil and gas other activities[27]	269,000 - 410,000	269,236	410,477	564,985[28]
Electricity	888,000 - 1,221,000	888,358	1,221,148	1,100,000[29]
Other[30]	21,000 - 27,000	20,593	26,669	n.a.
Total	1,500,000 - 2,200,000	1,520,759	2,190,233	1,994,950

Sources: European Commission (2013), Eurostat (2013a and 2013b) and industry associations.

As regards the employment structure of the energy system, the European Centre for the Development of Vocational Training (Cedefop) reports that in general around 10% of the labour force employed in the energy sector in 2012 were low-qualified workers, around 50-60% were medium qualified, and around 40% were highly qualified.[31] Oil and gas extraction and the manufacture of fuels have the highest share of highly qualified workers (around 43%), while coal and lignite mining activities employ by far the lowest share of highly qualified workers (some 15%). All of the studies surveyed by Behrens et al. indicate that that the share of highly qualified workers employed in the renewable energy sector is substantially higher than in coal mining (33-75% in the renewables sector compared with 15% in coal and lignite mining activities).[32] In a scenario in which fossil fuel-based power generation would be mainly replaced by electricity from renewable energy sources (RES-E) after 2020, low- and medium-qualified jobs in coal mining are likely to be replaced by highly qualified jobs in RES.

Around 10% of the labour force employed in the energy sector in 2012 were low qualified workers, around 50% were medium qualified, and around 40% were highly qualified.

Regarding the labour intensity of primary energy activities (expressed in jobs per ktoe, or kilotonnes of oil equivalent), mining of coal and lignite is the most labour-intensive activity (1.37-2.06 jobs per ktoe). Compared to coal, the extraction of oil and gas is about 66% less labour intensive per unit of energy extracted (0.49-0.81 jobs per ktoe). Downstream activities (refining, manufacturing and distribution of fuels) are the least labour-intensive activities, with a labour intensity of about 0.27-0.41 jobs per ktoe. Turning to the power sector, where labour intensity is expressed in jobs per MW installed capacity, the analysis presented in Behrens et al. shows that some renewables, in particular biomass (8.22 jobs per MW) and to a lesser extent solar PV (2.35), are more labour intensive than fossil fuel-based power generation (1.21-2.11).[33] Wind power (1.45) is in the same range, while small hydropower (1.08) is slightly less labour intensive. The labour intensities presented in this paragraph are equivalent to the employment factors referred to in the next section for calculating future employment in the energy sector.

2.6 A positive net effect: Jobs destroyed in primary energy activities may be overcompensated by job creation in the power sector

In order to estimate changes in the employment level, Behrens et al. (2014b) developed a simple but robust methodology based on employment factors. It allows employment impacts to be calculated by multiplying (future) energy units (in ktoe for primary fuels and MW for the power sector) by technology-specific employment factors. These employment factors are equivalent to labour-intensity ratios expressed in jobs per ktoe or jobs per MW (see above). They are calculated on the basis of current energy sector figures and then used to calculate the number of jobs linked to the projected future volumes of primary energy and levels of installed electric capacity in the years 2020, 2030 and 2050.

Regarding the results, three things should be noted. First, and as observed above, the methodology is applied only to direct employment in the energy-supply sector, i.e. to primary energy activities linked to fossil fuels and to the power sector. Second, the results below will be presented in a lower range and in an upper range. This results from the fact that the job figures (current direct employment levels) for primary fuels and the power sector are derived from different sources, thus showing some variance (see above). In order to account for this variance, we utilise the minimum and maximum employment levels linked to a fuel. Therefore, there is a lower and an upper range for the employment factors in fossil fuels, leading to a lower and upper range of results for the projected employment levels for each scenario. Third, projections are based on the reference scenario and two decarbonisation scenarios (Diversified Supply Technologies and High-RES) of the European Commission's Energy Roadmap 2050 (European Commission, 2011a).

The reference scenario (Ref) is based on the continuation of current economic and demographic trends. The '20-20-20' targets regarding GHG emissions reductions and RES deployment are achieved, but no future objectives are set beyond 2020, and investment decisions thereafter are largely driven by market forces. It is not a decarbonisation scenario, and therefore is not in line with the new SET away from fossil fuels. However, it serves as a baseline for the evaluation of the two decarbonisation scenarios. In contrast to the reference scenario, the decarbonisation scenarios both allow for a decrease in domestic EU GHG emissions by at least 80% compared to 1990. The diversified supply technologies scenario (DST) is neutral from a technological perspective. Decarbonisation is achieved by means of carbon pricing (i.e. an undefined proxy for policy measures that bring about emission reductions), which is applied to all sectors (ETS and non-ETS). The scenario assumes societal support (of member states, investors and citizens) for nuclear energy (except for declared 'nuclear sceptics' such as Germany), CCS and renewables facilitation policies. This scenario is interesting to assess, as it encompasses the application of a wide range of low-carbon technologies without preference for a specific type of technology. The high renewable energy sources scenario (High-RES) focuses on achieving a very high share of renewables (97% of electricity consumption by 2050). Technologies deployed include wind (both on- and offshore), solar PV and concentrated solar power (CSP) and storage, increased uptake of heat pumps, and so on. Given the key role of renewables in achieving an effective reduction of CO_2 emissions, scrutinising this decarbonisation scenario seems particularly important.

Taking into account all uncertainties related to the methodology and the available data, there is clear evidence that decarbonisation will lead to job losses in the primary fuels sector (see Table 2.2). Based on current employment levels of between 611,000 (lower range of labour intensities) and 943,000 (upper range of labour intensities), decarbonisation may destroy between 96,000 and 153,000 jobs by 2020, between 213,000 and 350,000 jobs by 2030, and between 380,000 and 686,000 jobs by 2050, depending on the decarbonisation scenario and the range chosen. Total employment in primary fuels may thus decrease to some 512,000-794,000 in 2020, 385,000-

Decarbonisation will lead to job losses in the primary fuels sector.

613,000 in 2030, and 170,000-347,000 in 2050. Generally, employment in primary fuels in the decarbonisation scenarios seems to be lower than in the reference scenario, pointing to the possibility of higher job losses in primary activities as the energy sector decarbonises.

Table 2.2 Direct employment in primary fuels in 2011, 2020, 2030 and 2050 (million jobs)

	2011	2020			2030			2050		
		Ref	DST	High-RES	Ref	DST	High-RES	Ref	DST	High-RES
Lower	0.6	0.6	0.5	0.5	0.5	0.4	0.4	0.4	0.2	0.2
Upper	0.9	0.9	0.8	0.8	0.7	0.6	0.6	0.7	0.3	0.3

Source: Behrens et al. (2014a).

In contrast to primary fuels, Table 2.3 shows that the power sector is likely to create jobs. Based on current employment levels of between 0.9 million (lower range of labour intensities) and 1.2 million (upper range of labour intensities), decarbonisation may create between 800,000 and 900,000 additional jobs by 2020, between 900,000 and 1.6 million additional jobs by 2030, and between 2.2 and 4.1 million additional jobs by 2050, depending on the decarbonisation scenario and range chosen. The total number of jobs in the power sector could thus increase to between 1.8 and 2 million in 2020, between 2 and 2.5 million in 2030, and between 3.2 and 5.2 million in 2050, depending on the decarbonisation scenario. Compared with the reference scenario, this means additional jobs in the ranges of 32,000 to 55,000 in 2020, 138,000 to 669,000 in 2030 and 800,000 to 2.6 million in 2050.

The increase in employment in the power sector is driven by jobs in construction, installation and manufacturing (CIM) and by jobs in operation and maintenance (O&M), and the share of each in total jobs (about 60% for CIM and about 40% for O&M) remains roughly constant over the entire period until 2050.

Table 2.3 Direct employment in the power sector in 2011, 2020, 2030 and 2050 (millions of jobs)

	2011	2020			2030			2050		
		Ref	DST	High-RES	Ref	DST	High-RES	Ref	DST	High-RES
Lower	0.9	1.8	1.8	1.8	1.8	2.0	2.4	2.4	3.2	5.0
Upper	1.2	1.9	2.0	2.0	1.9	2.1	2.5	2.6	3.4	5.2

Source: Behrens et al. (2014b).

2.7 Projected future employment increases in the power sector are mainly due to the higher labour intensity of renewables

Aggregating the employment effects in primary fuels and in the power sector reveals that decarbonisation in the context of a new SET may lead to substantial employment creation, particularly in the long term. As shown in Table 2.4, compared with current employment levels of about 1.5-2.2 million, decarbonisation may create up to 800,000 additional jobs in the energy system by 2020, up to 1.3 million additional jobs by 2030 and up to 3.7 million additional jobs by 2050, depending on the decarbonisation scenario and range chosen. The results also show that more jobs are created in the High-RES scenario than in any other scenario. While the results of the two decarbonisation scenarios are similar to those of the reference scenario until 2020, differences begin to materialise by 2030, and in particular by 2050. However, the results for 2050 are subject to high uncertainty, as described below.

Decarbonisation will have substantial employment effects in primary fuels and in the power sector.

Table 2.4 Direct employment in the energy sector in 2011, 2020, 2030 and 2050 (millions of jobs)

	2011	2020			2030			2050		
		Ref	DST	High-RES	Ref	DST	High-RES	Ref	DST	High-RES
Lower	1.5	2.3	2.3	2.3	2.3	2.4	2.8	2.9	2.5	5.2
Upper	2.2	2.8	2.8	2.8	2.7	2.7	3.1	3.3	3.7	5.4

Source: Behrens et al. (2014b).

Apart from changes in the quantity of direct jobs associated with the energy transition, Behrens et al. also analyse how required qualification levels may change.[34] They do this by applying the current distribution of low, medium and highly qualified jobs in various energy technologies to the changed mix of primary (fossil) fuels and of power sources in the future.

In all three scenarios, the amount of jobs created in the RES sector is more significant than the number of jobs lost in primary fuels. RES may not only maintain the distribution of qualification levels, but

The increase of renewables may actually increase the demand for highly qualified workers.

may actually increase the demand for highly qualified workers. Considering that the renewable energy sector has a higher share of highly qualified workers (33-75%) than most activities in primary fuels (see above), this results in a net increase of highly qualified workers.

With the level of qualifications in the energy sector going up, there may be a risk of skills shortages. Indeed, as the share of highly qualified workers in the general labour market increases,[35] the energy sector could be in competition with other sectors for the recruitment of a highly qualified workforce. In particular, shortages of engineers and technicians are common in the renewable energy sector.[36] The problem can be traced back upstream, with a lack of qualified trainers for renewable technologies.[37] Fortunately, dynamics recently at play in the labour market are easing the risk of skill shortages. First, an increase in the supply of highly skilled workforce is observed in Europe. The growth in the supply of medium and highly skilled workers is even expected to outpace the growth in demand for highly skilled workers.[38] Second, the economic crisis has had a positive effect on skills shortages by facilitating the filling of vacancies in some occupations.[39] Finally, certain existing skills are transferable to the renewable energy sector, either with or without the need for retraining. Examples of portable skills include welding, surface treatment and outfitting skills in the oil and gas industry that are applicable in the wind turbine sector.[40] Examples of areas of upskilling include skills in the assembly and installation of parts for industrial operators and industry electricians to work as wind turbine operators, and training on solar PV for electricians and roofers to work as solar PV installers and designers.[41]

2.8 The key to the impact of the SET on employment lies in the labour productivity of renewable energy sources

Even though the EU can hardly be considered a decarbonised economy, the process is slowly underway. The production of renewable energy in Europe has increased by over 80% since 2000, and the share of renewables in final energy consumption is continuing to increase in almost all European countries. Energy efficiency is also improving in most countries in Europe, whether in energy-intensive manufacturing industries or in service sectors. The impact of this on economic growth has been relatively small.

When looking at all economic inputs, energy had the smallest cumulative impact on economic growth in the six large European economies studied, which means that reductions in energy inputs are unlikely to have a large direct impact on economic growth. However, when taking the indirect effects into account, we find that energy reductions also impact material use and capital. More importantly, we find that energy efficiency gains improve technological progress and, with that, economic growth. With currently known technologies, society is already advanced enough to decarbonise. The overall effects of the SET on the macro-economy have therefore been minor and are unlikely to be enormous in the future, if the process moves gradually.

This is also the case for employment, which usually moves together with the economy in the long run, unless the SET results in large shifts in labour productivity due to changes in the types of employment that are needed to support the economy. When the energy sector becomes much more labour intensive, the productivity of the sector declines and therefore more employment is needed for the same energy production. This could be the case for Europe, as changes in the composition of the energy mix due to the SET are likely to result in significantly higher employment in the energy sector. At current employment factors, employment in the energy sector could increase by more than three million in 2050 if a rapid shift to renewable energy sources were to occur. If the share of renewables were to increase at a slower pace, more than a million extra jobs would still be created in the sector.

Even though this is great news from a job-creation perspective, there are also downsides. The resulting decline in labour productivity would have an impact on prices, assuming that other economies would not go through a similar radical change, which would make importing energy or outsourcing more attractive. Therefore, efficiency gains are key to the success of the SET in a growing economy. Without such gains, alternatives for the more expensive energy solutions would likely be sought. Technological progress is also taking place rapidly in the renewables sector. When looking at the jobs that can currently be classified as 'green' in the European economy, we see that most of the green jobs are in research and development of solar and wind technologies.[42]

Efficiency gains are key to the success of the SET in a growing economy.

Technological developments in the renewables sector will likely result in more cost-efficient production, especially from the employment side as productivity is likely to improve. This will be necessary for the SET to succeed and would still generate more employment in the energy sector, albeit at a slightly lower level than current employment factors would suggest. Overall, it seems likely that the improvements coming from the SET through decarbonisation will not come at the cost of a large effect on Europe's economic growth projections, but instead that the technological advancement in the energy sector is likely to impact the economy positively. This in turn will have its effects on overall macroeconomic employment growth, but these will also likely remain small. When focusing on the energy sector itself, it seems that large net employment opportunities will arise. These opportunities will likely decrease when the necessary efficiency gains in RES are made, which in turn will increase the chances for success of the socio-ecological transition in Europe.

Bibliography

Behrens, A. and C. Coulie (2015), "Options to Address Labour Market Issues During the Transition to a European Low-Carbon Economy", NEUJOBS Policy Brief No. D11.3, NEUJOBS Project (www.neujobs.eu).

Behrens, A., C. Coulie and J. Teusch (2014a), "The potential evolution of the European energy system until 2020 and 2050", CEPS Working Document No. 392, Centre for European Policy Studies, Brussels.

Behrens, A., C. Coulie, F. Genoese, M. Alessi, J. Wieczorkiewicz and C. Egenhofer (2014b), "Impact of the Decarbonisation of the Energy System on Employment in Europe", NEUJOBS Working Paper No. D11.2, NEUJOBS Project (www.neujobs.eu).

Bukowski, M. (2014), "On the endogenous directed technological change in multi sector DSGE model: the case of energy and emission e-ciency", NEUJOBS Working Paper No. D3.8, NEUJOBS Project (www.neujobs.eu).

Burton, A. and K.H. den Haan (2013), "European downstream oil industry safety performance: Statistical summary of reported incidents - 2012", Report No. 5/13, CONCAWE, Brussels, August.

Cedefop (2010a), "Skills for green jobs", Briefing note, European Centre for the Development of Vocational Training, Publications Office of the European Union, Luxembourg, July.

____ (2010b), "Skills for Green Jobs. European Synthesis Report", European Centre for the Development of Vocational Training, Publications Office of the European Union, Luxembourg.

_____ (2011), "Labour market polarisation and elementary occupations in Europe. Blip or long-term trend?", Research Paper No. 9, European Centre for the Development of Vocational Training, Publications Office of the European Union, Luxembourg.

_____ (2012), "Green skills and environmental awareness in vocational education and training", Research Paper No. 24, European Centre for the Development of Vocational Training, Publications Office of the European Union, Luxembourg.

_____ (2013), "Skills Forecasts", European Centre for the Development of Vocational Training (www.cedefop.europa.eu/EN/about-cedefop/projects/forecasting-skill-demand-and-supply/skills-forecasts.aspx).

Cleveland, C.J., R. Costanza, C.A.S. Hall and R. Kaufmann (1984), "Energy and the U.S. Economy: A Biophysical Perspective", *Science*, Vol. 225, No. 4665, pp. 890-897.

Colijn, B. (2014), "Green Jobs in Europe and the Increasing Demand for Technical Skills", NEUJOBS Working Paper No. 4.2, NEUJOBS Project (www.neujobs.eu).

Colijn, B. and B. van Ark (2014), "Energy Productivity and Economic Growth in Six European Countries", NEUJOBS Working Paper, NEUJOBS Project (www.neujobs.eu).

Colijn, B., K. Jaeger and B. Van Ark (2013), "The Conference Board EU KLEMS Update for NEUJOBS", NEUJOBS methodological note, NEUJOBS Project (www.neujobs.eu).

Corrado, C., C. Hulten and D. Sichel (2005), "Measuring Capital and Technology: An Expanded Framework", in C. Corrado, J. Haltiwanger, and D. Sichel (eds), *Measuring Capital in the New Economy*, Chicago, IL: University of Chicago Press, pp. 11-41.

Diamond, J. and P. Bellwood (2003), "Farmers and Their Languages: The First Expansions", *Science*, Vol. 300, pp. 597-603.

Euracoal (2013), "Manpower in 2010 and 2012", Brussels.

Eurelectric (2012), "Power Statistics and Trends 2012", Brussels, December.

Eurogas (2012), "Statistical Report 2012", Brussels, December.

European Commission (2011a), "Energy Roadmap 2050. Impact Assessment. Part 1", SEC(2011) 1565 final, Brussels.

_____ (2011b), "Employment and Social Developments in Europe 2012", DG Employment.

_____ (2013), "EU Energy in Figures: Statistical Pocketbook 2013", Publications Office of the European Union, Luxembourg.

Eurostat (2013a), Labour Force Survey.

_____ (2013b), Structural Business Statistics.

_____ (2013c), National accounts.

Fischer-Kowalski, M., W. Haas, D. Wiedenhofer, U. Weisz, I. Pallua, N. Possanner, A. Behrens, G. Serio, M. Alessi and E. Weis (2012), "Socio-ecological transitions: definition, dynamics and related global scenarios", NEUJOBS State of the Art Report No. 6/D1.1 and Working Paper D1.2, NEUJOBS Project (www.neujobs.eu).

Hao, J.X. and B. Van Ark (2013), "Intangible Investment and the Intensity of Energy Use by Industry", NEUJOBS Working Paper, NEUJOBS Project (www.neujobs.eu).

ILO and EU (2011), "Skills and Occupational Needs in Renewable Energy", International Labour Organization, Geneva.

Jorgenson, D.W. (1984), "The role of Energy in Productivity Growth", *American Economic Review*, Vol. 74, No. 2, pp. 22-30.

Ketteni, E., T. Manumeas and P. Pashardes (2012), "ICT and Energy Use: Patterns of Substitutability and Complementarity in Production", NEUJOBS Working Paper D3.5, NEUJOBS Project (www.neujobs.eu).

Kümmel, R. (2011), *The Second Law of Economics: Energy, Entropy and the Origins of Wealth*, New York, NY: Springer.

Maselli, I. (2012), "The Evolving Supply and Demand of Skills in the Labour Market", *Intereconomics*, January.

Massari, R., P. Naticchioni and G. Ragusa (2013), "Unconditional and Conditional Wage Polarization in Europe", NEUJOBS Working Paper No. D3.6, NEUJOBS Project (www.neujobs.eu).

Mulder, P. and H. de Groot (2007), "Sectoral energy- and labour-productivity convergence", *Environmental and Resource Economics*, Vol. 36, pp. 85-112.

_____ (2011), "Energy Intensity across Sectors and Countries: Empirical Evidence 1980-2005", CPB Discussion Paper No. 171, The Hague.

NEUJOBS (2013), "Summary info about the project", NEUJOBS Project (www.neujobs.eu).

Poupard, J.-F. and D. Tarren (2011), "Towards a low carbon electricity industry: employment effects and opportunities for the social partners", EPSU/Eurelectric/EMCEF, Brussels.

Sieferle, R.P., F. Krausmann, H. Schandl and V. Winiwarter (2006), *Das Ende der Fläche – Zum gesellschaftlichten Stoffwechsel der Industrialiserung*, Cologne: Böhlau.

Stern, D.I. (2003), "Energy and economic growth in the USA: A multivariate approach", *Energy Economics*, Vol. 15, pp. 137–150.

Weisz, H. (2006), "Accounting for raw material equivalents of traded goods: A comparison of input-output approaches in physical, monetary, and mixed units", Social Ecology Working Paper No. 87, Institute of Social Ecology, Vienna.

[1] Fischer-Kowalski et al. (2012).

[2] Diamond and Bellwood (2003).

[3] Fischer-Kowalski et al. (2012).

[4] European Commission (2013).

[5] Sieferle et al. (2006).

[6] This section is based on Behrens et al. (2014a).

[7] A database that comprises historical data of economic inputs and output for a large number of sectors and countries: www.euklems.net.

[8] Colijn et al. (2013).

[9] Colijn and Van Ark (2014).

[10] Hao and Van Ark (2013).

[11] Kümmel (2011); Ketteni et al. (2012).

[12] Colijn and Van Ark (2013).

[13] Stern (2003).

[14] Cleveland et al. (1984).

[15] Mulder and De Groot (2007).

[16] Weitz et al. (2006).

[17] Behrens et al. (2014a).

[18] 'Absolute decoupling' refers to a situation in which energy demand declines in absolute terms while the economy grows. In contrast, relative decoupling refers to a situation in which energy demand may increase, but at a lower rate than economic growth.

[19] Ketteni et al. (2012).

[20] Maselli (2012) and Massari et al. (2013).

[21] Ketteni et al. (2012).

[22] See Behrens et al. (2014b).

[23] For activities linked to primary energy carriers, only fossil fuels are considered because RES such as wind, solar and hydropower do not require combustibles. Therefore, there is no fuel that needs to be extracted and/or processed. Regarding biomass and nuclear, no separate job figures are available for primary activities. Jobs related to RES are accounted for in the power sector/electricity statistics.

[24] For 2012 (Euracoal, 2013).

[25] Oil and gas are aggregated to reflect the nature of the production fields, which most of the time produce both oil and gas. Figures from DG Energy and LFS include jobs in extraction and activities in support of extraction.

[26] Derived from unpublished data obtained during an interview with an OGP expert in 2013.

[27] Other activities in oil include refining and marketing, and other activities in gas include manufacture of gas, distribution of gas, and trade of gas through mains.

[28] 285,256 jobs in oil, derived from 534 million hours worked in the downstream oil sector in 2012 (Burton and den Haan, 2013), assuming that people worked 36 hours per week; 279,729 jobs in gas (Eurogas, 2012).

[29] Estimation based on Eurelectric data (Eurelectric, 2012). The estimate includes people employed in all power generation sources; it may double-count workers that are already included in figures for employment in fossil fuels.

[30] Manufacture of coke oven products, and extraction of peat.

[31] Cedefop (2013).

[32] Behrens et al. (2014b).

[33] Ibid.

[34] Ibid.

[35] Cedefop (2011).

[36] ILO and EU (2011)

[37] Ibid.

[38] European Commission (2011b).

[39] Cedefop (2012).

[40] Cedefop (2010a).

[41] Cedefop (2010b).

[42] Colijn (2014).

3. BIKING TO WORK? TRANSPORT POLICY, SUSTAINABILITY AND EMPLOYMENT

*CHRISTOPHE HEYNDRICKX, RODRIC FREDERIX AND JOKO PURWANTO**

The transport sector consumes 32% of the total energy and three quarters of all petroleum products in the EU.[1] In 2012, the transport sector was responsible for 20% of EU28 greenhouse gas (GHG) emissions (a total of 0.893 Mt CO_2 eq.), which is around 20% more than in 1990 and up from a share of around 16% of total emissions.[2] Whereas other economic sectors achieved reductions in greenhouse gas emissions of up to 20%, emissions from the transport sector only started to follow a decreasing trend in 2007. Looking at the developments within the sector, it is obvious that road transport is the major culprit - with a share of over 70%, it generated by far the largest quantity of GHG emissions within the transport sector in 2012. Navigation and civil aviation, both including international bunker fuels,[3] generated about 16% and 15%, respectively.

The rather sluggish reduction of overall transport emissions is difficult to reconcile with the EU climate policy, which aims to reduce GHG emissions to 20% below 1990 levels by 2020, or 30% in case of a joint global agreement similar to the Kyoto Protocol. The 2011 European Commission Communication "Roadmap for moving to a competitive low-carbon economy in 2050" suggests that by 2050, the EU should cut its emissions to 80% below 1990 levels through domestic reductions alone. To reach this target, emissions from the transport sector by 2030 should be reduced by at least 30% compared to 2010.[4] However, significant reductions of GHG emissions over the next four decades will have important consequences for

* Christophe Heyndrickx, Rodric Frederix and Joko Purwanto: Transport & Mobility Leuven.

both private households (i.e. the labour supply) and the transportation sector (i.e. the labour demand). The question we try to answer in this chapter is therefore: Are there policies that can reduce our carbon footprint and, at the same time, create jobs?

3.1 The transport sector accounts for 4.5% of employment in the EU

In several European countries, the production of motor vehicles and other forms of transport equipment has long been a crucial part of the industrial economy, generating both income and employment. There is also an extensive range of jobs associated with transport, covering those employed in airlines and other forms of public transport, as well as a range of maintenance and associated services.

The transport sector directly employs more than 10 million people, accounting for 4.5% of total employment in the EU. Around 55% of these people work in land transport, 2% in sea transport, 4% in air transport, and 22% in warehousing and supporting transport activities (cargo handling, storage and warehousing), with the remaining 17% in postal and courier activities. With around €533 billion in gross value added (GVA) at basic prices, the transport and storage services sector - including postal and courier activities - accounted for about 5.1% of total GVA in the EU27 in 2009 and represents 4.6% of EU gross domestic product (GDP). Manufacture of transportation equipment provides an additional 1.7% of GDP and 1.5% of employment.

Beyond its role as a direct employer, a well-functioning transport sector is necessary for logistics and distribution, as well as allowing employees to commute to their workplaces. In 2010, private households in Europe spent €904 billion, or roughly 13% of their total consumption, on transport-related items. More specifically, 30% of this sum (around €260 billion) was spent on vehicle purchase, slightly more than 50% (€477 billion) on the operation of personal transport equipment, and the rest (€168 billion) on transport services (e.g. bus, plane or train tickets).

3.2 The transition away from fossil fuels will impact the transport sector

The socio-ecological transition away from fossil fuels will have important consequences for the transport sector as an employer. The changes in the transport sector will be the result of a number of drivers, including climate policy, fossil fuel scarcity, the introduction of new propulsion technologies and changes in logistics chains. The number of drivers, as well as the complexity of the expected changes, is such that it is unclear how fast and how radical the transition will be. The background scenarios discussed in the Introduction therefore differentiate between 'friendly' and 'tough' future global scenarios. The former is characterised by a slow rate of change that is less challenging for Europe, whereas the latter is characterised by a more radical and rapid rate of change. With regards to the transport sector, the tough scenario assumes greater resource scarcity, higher prices of resources and slower economic growth compared with the friendly scenario. The three possible policy responses to the socio-ecological transition differ in the rate of change that is induced by the response strategy - low ('status quo'), medium ('modernisation'), or high ('sustainability'). The combination of the two background global conditions with the three policy response strategies enables us to define six separate scenarios, which we classify into two broad groups: 1) policies aimed at using energy more efficiently in transport; and 2) policies oriented towards behavioural change (see Table 3.1).

Table 3.1 Policy strategies and scenarios combined

	Friendly	Tough
Strategy 1: No policy changes	'Careless and globalised world'	'Constrained and ignorant world'
Strategy 2: Ecological modernisation and eco-efficiency	'Ecologically aware and globalised world'	'Restricted, but ecologically aware world'
Strategy 3: Sustainability transformation	'Sustainable and globalised'	'Challenged and sustainable world'

The first set of policies aims to make significant changes to propulsion technology and the relative carbon intensity of transport, and a number of technological options are available to accomplish this. The first option relates to any kind of *electrification* of road transport, be it plug-in hybrid vehicles, battery electric vehicles or hydrogen fuel cell vehicles. The second option is the increased use of biomass (biomassification), although this requires that the biomass be grown in a sustainable manner and does not compete with food. Examples are second-generation biofuels (e.g. Fischer-Tropsch fuels[5] from full energy plants or plant residues) and third-generation biofuels (e.g. algae). The third technological option (the efficiency revolution) would involve lightweight solutions for vehicles and/or downsizing of vehicles such that 1-litre or 2-litre cars become more prevalent.

A second path for structural change focuses on behavioural change. This is absolutely essential, as many of the technological options presented above tend to increase the cost of acquiring a car, but reduce the actual cost of driving. Without any correction to the demand for transport services, technological options will not be sufficient to reduce overall transport emissions. Adjusting the tax system to better reflect the damage that transport inflicts on the environment (i.e. the internalisation of external cost), stimulating the use of public (collective) transport and reducing the need for 'physical interaction' (by use of information technology) are essential steps to achieve this goal.

3.3 The socio-ecological transition will lead to GHG reductions and job creation

Using the 'status quo' scenario as a reference, we analyse the extent to which the implied scenarios allow reductions in GHG emissions at the level of the transport sector and the full economy, given friendly or tough background conditions, in eight European countries: Austria, Belgium, Bulgaria, Finland, Germany, Greece, Poland and Spain. At the same time, we study the impact of these scenarios on the job market.[6]

We start by showing the aggregate impact on total GHG emissions (the total for the eight countries under study) for 2030, compared to 2010, for all six scenarios. We distinguish the background ('no policy') impact, the 'status quo', 'modernisation' and 'sustainability' impacts and the relative contribution of each scenario to total emissions reduction. Disaggregating the impact of each scenario and taking into account the impact of background scenario, we find that a considerable decrease in transport sector emissions is already realised in the reference scenario,[7] especially in the 'tough' scenario. The 'modernisation' and 'sustainability' scenarios reduce overall emissions from households ('private transport'), which fall by almost 55% in the tough scenario of 2030. With respect to the total economy, total economy-wide emissions fall by 12% in the friendly and 16% in the tough scenario.

Figure 3.1 Impact of different scenarios on transport and total GHG emissions in eight countries

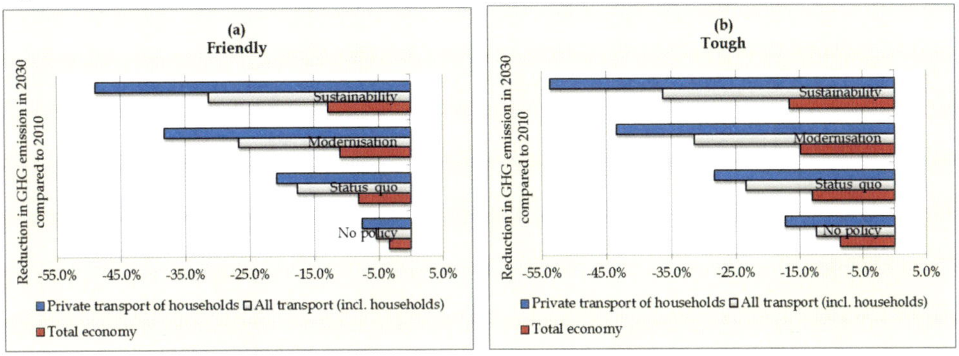

Source: Heyndrickx et al. (2013a).

We distinguish the job gains and losses for the entire economy and the shifts within the job market for the transport sector itself. The general impact is a shift from employment in transport manufacturing industries towards jobs in transport services. The proposed policy scenarios are mildly stimulating for the job market, independent of friendly or tough background conditions, and more so for the 'sustainability' scenario than for the more moderate 'modernisation' scenario. On average, for each job lost in manufacturing, around two jobs are generated in the service sector. This is based on the assumption that policy shifts from fuel-based to driving-based taxation, cutting demand for private vehicles. At the same time, increased urbanisation leads to a further realignment in preferences toward public transit solutions. This change is only partially counteracted by a reduction in the variable cost of driving attributable to the electrification of transport and increased fuel efficiency. As a result, fewer people are driving or employed in making cars, but more are engaged as drivers or operators of transport systems in the more sustainable society.

For every job lost in manufacturing, about 2 are created in transport services

The result is a net increase in employment of around 400,000 jobs in the 'sustainability' scenario and just under 200,000 jobs in the 'modernisation' scenario in the eight countries under study. This represents a decrease in unemployment of 4.4% and 2.4%, respectively. Extrapolation of this result to the whole of Europe leads to a net job creation of around 1 million full-time equivalents (FTEs) in the 'sustainability' scenario and just below 500,000 in the 'modernisation' scenario. To put things into perspective, this is a quarter to a half of the current employment in car manufacturing.

Figure 3.2 Net yearly job creation (in FTEs) compared with the reference scenario (ΔMO = change in modernisation and ΔSU= change in sustainability) in all countries, 2010 versus 2030

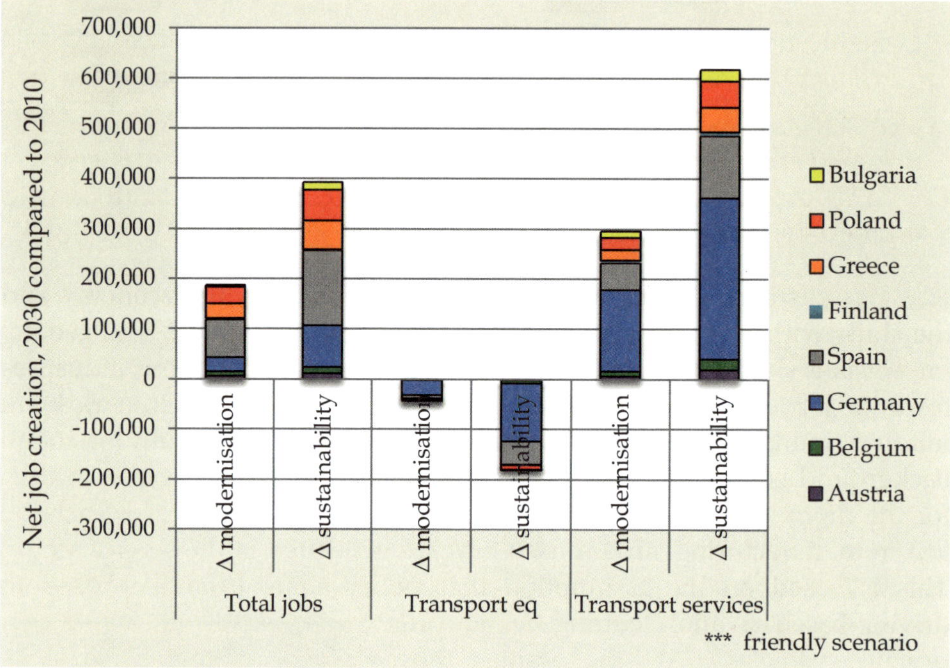

Source: Heyndrickx et al. (2013a).

The net positive impact on job creation is interesting, as the proposed 'modernisation' and 'sustainability' scenarios show significant reductions in emissions above the reference ('status quo') scenario (Figure 3.1). This is hardly surprising, since almost all transport policies directly aim to decrease energy and fuel consumption. Figures 3.3 and 3.4 present the relative contribution of various policy sub-scenarios to employment and GHG emissions.[8] These transport policy sub-scenarios include:

- an increase in energy efficiency (a reduction in the total energy use per unit of value due to technological policy and government stimulation);
- an increase in fuel efficiency (autonomous gains in productivity and a larger gain in fuel efficiency due to active government intervention in the 'modernisation' and 'sustainability' scenarios);

- electrification of transport (an increase in the use of electrified transport for households from approximately zero in most European countries up to 10% in the 'modernisation' and 20% in the 'sustainability' scenario);
- the internalisation of external costs of transport (through fuel taxes or smart charging on all roads);
- reduced use of own transport (a shift in preferences towards public transport as a result of increased urbanisation, car-sharing, measures to discourage car transport or improvements in quality and coordination of public transport services); and
- a reduction in administrative inputs for freight transport (following the e-Freight initiative of the EU).

Figure 3.3 Relative impact of each policy sub-scenario on job creation (in terms of the percentage of the final result) for the friendly 'modernisation' (left) and 'sustainability' (right) scenarios

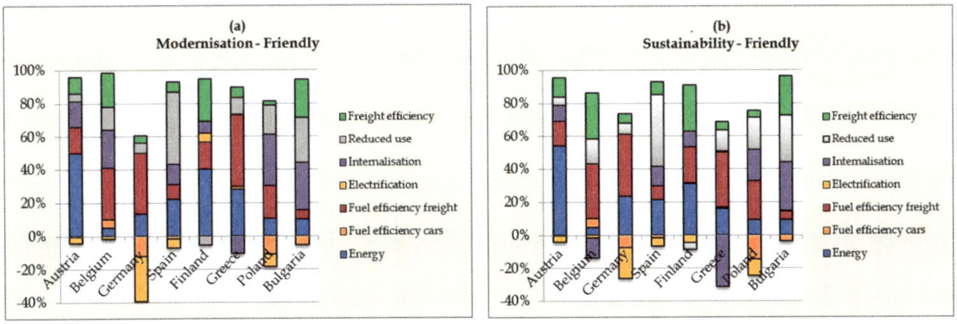

Source: Heyndrickx et al. (2013a).

Figure 3.3 suggests that the policies with the largest impact on employment are the 'energy efficiency', 'reduced use of private transport' and 'transport efficiency' sub-scenarios. Gains in fuel efficiency for freight transport have a much more positive impact on employment than fuel efficiency for passenger transport. This is because lower costs for fuel lead to substitution to labour. By far the most effective strategy for net job creation was related not directly to transport but to increased energy efficiency in the economy as a whole. Energy-efficiency improvements and transport subsidies deliver about three times more jobs in the eastern European countries (Group 2) than in the other countries. We shows that there is a big difference between jobs created within the richer and more developed western and northern EU countries (Belgium, Germany, France,

Finland, Denmark, etc.), the southern EU countries (Spain, Italy, Greece, etc.) and the eastern EU countries (Poland, Bulgaria, Czech Republic, etc.).[9] We are not the first to note this difference in the relative impact of improvements in energy efficiency - both the Green Jobs Initiative[10] and the Energy Efficiency Industrial Forum[11] found similar differences when studying the impact of a number of renovation projects across the EU and the US. This runs parallel to the relative labour intensity of the economy, wage rates and current unemployment rates. This would imply that job creation is quite different in the developing EU economies.

No such differences between countries become apparent in fuel economy and electrification. If there is any difference at all, the model implies a lower effectiveness of fuel economy standards and electrification on job creation than gains in energy efficiency in other sectors. This is also reflected in lower and even negative impacts on GDP when moving towards less-polluting vehicles. The reason for these negative values is mainly explained through the interaction with government tax income.[12]

Figure 3.4 Relative impact of each policy sub-scenario on GHG emissions (in terms of the percentage of the final result) for the friendly 'modernisation' (left) and 'sustainability' (right) scenarios

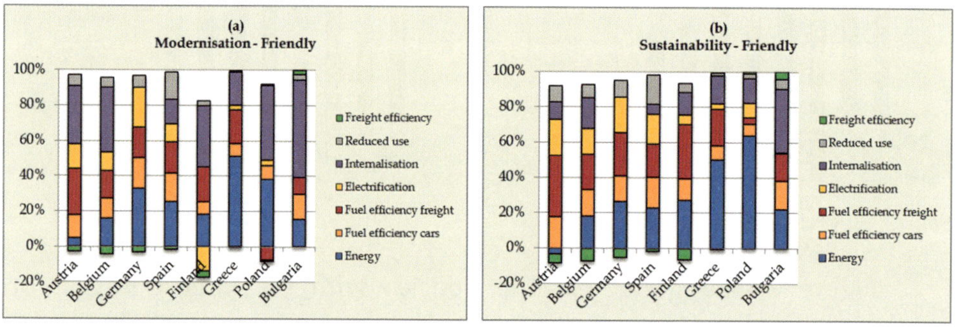

Source: Heyndrickx et al. (2013a).

The modelled fuel efficiency measures had only a limited positive impact on job creation. The influence of electrification on employment is negative, for a number of reasons.[13] First, electric vehicles require less in the way of maintenance services compared with the fixed cost of the car, and therefore have a dampening effect on service employment. Second, they reduce the variable cost of driving, but also the tax revenue from fuels. This is compensated by an increase of jobs

Job losses induced by labour-efficient technologies are compensated by employment gains in other sectors.

in the energy sector and car manufacturing. While some countries like Germany and the UK can potentially gain, the net effect is slightly negative or, in the best case, close to zero.

Figure 3.5 Total impact on employment (measured in million euros) in the top four 'winning sectors' and top four 'losing sectors' when moving towards electric mobility

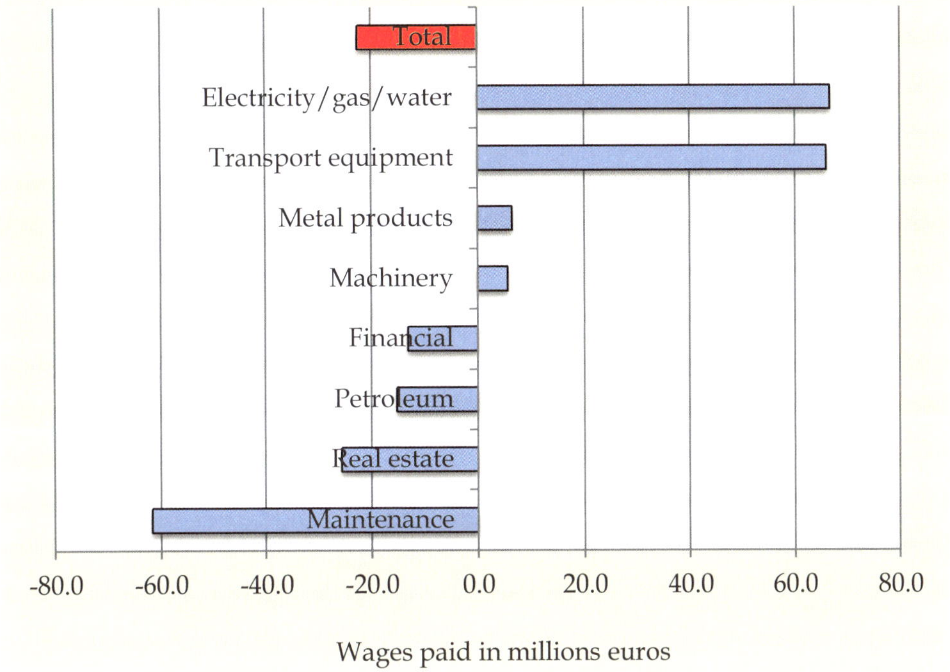

Source: Heyndrickx et al. (2013b).

The impact of electrification on employment is negative, but it contributes positively to the environment.

This does not mean that moving towards electric propulsion for vehicles is necessarily a bad policy. Figure 3.4 shows that increased fuel efficiency and electrification can contribute significantly to making transport more environmentally friendly, even when the net consumption of electrical energy increases. However, it entails a trade-off between the environmental and the job creation goals.

In contrast, behavioural changes and improvements in the administrative efficiency of transport are effective in creating new jobs. The administrative simplifications implied by e-Freight lead to job losses in auxiliary transport services – for this reason, transport operators are often reluctant to promote labour-efficient technologies – but these are compensated by gains in other sectors. This finding runs parallel to the conclusion of the draft impact assessment of the new European Single Sky initiative[14] for improvements in the auxiliary air transport sector. Further analysis of the cross-country differences showed that the relative size of the land and air transport sector (and water transport to a minor degree), the auxiliary transport sector and wholesale trade contributed to a more positive result in terms of job creation.[15] The size of the machinery and basic metal sectors contributed negatively. By far the largest impact was caused by the size of the land transport sector and the auxiliary transport sector. This is not that surprising, as it reflects the dependence of the economy on transport services. Our results imply that if the auxiliary transport sector is relatively large, so are the potential gains from administrative efficiency.

Measures to discourage private transport lead to a pickup in jobs for drivers and operators. We assume a relatively large shift towards public transit systems, which would reflect a behavioural change by consumers over the coming decades. This makes a notable difference to employment in transport services.

3.4 Policies aimed at energy efficiency, cycling and public transit are most likely to boost both employment and sustainability

The urban system provides an excellent case study for sustainable strategies and green job creation. Adaptive and better urban (transport) planning and the quest for innovative solutions could be a stimulus for green jobs. The size and growth of urban areas is an important aspect of the socio-ecological transition[16] and is a main driver for changes in the transport system. By 2050, urban regions will have absorbed 3 billion new dwellers. The growth of urban regions is strongest in the developing countries, but is also far from over in the most developed countries. By 2050, more than 85% of the European population will live in urban (or urbanised) regions.[17]

The form, and in particular the density, of urban regions plays a decisive role in transport energy requirements and hence in a move towards sustainability. For example, an analysis of Dutch CO_2 emissions by transport activity documented that average emissions were 47% lower in the high urban density class, compared with the low urban density class.[18] In the US, a combination of avoiding a further reduction of urban density and a 1% annual improvement in energy efficiency could reduce urban automobile emissions by as much as 18 GT[19] by 2054.[20] One way to reduce material and energy flows in the city would be to reduce car dependence and the material and energy requirements for buildings.[21] The rationale behind this is simple: suburban dwellers are much more dependent on automobiles.[22] It is therefore possible to argue that urban sprawl in Europe is detrimental to sustainable development and deserves more attention within the EU.[23]

Table 3.2 summarises a number of policies that are being implemented at the city level today and that may be drivers for a generally more sustainable transport system in Europe. For each policy, we assess its impact on seven important indicators: employment, size of city (sprawl), prices (transport and housing), pollution, traffic congestion and public finances. In the absence of hard quantitative evidence, we discuss the most likely direction of the effect of each policy on the chosen indicators.

When the private cost of transport does not reflect the total social (external) cost of transport, the city density will be lower than optimal, congestion higher and the total commuting distance longer. The link between environmental costs and excess private transport is self-evident. However, the costs of commuting go well beyond the purely economic one. Long commuting distance is associated with psychological and health-related illness[24] and higher separation rates.[25] Strategies to correct private incentives and achieve optimal city density, as well as to avoid excessive traffic congestion and pollution, are therefore of great importance.

To limit city expansion, cities have predominantly used restrictive strategies such as urban growth boundaries. These are effective in restricting the growth of the city to certain areas and preserving green areas to some extent, but impose costs on the city population in terms of higher housing prices.[26] Cost-benefit evaluations of urban growth boundaries in empirical situations are often negative, especially when development is easily relocated to uncontrolled regions and causes suburbanisation beyond the city borders.[27]

Table 3.2 City-level policy and estimated impacts on sprawl, price of housing and transport, pollution, congestion, municipal finances and employment

Policy	Urban sprawl	Housing prices	Transport costs	Pollution	Congestion	Public finances*	Employment
General energy efficiency standards	0	+	0	-	0	+	++
Fuel efficiency standards	≈	0	≈	-	+	-	+
Electrification of transport	≈	0	≈	-	+	-	≈
Low Emission Zones	≈	≈	+	-	-	+	≈
Road charging (tolls)	-	≈	+	-	--	+	-
Access restrictions for freight**	0	≈	+	≈	≈	0	-
Urban growth boundaries	--	++	0	≈	≈	-	-
Parking policy	0	≈	+	-	≈	+	≈
Pro-Cycling policies	0	0	0	-	-	+	+
Investments in public transport	+	≈	0	-	-	--	+
Promoting public transport	0	0	0	-	-	≈	+
Urban delivery centres	0	0	≈	≈	≈	-	≈
Dynamic transport management	0	0	-	≈	-	≈	0
Investments in road infrastructure	++	-	-	++	≈	--	+
Work-at-home incentives	+	-	-	≈	-	0	+

* A positive sign reflects an increase in public budget (public revenues).

** This entails any type of regulation that limits the access of vans and other freight transport for deliveries in the city centre. In many cities this confines deliveries to either night-time or business hours.

Notes: 0 = No discernible impact. ≈ = Questionable impact (either a positive or negative direction is possible). - = Reduction. -- = Strong reduction. + = Increase. ++ = Strong increase.

Source: Heyndrickx et al. (2013b, p. 45).

A form of road-charging provides incentives to alleviate congestion and increase the price of transport to better reflect the damage that transport imposes on the environment. In the long run, higher transport prices will increase urban density and house prices in the urban centres. Road-charging gives cities a flexible tool for redirecting traffic flows and provides cities with revenues that can be used for improving public transit or redistributed for other social needs. Furthermore, employment can be impacted positively when the revenue is recycled (partially) towards the reduction of labour taxes.[28]

Plans to introduce road-charging have generally been met with considerable public opposition. Nevertheless, the idea of access restrictions and charges is slowly working its way into people's minds. In the cities where road-charging, or a similar type of charge, has been introduced (London, Milan and Stockholm), public acceptance grew substantially after introduction.[29] In the case of London, earmarking the taxes from the road charge has substantially helped to gain public acceptance for the scheme. It also creates a direct link between the revenues collected from road charges (and thus from congestion) and investments in public roads and public transport. In general, public acceptance for establishing low emission zones (LEZs) is higher, due to the focus on environmental benefits and the lower reach of the policy. The main difference is that in LEZs, decreasing congestion is generally a secondary goal, while it is the primary objective in the case of road-charging. In their operation, however, LEZs are very similar to a road-charging system.

Road-charging zones or low emission zones would allow cities greater control over urban traffic.

Parking charges can be a potential second-best strategy for road-charging, especially when combined with advancements in parking technology to allow different rates to be charged for vehicles according to their arrival time and emission intensity.[30] However, parking charges that are too stringent may reduce the efficiency of the policy and lead to extra cruising, causing additional traffic congestion in the city.[31] The presence of private parking spots or parking at the workplace as an extra-legal benefit also reduces the effectiveness of this type of policy.

Road charging positively impacts employment by increasing the efficiency of commuting and generating revenue for public investment and tax cuts.

One of the more effective policies to combine sustainable development with growth is the promotion of cycling. Cycling is the fastest intra-urban transport mode and has strong health benefits. Commuting by bike is also associated with higher work productivity and fewer sick days.[32] Many cities have started subsidising bike programmes and improving the traffic infrastructure for cycling; Copenhagen is a forerunner in this aspect.

Large (public) transport infrastructure works are generally proposed as means to stimulate the labour market, as well as providing better accessibility. While in some cases new road capacity may be necessary, this should be weighed against its negative impact on sustainability. Investments in road infrastructure are costly to the public budget, increase urban sprawl,[33] the private use of cars and traffic pollution, and only have a transient effect on congestion, due to induced travel demand effects.[34] Investments in public transit may stimulate public transport use, but should be carefully planned and executed, and focused on demand. Dynamic transport management is an efficient way to improve traffic flows without creating new and costly infrastructure.[35] However, it is unable to create any structural change to the urban environment.

Promotion of public transit is a soft measure that has been shown to stimulate the use of public transit to some degree. Publicly funded training programmes may help to familiarise new users with public transit, but may not lead to any structural change towards public transit use. Other measures to promote public transport, such as establishing a unified ticketing system for public transit or improving and visualising transport schedules, are more likely to lead to long-term results. For example, the simplification of ticketing through the introduction of the Oyster card system in London has proved a very effective way to reduce waiting lines and the cost of taking public transit.[36]

Teleworking is often cited as a potential 'cure' for excess commuting. Some experts are especially positive about this sort of incentive, pointing out that the reduced demand for office space would lead to lower energy consumption and lower land use in the city.[37] The positive impact of the scheme is reduced when a large proportion of commuters are already taking public transit.[38] Furthermore, teleworking can have negative consequences. The specific 'Dutch' practice of working at home during the morning and leaving for work later can balance traffic flows more evenly during the morning, but it may also affect the work-life balance and lead to congestion during evening hours.[39] Hyok-Joo Rhee finds that work-at-home incentives can lead to more urban sprawl.[40] Finally, the presence of rebound effects in energy use at home and the latent demand of non-teleworkers make it questionable whether teleworking can really have any significant results on pollution.

Freight transport within and between cities is a large consumer of energy, as well as a cause of congestion at the city level. Traditionally, there has not been so much attention on urban freight in transport planning; however, access of goods to business districts is an important part of the demand for travel in any city. Freight vehicles typically represent 15% of total traffic flow in urban areas, but when they park to make collections or deliveries outside designated parking spaces they can reduce road capacity and contribute to congestion.[41] One idea, which has been popular in the last decade, is to increase the bundling of urban freight by creating urban consolidation centres (UCCs).[42] The idea is that a central, publicly operated company collects urban freight outside the city centre. In a second stage, the packages can be transported by low-emission vehicles or by bike. Theoretically, this can increase bundling of freight and draw some of the heavy goods transport out of the city. This may also have some job effects, through employment connected to the centres. Many cities, particularly in Italy, have experimented with UCCs. The Italian experience reveals rather mixed results, as most of the centres were costly to public finances and had too little impact on city traffic to be effective.[43]

Access restrictions for freight transport reduce the efficiency of deliveries within the city and will generally have an economic cost and reduce employment in the distribution sector. Imposed delivery windows in cities restrict freight to either daytime (London) or night-time (Paris) deliveries. These reflect city-level preferences for congestion avoidance during the day or noise avoidance at night for urban freight. Therefore, the impact on either congestion or noise avoidance is somewhat ambivalent and depends upon the type of scheme imposed.

3.5 Behavioural policy is better suited to meet employment targets

Sustainable transport policies can be classified into two broad groups: 1) policies aimed at using energy more efficiently in transport; and 2) policies oriented towards behavioural change. A combination of these policies reduces structural emissions of greenhouse gases and related pollutants by 1%-8% by 2030, compared with the status quo. The proposed 'sustainability' scenario reduces household emissions (private transport) by over 50% and total transport emissions (including freight) by over 30%; this is in line with the Roadmap 2050 goals for transport emissions in 2030.[44] All eight countries analysed in our study showed net job creation under both the 'modernisation' scenario (an additional 200,000 jobs) and the 'sustainability' scenario (an additional 400,000 jobs). Extrapolated to the whole of Europe, this reflects a gain of between 500,000 and 1 million jobs, or about half of the current employment in car manufacturing. The impact of each policy is similar under both the friendly and tough background scenarios, even though the overall impact on the EU economy of these two background scenarios differs greatly.

The impact of teleworking on pollution is ambivalent at best.

When analysing each policy option, we find that no single transport policy could match the effectiveness of a general improvement in energy efficiency standards while at the same time stimulating the labour market. For instance, fuel efficiency standards and the introduction of electric vehicles lead to environmental benefits but have only modest impacts on job creation. In the case of electric vehicles, the impact on employment may even be negative for many countries.

Policies oriented towards behavioural changes, such as changing the tax base to discourage private motor vehicle use or improvements in transport efficiency, lead to more positive labour market outcomes but have less impact on pollution and emissions. Improving the efficiency of transport even has a noticeable positive impact on transport demand, which may increase emissions to some degree. However, this only partially reduces the environmental benefits of improved fuel efficiency. Investments in public infrastructure, increased transport efficiency and improvements in energy efficiency have the largest impact on employment per million euros spent, especially in eastern and southern European countries. A reduction of private car use leads to slightly positive labour market outcomes through increased employment in public transport.

Overall, in moving towards a more sustainable economy, the relative importance of the transportation manufacturing sector in the EU diminishes in favour of transport services. Our society, as it becomes more environmentally conscious, has less need for privately owned vehicles but more need for transport and service operators. Increased efficiency (such as the introduction of measures to reduce the administrative burden in transport) leads to job losses in sectors providing auxiliary services to transport, but at the same time benefits employment in other sectors.

Bibliography

Anas, A. and H.-J. Rhee (2006), "Curbing excess sprawl with congestion tolls and urban boundaries", *Regional Science and Urban Economics*, Vol. 36, No. 4, pp. 510-541.

Arnott, R. and E. Inci (2010), "The stability of downtown parking and traffic congestion", *Journal of Urban Economics*, Vol. 68, No. 3, pp. 260-276.

Baum-Snow, N. (2007), "Did Highways Cause Suburbanization?", *The Quarterly Journal of Economics*, Vol. 122, No. 2, pp. 775-805.

Beblavý, M, I. Maselli and M. Veselková (2014), *Let's Get to Work! The Future of Labour in Europe, Vol. 1*, CEPS Paperback, Brussels.

Browne, M., A. Woodburn and J. Allen (2007), "The potential for urban consolidation centers", *European Transport/Trasporti Europei*, No. 35, pp. 46-63.

Calthrop, E. and S. Proost (2000), "Regulating urban parking space: the choice between meter fees and time restrictions", Energy, Transport and Environment Working Papers Series, KU Leuven.

Danielis, R., L. Rotaris and E. Marcucci (2010), "Urban freight policies and distribution channels", *European Transport/Trasporti Europei*, No. 46, pp. 114-146.

Energy Efficiency Industrial Forum (2012), *How Many Jobs? A Survey of the Employment Effects of Investment in Energy Efficiency of Buildings*, May.

European Commission (2011), Roadmap for moving to a competitive low-carbon economy in 2050, Communication from the Commission to the European Parliament, the Council, The European Economic and Social Committee and the Committee of the Regions, Brussels, 8 March.

_____ (2012a), *EU Transport in Figures 2012 – Statistical Pocketbook*, Directorate General for Mobility and Transport, European Commission, Brussels.

_____ (2012b), *Study on Urban Freight Transport*, final report by MDS Transmodal Ltd. and CTL, Directorate General for Mobility and Transport, European Commission, Brussels.

_____ (2013), Draft impact assessment on Single European Sky – SES2+, COM(2013) 410 final and SWD(2013) 206 final, Brussels.

Fischer-Kowalski, M., W. Haas, D. Wiedenhofer, U. Weisz, I. Pallua, N. Possaner, A. Behrens, G. Serio, M. Alessi and E. Weis (2012), "Socio-ecological transitions: definition, dynamics and related global scenarios", NEUJOBS Deliverable D1.1, NEUJOBS Project (www.neujobs.eu).

Fuhr, J. and S. Pociask (2011), "Broadband and Telecommuting: Helping the U.S. Environment and the Economy", *Low Carbon Economy*, Vol. 2, No. 1.

Grazi, F., J. van den Bergh and J. van Ommeren (2008), "An empirical analysis of urban form transport and global warming", *The Energy Journal*, Vol. 29, pp. 97-122.

Heyndrickx, C., O. Ivanova, A. Van Steenbergen, F. Witlox and B. Hamaide (2009), "Development of a spatio-ecological-economic model for Belgium", Final report ISEEM project (www.tmleuven.be/project/iseem/Final%20report%2020090302.pdf).

Heyndrickx, C., O. Purwanto and R. Frederix (2013a), "Effects of the main global scenarios on the transport sector", NEUJOBS Deliverable D15.2, NEUJOBS Project (www.neujobs.eu).

Heyndrickx, C., O. Purwanto and R. Frederix (2013b), "Sustainable urban transport strategies and job creation", NEUJOBS Deliverable D15.3, NEUJOBS Project (www.neujobs.eu).

ILO (2012), *Working towards sustainable development - Opportunities for decent work and social inclusion in a green economy*, Geneva: International Labour Office.

Jun, M.-J. (2004), "The Effects of Portland's Urban Growth Boundary on Urban Development Patterns and Commuting", *Urban Studies*, Vol. 41, No. 7, pp. 1333–1348.

Litman, T. (2013), *Generated Traffic and Induced Travel: Implications for Transport Planning*, Victoria, BC: Victoria Transport Policy Institute.

Macharis, C., A. De Witte, F. Van Malderen and T. van Lier (2011), "Telework. Studie betreffende de milieu-, de mobiliteits- en de socio-economische impact van het telewerken in grote bedrijven in het Brussels Hoofdstedelijk Gewest" [Telework. Study of the environmental, mobility, and socio-economic impact of telework in large companies in the Brussels Capital Region], study for the Brussels Institute for the Environment (BIM).

Marshall, J.D. (2008), "Energy-efficient urban form", *Environmental Science and Technology*, Vol. 42, pp. 3133-3137.

Novaco, R.W. and O. Gonzalez (2009), "Commuting and well-being", in Y. Amichai-Hamburger (ed.), *Technology and Well-being*, Cambridge: Cambridge University Press, pp. 174-205.

Piorr, A., J. Ravetz and I. Tosics (2011), *Peri-urbanisation in Europe: Towards European Policies to Sustain Urban Rural Futures*, Copenhagen: University of Copenhagen/Academic Books Life Sciences.

Rabl, A. and A. de Nazelle (2012), "Benefits of shift from car to active transport", *Transport Policy*, Vol. 19, No, 1, pp. 121–131.

Rhee, H.-J. (2009), "Telecommuting and urban sprawl", *Transportation Research Part D*, Vol. 14, pp. 453-460.

Rietveld, P. (2011), "Telework and the transition to lower energy use in transport: On the relevance of rebound effects", *Environmental Innovation and Societal Transitions*, Vol. 1, pp. 146-151.

Sandow, E. (2013), "Till work do us part: the social fallacy of long-distance commuting", *Urban Studies*, Vol. 51, No. 3, pp. 526-543.

Santos, G. (2008), "The London experience", in E. Verhoef et al. (eds), *Pricing in Road Transport: A Multi-Disciplinary Perspective*, Cheltenham: Edward Elgar, pp. 273-292.

Schoemaker, J., J. Allen, M. Huschebek and J. Monigl (2006), *Quantification of Urban Freight Effects*, Best Urban Freight Solutions (BESTUFS) Project.

Steininger, K.W., B. Friedl and B. Gebetsroither (2007), "Sustainability impacts of car road pricing: A computable general equilibrium analysis for Austria", *Ecological Economics*, Vol. 63, No. 1, pp. 59-69.

United Nations (2012), *World Urbanization Prospects: The 2011 Revision*, New York: United Nations Population Division.

Van Dender, K. and P. Crist (2011), "What Does Improved Fuel Economy Cost Consumers and What Does It cost Taxpayers? Some Illustrations", International Transport Forum Discussion Papers No. 2011/16, OECD/ITF Joint Transport Research Centre, Paris.

Van de Weghe, J. and C. Kennedy (2007), "A Spatial Analysis of Residential Greenhouse Gas Emissions in the Toronto Census Metropolitan Area", *Journal of Industrial Ecology*, Vol. 11, pp. 133-144.

Wiedenhofer, D., M. Lenzen and J.K. Steinberger (2013), "Energy requirements of consumption: Urban form, climatic and socio-economic factors, rebounds and their policy implications", *Energy Policy*, Vol. 63, pp. 696-707.

Notes

1 See www.eea.europa.eu/data-and-maps/indicators/final-energy-consumption-by-sector-5/assessment.

2 Extracted from Eurostat (based on EEA data) update 11 June 2014.

3 Bunker fuels are a type of crude oil that is often used by vessels (maritime transport).

4 See http://ec.europa.eu/clima/policies/2030/index_en.htm - climate policies for 2030. The text states a 43% reduction in ETS sectors and a 30% reduction in non-ETS sectors compared to 2005. Note that the transport sector is not a part of the EU ETS sectors and transport emissions in 2010 are only 1% higher than in 2005.

5 Fischer-Tropsch fuels refer to the process developed by Hans Fischer and Franz Tropsch that is used to convert carbon monoxide and hydrogen into hydrocarbons. It is commercially used to produce synthetic oils out of coal, natural gas and biomass.

6 We base our results on a full-scale general equilibrium model called European Model for the Assessment of Income Distribution and Inequality Effects of Economic Policies (EDIP) (Heyndrickx et al., 2007). An analysis of the impact of the proposed transport policies was performed in two parts. The first part was a top-down analysis using the NEUJOBS scenarios defined above and applied to eight European countries (Austria, Belgium, Bulgaria, Finland, Greece, Germany, Poland and Spain), which are presented in Heyndrickx et al. (2013a). The second part of the analysis is presented as a relative comparison of the effective contribution of small shocks in transport policy on larger set of European countries. Results from EDIP were thoroughly analysed and compared in an extensive literature review of the job market effects of sustainable transport strategies in Heyndrickx et al. (2013b). Then, country- and policy-specific multipliers were calculated to measure the relative impact of different policies on job creation (in FTE per million euros) and GDP.

7 The reference scenario is defined as the sum of the background ('no policy') and the 'status quo' scenario.

8 We show only the friendly scenario, as the conclusions from the tough scenario are similar. See Heyndrickx et al. (2013a) for other indicators and a more detailed analysis of the results.

9 Heyndrickx et al. (2013b).

10 ILO (2012).

11 Energy Efficiency Industrial Forum (2012).

12 See also Van Dender and Crist (2011).

[13] See Heyndrickx et al. (2013b).

[14] European Commission (2013).

[15] Heyndrickx et al. (2013b).

[16] Fischer-Kowalski et al. (2012).

[17] United Nations (2012).

[18] Grazi et al. (2008).

[19] GigaTonnes

[20] Marshall (2008).

[21] Wiedenhofer et al. (2013).

[22] Van de Weghe and Kennedy (2007).

[23] Piorr et al. (2011).

[24] Novaco and Gonzalez (2009).

[25] Sandow (2013).

[26] Anas and Rhee (2006).

[27] Jun (2004).

[28] See Steininger et al. (2007); Heyndrickx et al. (2009).

[29] Nevertheless, in neither of these cases was the incumbent mayor authorising the scheme voted back into office after elections.

[30] Calthrop and Proost (2000).

[31] Arnott and Inci (2010).

[32] Rabl and de Nazelle (2012).

[33] Baum-Snow (2007).

[34] For example, see Litman (2013).

[35] Schoemaker et al. (2006).

[36] Santos (2008).

[37] Fuhr and Pociask (2011).

[38] Macharis et al. (2011).

[39] Rietveld (2011). A discussion on innovative practices at the workplace can be found in the first NEUJOBS book: *Let's Get to Work! The Future of Labour in Europe, Vol. 1.*

[40] Rhee (2009).

[41] DG MOVE (2012b).

[42] Browne et al. (2007).

[43] Danielis et al. (2010).

[44] The range of the overall reduction in emissions per capita under the sustainability scenario.

4. DEMAND AND SUPPLY OF LABOUR IN THE HOUSING SECTOR

*KEES DOL, JOHN DOLING, MARJA ELSINGA, NICHOLAS HORSEWOOD, FRITS MEIJER AND HENK VISSCHER**

The housing sector is large and significant in all aspects of human life, making the task of the policy-maker especially complex. Homes constitute the largest single land use in the 'built environment', they are generally the largest single item of expenditure in household budgets and the largest form of household wealth, and they are instrumental in our social networks and our psychological wellbeing. The scale and extent of the connections have complex impacts on, and are impacted by, both the demand for and supply of labour and the socio-ecological transition. The ageing of European populations, for example, will continue to influence the demand for housing in terms of location, size and services, which in turn will create jobs in construction, raw material acquisition and delivery, infrastructure (ranging from roads to medical services) and transaction activities (such as legal services, new furniture and fittings). The link between the geographical location of the family residence and of the workplace will be altered by further developments of ICT and home working, influencing the impact of housing sectors on the direct supply of labour.

Of the many possible linkages and considerations for policy-makers in relation to the housing sector, this chapter focuses on three specific aspects. Section 4.1 examines the likely impact of energy renovation of the

* Kees Dol, Marja Elsinga, Frits Meijer and Henk Visscher: Technische Universiteit Delft; John Doling and Nicholas Horsewood: University of Birmingham.

housing stock on jobs in the construction industry. Section 4.2 looks at possible developments in direct employment in mortgage markets. Section 4.3 examines how home ownership shapes the supply of labour. The final section offers policy recommendations.

4.1 Energy renovation is crucial to achieve energy-efficiency targets

The building stock is important to energy-efficiency targets in Europe, being responsible for some 40% of overall energy usage and 36% of CO_2 emissions across the region.[1] There are currently around 230 million dwellings in the EU and, measured in floor space, they account for 75% of the total building stock. In any one year, new house building typically adds no more than 1% to the existing stock. One consequence of this is that perhaps as much as 75% of the housing stock that will be in use in 2050 has already been built, and was built at a time when energy conservation was not an important objective. Therefore, it is the existing buildings, and not new buildings, that present the major challenge to achieving the energy-saving goals. The renovations necessary to achieve energy-efficiency goals covering a range of targets - including greenhouse gas emissions, renewable energy and energy consumption - can lead to job creation in the housing sector. For every €1 million invested in upgrading the energy efficiency of the existing building stock, as many as 17 new direct jobs could be generated.[2]

The building stock is responsible for some 40% of overall energy usage and 36% of CO_2 emissions

While there is general agreement that progress towards realising EU and member state energy-saving targets has been slower than was expected and hoped for, there is actually a lack of unambiguous data on almost all relevant parameters - about the physical characteristics of the European housing stock, the renovation rate, the extent of the measures being undertaken, the investment that has been made, the results of this investment in terms of energy efficiency and the impact on employment.

Across the member states, there are many programmes of improvement and renovation to bring existing dwellings up to acceptable standards of energy efficiency. Estimates of the exact number of renovations vary, but it seems likely that they are being applied to

The renovation rate would have to triple to achieve set energy-efficiency goals.

approximately 1% of the stock per year. In order to realise the energy goals that have been set, the renovation rate must be tripled, while the number and type of renovation measures should also be increased significantly.

There are several reasons why the renovations expected (and needed) will most likely not materialise. First, there is evidence of market failures, including a poor reflection of environmental and social costs in energy market prices, as well as poor incentive structures and a general lack of adequate training and knowledge of many actors in the building sector. Second, there are financial barriers to the renovation of the housing stock. Given the high level of initial costs, housing investments must provide returns over a long period of time to be financially viable. Equally, the lack of awareness among lenders of the benefits of housing renovation limits households' access to credit. Third, the regulatory frameworks in many member states are often inadequate to achieve the energy targets. In many countries, there is a lack of administrative capacity to develop effective energy-efficiency legislation, as well as a lack of enforcement.

Looking to the future, our investigations indicate that the ageing of European populations may depress the demand for energy renovation, which is not necessarily intuitive as the elderly tend to feel the cold and suffer ill health through poor-quality housing. Many studies find that older people - perhaps as a result of low income, but also perhaps due to having more limited time horizons than younger people - may be less responsive to the poor condition of their housing and more likely to make a calculation that investments will not generate a return for them.[3]

A comprehensive review of national and EU-wide studies on energy renovation conducted by Meijer et al. offers insights into the number of jobs that may be created and the skills that will be demanded.[4] Looking to 2020, estimates of the total number of jobs created by energy renovations in the housing stock vary from 0.28 million to 1.40 million. In part, the variation reflects the level of activity, with a continuation of the current rate of energy renovation being likely to create a number of jobs at the lower end of the range of the estimates. On average, 12 to 17 new jobs can be created per €1 million invested. Even at the bottom end of this range, however, job creation could be considered the main motivation for investing in energy efficiency, with energy saving itself being an important corollary effect. Additional benefits would be a reduction in spending on government subsidies for presently unemployed workers, and improved health of citizens because of the reduction in air pollution and a better indoor climate, both of which would mean fewer hospitalisations and improved worker productivity.

The jobs themselves would include those in industries that produce materials, components and products needed to improve the energy performance of buildings, those in the construction sector fitting new materials and products, energy auditors and certifiers, and inspectors of heating and air-conditioning services, for example. There could be others, such as those supplying financial packages enabling investments to be made. Against this, jobs could be lost in the energy sector because of the relative reduction in energy consumption, compared to what it would have been.

With respect to the construction industry, there appears generally to be a shortage of skills, which has both qualitative and quantitative aspects. Qualitative skills mismatches are of particular importance: the introduction of advanced green technologies and practices makes previously demanded skill sets obsolete. Many workers will therefore have to undergo training to upgrade their skills. For example, renovation work is relatively labour-intensive and more demanding in terms of craftsmanship than new construction. As a result, the skills of construction workers without previous experience in renovation work will have to be upgraded. This applies not only to manual operatives working on-site, but also to professional staff such as architects and engineers. There will also be a need for people to carry out 'new' jobs, such as energy-efficiency analysts or energy auditors.

4.2 Employment in mortgage markets in 2025 will be the same as or lower than in 2007

The importance of the housing market for the labour market goes beyond the construction/renovation sector. Given the increasing weight of the financial sector in advanced economies, especially up to 2007, employment in mortgage markets also needs to be considered for completeness. Moreover, the financial crisis demonstrated that mortgage markets can undermine economies.

Although existing statistical sources do not allow the identification of the precise number and nature of the jobs generated by mortgage activities, it is clear that not only are the numbers large, but they are also skewed towards workers with higher levels of education and training and earning higher wages. For these reasons, the future of mortgage markets and employment within them, particularly in the context of the post-2007 reductions in the size of mortgage markets in most of the EU, are important.

Analysis of the sector is limited not only by the limitations of existing statistical sources, but also by the paucity of studies of mortgage markets, and especially of the links between mortgage market activity and size on the one hand, and jobs on the other. Nevertheless, an examination of existing written sources, as well as interviews conducted with key informants in three countries with very distinctive mortgage markets (the Netherlands, Poland and the UK), provide insights into the key future developments in employment supported by mortgage market activity.[5]

On the face of it, there is considerable capacity for further growth of mortgage activity, and with it employment. Across Europe, mortgage debt in the mid-2000s was equivalent to about 50% of total GDP, and in some countries it was as high as 100%. Whereas the latter figure may not be achievable in all countries, in many there may nevertheless be great growth potential. However, the willingness of households to take on such large debt has been affected by the financial crisis, at least in the short term.

There is the general recognition that a high debt-to-income ratio is not sustainable in the long run and could have serious macroeconomic implications when faced by an adverse shock. Hence, it should not be assumed that levels of mortgage activity and employment will automatically grow to pre-crisis levels. Rather, the evidence from our investigations is that the future will be determined by a set of drivers, the first of which is the route out of the current economic crisis. Mortgage market activity in member states since 2007 has broadly matched changes in GDP; in other words, activity has declined where GDP has declined, and increased where GDP has increased. A key to the future, then, is how quickly and in what ways the present crisis is resolved. Given the economic turmoil in the eurozone, it seems unlikely that this will happen quickly; instead, a return to what might be called 'normal' market conditions and market growth - and normal levels of employment - might perhaps be delayed until the end of the current decade.

The issue of what is meant by 'normal' and whether mortgage markets - and more generally, financial markets - will return to anything like their former nature is unknown. One element of this lies in the development of new regulatory regimes being drawn up by member states, the EU and international authorities. Although much is yet to be agreed on and put in place, it is difficult to conclude anything other than that financial institutions will face a greater degree of regulation in future, with greater capital and liquidity requirements and less exposure to risk. Broadly, the emphasis of mortgage markets is being switched from growth in new lending towards stability and safety.

For those involved in providing mortgages, this will mean more information, more verification and more monitoring, and all with greater responsibility placed on lenders to assure the accuracy of the evaluations. This suggests that more labour input will be required per unit of mortgage activity. It also seems likely that lending institutions will develop new operational models that might imply, for example, more or less use of outsourcing through intermediaries. In turn, this might lead to different configurations of skills. But while the overall increase in labour input will enhance total employment for a given level of lending activity, it will also increase costs which, passed onto customers, could lead to an overall reduction in demand. And so, on balance, new regulation seems likely to increase costs, but will not necessarily increase the numbers employed in mortgage industries significantly. It may be expected that these effects will be greater in those countries where regulation has previously been the loosest, for example in the liberal UK market as opposed to the more regulated German one.

A further set of drivers relates to the development of new products serving different household needs. A large proportion of the personal net wealth of European households is held in the form of housing equity, net of mortgage debt. In certain member states, there is evidence that households previously accessed this net housing wealth to fund consumer expenditure.

In a context in which governments are presented with challenges of meeting the costs of established welfare models and entitlements – challenges that are exacerbated by a combination of the present crisis and demographic ageing – one potential approach is to encourage households to draw on their own resources embedded in mass home ownership. In this way, a part of tax-based state expenditure may be replaced by schemes in which European households take greater responsibility for the costs of meeting their needs in later life. In doing so, there is the potential to extend what, in most European countries, has been an emphasis on forward mortgages that enable households to invest to an associated emphasis on reverse mortgages that allow households to dis-invest. The theoretical potential for the expansion of mortgage business, and therefore of employment, is considerable.

Another direction of expansion for housing finance markets is supporting energy-reduction activity, i.e. expanding the opportunities for households to participate by taking loans against the collateral of their homes. As this is additional business rather than a diversion from lending to purchase housing (or indeed, lending to extract equity), it could mean an expansion of overall lending activity.

Set against these possibilities for employment growth are productivity gains. In recent years, increasing use of the internet and ICT has reduced the number of employees needed to process each unit of mortgage activity. The extent of such developments clearly varies across the member states, but with continuing restrictions on the amount of lending, many lenders are trying to reduce costs further, and in so far as such systems continue to be developed, they will continue to depress the workforce across all European mortgage markets. Furthermore, ICT developments could lead to changes in the patterns of skills required in the industry, and perhaps to a reduction in skills, by replacing the discretion previously vested in frontline staff with more automated and centralised monitoring and decision systems. This in turn could lead to further job and remuneration polarisation within the industry, with an increasing divide between highly skilled and highly remunerated central office staff and lesser skilled, more modestly remunerated staff interacting with the public.

Increasing use of IT will reduce employment in mortgage markets and exacerbate job polarisation.

The effect of these drivers in the member states, each of which has a different starting point, will be different. For example, based on six scenarios for the UK, with different levels of future mortgage activity, productivity increases and impacts of regulation, projections by Doling indicate that only in the case of the market quickly recovering to its 2007 level and regulation imposing significant additional labour inputs would overall employment be likely to exceed its 2007 peak.[6] A more general rule-of-thumb estimate is that in 2025, activity in the mortgage market in each member state will be at a similar level to 2007, adjusted by the changes in the 2007-2010 period. Broadly speaking, activity, and therefore employment, could be at the same or a lower level compared to 2007 in the Anglo-Saxon and Mediterranean countries (and also perhaps the Netherlands), and perhaps higher in Scandinavian and the northern mainland countries, with a mixed picture across the eastern countries.

4.3 Home ownership influences small business formation, unemployment and retirement

A holistic approach to an analysis of the impact of the housing sector on the labour market requires a discussion of how home ownership influences the demand and the supply of labour. Over the decade leading up to 2007, the general pattern across the EU was one of home ownership sectors increasing in size, to the point at which about two-thirds of Europeans had become homeowners. The increases were generally supported by public policies that, for example, gave tax subsidies against interest payments and encouraged the sale of social housing to individual owners. The trends were also associated with expanding mortgage markets and increasing house prices. For households, this contributed to increasing levels of indebtedness – with housing costs, including loan repayments, frequently being the largest single item in the household budget – as well as wealth portfolios dominated by housing equity.

Our investigations point to two important general issues. The first is whether home ownership will continue to grow, or if it will in fact decline. A trend-based projection for the UK, for example, suggests a 10 percentage-point reduction by 2020.[7] EU-wide, the impact of demographic ageing, international migration, insecure labour markets, fiscal pressures on governments leading to the withdrawal of tax breaks for homeowners, and depressed mortgage markets could all combine to result in decreasing home ownership.

Second, as household finance correlates with home ownership, it influences the ability and willingness of European households to participate in labour markets. In this respect, the pattern of constraints and opportunities facing homeowners places them in a different position from those who rent their homes. There are many dimensions to this tenure divide, of which we considered three: small business formation, unemployment and retirement.

i) Small business formation

The European Commission has acknowledged entrepreneurship as an economic driver and actively supports small and medium-sized enterprises. But a persistent problem is that while many Europeans express an interest in doing so, in practice relatively few actually start a business, with one of the major constraints being access to finance. Here, it might be expected that housing equity would provide collateral, thus overcoming credit restrictions set by formal financial institutions. In this respect, having a house, whether owned outright or with a small outstanding mortgage debt, may be important.

However, Horsewood and Dol argue that the relationship between home ownership and small business formation is more complex.[8] While there is evidence that funds to support entrepreneurial initiatives may come from housing markets, via homeowners increasing the size of their mortgages, a statistically stronger effect is that high returns from home ownership appear to discourage households from starting a new business. Policies encouraging people to become homeowners and that lead to rises in house prices may have the effect of diverting enterprise and funds away from industry and instead encouraging speculation in the housing market. Furthermore, high levels of mortgage indebtedness also appear to discourage new business formation. This effect is not completely clear, since increases in loans may reflect at least some households taking on a mortgage, or increasing their current one, in order to finance their business objectives, but it could also be that high leverage in the housing market reduces the ability of people to borrow additional money to support those objectives. To sum up, employment should increase in those countries where home ownership fuels growth in small business formation, but the loss of employment in larger industries needs to be taken into consideration. The net effect will be positive, especially in the more dynamic economies.

High house prices divert funds away from industry and encourage speculation in the housing market.

ii) Unemployment

A widely held, but also widely contested view is that labour mobility is lower for homeowners than for renters, because homeowners' higher transaction costs lead to a disincentive to relocate to areas where jobs are more abundant. As a consequence, the housing market could be responsible for a mismatch between vacancies and the unemployed within a country, and also across nations. This mismatch could therefore be larger in countries with higher rates of home ownership.

The findings of Horsewood and Dol indicate that, although there is some evidence that an economy with a high proportion of homeowners will have a higher unemployment rate, the main influence of the housing market appears to be through the stock of outstanding mortgages.[9] It appears that when families take on large mortgages to finance dwellings, they are less mobile and the locations of their employment opportunities are effectively restricted. While this may not be a problem when adults are in continuous employment, difficulties may arise when a household needs to relocate for employment reasons. In effect, homeowners with mortgages may be less able to respond to changing circumstances. Thus, countries where home ownership (with a mortgage) is the dominant form of tenure appear to experience higher unemployment for a given demand shock.

Insofar as this is the case, it is an effect that may be modified by future trends in 'remote working'. The development of ICT, for example through use of the internet, has broken the previous relationship for many organisations and workers between home and work. Much productive activity, especially in the service industries, is now undertaken at the home of the worker, so that daily travel to the employer's premises is no longer necessary. Clearly, the greater the extent of such developments in technology and work practices, the less the location of the home will impact on the ability of the worker to get a job.

Development of ICT will break the relationship between home and work.

iii) Retirement

Although all countries have formal retirement ages at which entitlement to pensions can be taken up, in reality approximately half of European workers retire either early (i.e. before the formal retirement age) or late (after the formal retirement age), although with a marked skew towards early retirement. In recent years, governments have tried to reverse this trend and prolong working life by increasing the formal retirement age and creating both disincentives for early retirement and incentives for later retirement.

The housing circumstances of workers appear to impact on their ability to act independently of government objectives. Dol and Horsewood show that compared with households who rent or own with an outstanding housing loan, those who own their home outright are more likely to retire early.[10] A credible explanation is that those who own their own homes can effectively live rent-free and thus get by on a lower income, as well as sometimes having the opportunity to release equity - perhaps by moving down market - to create an income. Households with outstanding housing loans, in contrast, need a higher income in order to maintain repayments.

Those who own their home outright are more likely to retire early.

Consistent with this, labour market participation rates for 55-59 year olds and for 65-70 year olds are highest in those countries where there has been a high growth of mortgage debt. It is not clear from the analysis whether mortgage debt ties people into labour market participation, or whether access to mortgage finance is predicated on a decision to retire late anyway. Nevertheless, it leads to the conclusion that the objective of increasing labour supply by extending working life is dependent in part on developments in mortgage markets.

4.4 The complexity of the relationships between the housing sector and labour markets poses difficult policy challenges

i) Energy renovation

Overall, there seems to be agreement that progress in realising energy-efficiency goals set by the EU and its member states is lagging behind expectations. Policy-makers should act to ensure that this progress improves in the coming years. This raises questions over the desirability of energy-renovation targets themselves, but wider economic considerations are also important. Given the present economic conditions of high unemployment and low (even negative) GDP growth, energy-renovation measures offer a relatively low-cost way of expanding the demand for labour. While directly contributing to higher employment and lower social security expenditures, other potential economic benefits from energy-conservation measures include improved health (and lower healthcare expenditures) and improved productivity.

In order to achieve such goals, policy-makers will need to recognise and overcome the barriers to the expansion of energy renovation activity. Important here is the fact that expansion will require increased levels of investment, which will in turn require consideration of the balance between public and private investment. Insofar as investment will depend on the financial capacity of private owners, access to appropriate forms of loan financing will need to be developed. One way in which this could be achieved is through using housing finance markets, which would effectively allow owners to use existing equity in housing either directly or as collateral. This will require consideration not only of the supply of finance, therefore including the role of financial institutions, but also the demand from households. Here, the position of the growing number of older home-owning households is particularly important. As older people may be less willing to invest when the pay-back period is long, it may be appropriate for policies to emphasise the fact that, in addition to reductions in energy bills, energy-saving measures tend to enhance the comfort of the living environment.

There should also be an assessment of the existing ability of the public sector to draw up adequate legislation, codes and procedures, including regulation and stricter enforcement. Additionally, it is important to recognise that any increase in the amount of energy-renovation activity will, in many countries, come up against skills shortages. In some cases, these will arise because existing workers will need to enhance their skills to meet the new challenges imposed by energy renovation technologies, but new skill sets will also be needed to enable the undertaking of different jobs.

ii) Mortgage markets

In thinking about mortgage markets, macroeconomic outcomes - such as the contribution of housing finance to finance sectors in general - as well as the desirable levels of household debt need to be taken into account. Further, there are considerations about meeting the needs of those who want to purchase their homes. As these considerations affect the size of the mortgage sectors (as defined by their levels of new lending and outstanding loans), they also affect the number and type of jobs. It seems likely that the sectors will continue to be important in requiring highly skilled and highly paid workers.

However, the considerations of the extent to which housing equity should be utilised in order to fund household consumption and investment are much more complex. The large amount of housing equity - held in particular by older households, many of whom have paid off forward mortgages - could be utilised in order to meet important EU and member state agendas. Housing equity could, for example, provide the foundation for loans to enable a higher level of energy-renovation activity. Furthermore, it could contribute to the challenge of the fiscal requirements of meeting present social provision entitlements (on pensions and long-term care, for example) as these increase with the growing number of older people.

Housing equity could serve as collateral for loans to enable a higher level of energy-renovation activity.

Such developments would require consideration of whether subsidies and regulations that apply to established forward mortgage systems are appropriate for reverse mortgages or other types of lending based on housing. For example, should tax relief on interest payments also apply to energy-renovation loans? Further, in some countries where reverse mortgages are currently not allowed, legal frameworks would need to be amended, and other barriers overcome.

Alongside such activity and the related employment growth scenarios are regulatory issues. In the continuing aftermath of the 2007 financial crisis, new regulatory architecture and requirements are being set up and implemented. Reducing risks for individual borrowers and lenders, and also economies, will require additional labour inputs to evaluate and monitor lending decisions. But the greater the labour input, the higher the cost passed onto consumers in the form of more expensive products, and the lower the demand. The regulatory regimes themselves will therefore influence the size of the market and the number and type of jobs.

iii) Home ownership and labour supply

Since 2007, there has been a reversal of the previous long-lasting trend of increasing levels of new mortgage activity in most member states. As net mortgage indebtedness appears to have a positive impact on the unemployment rate and the duration of unemployment via its influence on labour mobility, a key consideration is the extent to which mortgage markets will return to their former trajectory. Insofar as they do, and insofar as this increases the levels of household indebtedness tied to housing, this suggests that in the future home ownership will impose an even greater barrier to labour mobility than in the past and thus to the optimum matching of workers with jobs.

The physical separation between the location of a worker's residence and workplace is critical here. The development of cheaper and quicker means of physical transport has enabled longer commuting distances, while IT developments have increasingly enabled remote working practices. Both of these developments reduce the importance of moving home in order to relocate the place of work. One issue for governments will be the extent to which they encourage further investment in transport and IT infrastructure.

Housing debt also appears to be an important factor in decisions over the timing of retirement. Outright home ownership may provide households with an investment that enables them to resist policy moves to encourage longer working lives - essentially, to facilitate early exit pathways. If it were thought desirable to counteract this effect, broad strategies could include encouraging tenure structures which are less skewed towards home ownership, encouraging longer repayment periods for housing loans or re-mortgaging possibilities, and imposing taxes on the capital value or imputed rent of homes so that owners do not live rent-free.

Finally, housing debt is important to new business formation. While housing equity has the potential to contribute to the financial basis for new businesses, high levels of housing debt contribute to a downward shift in new business formation. This may suggest that governments should act to reduce incentives to expand mortgage lending. And, insofar as mortgage lending may be diverted into small business formation and expansion, it would suggest that the appropriate response would be to promote lending to entrepreneurs.

These notions provide further support for the actions of member state governments and their regulatory bodies in monitoring the build-up of net residential debt and considering the imposition of limits in relation to income. Such actions may include reconsidering inducements for households to maximise their mortgage debt and phasing out incentives such as mortgage interest tax relief, which still exist in some EU countries.

Bibliography

ACE (2000), "National and Local Employment Impacts of Energy Efficiency Investment Programmes", Association for the Conservation of Energy, London.

Clapham, D., P. Mackie, S. Orford, K. Buckley and I. Thomas (2012), "Housing options and solutions for young people in 2020", Joseph Rowntree Foundation, York.

Dol, K. and N. Horsewood (2013), "Home ownership and the retirement decision", NEUJOBS Working Paper No. 14.3C, NEUJOBS Project (www.neujobs.eu).

Doling, J. (2012), "Employment in European Mortgage Markets", NEUJOBS Working Paper No. D.14.1, NEUJOBS Project (www.neujobs.eu).

Horsewood, N. and K. Dol (2013a), "The housing market and business starts", NEUJOBS Working Paper No. 14.3B, NEUJOBS Project (www.neujobs.eu).

_____ (2013b), "Home ownership, mobility and unemployment: A re-evaluation of the Oswald thesis", NEUJOBS Working Paper No. 14.3A, NEUJOBS Project (www.neujobs.eu).

Itard, L., F. Meijer, E. Vrins and H. Hoiting (2008), "Building renovation and modernization in Europe: State of the art review", Delft University of Technology, OTB Research Institute.

Janssen, R and D. Staniaszek (2012), "How Many Jobs? A Survey of the Employment Effects of Investment in Energy Efficiency of Buildings", Energy Efficiency Industrial Forum, Brussels.

Meijer, F., H. Visscher, N. Nieboer and R. Kroese (2012), "Jobs creation through energy renovation of the housing stock", NEUJOBS Working Paper D14.2, NEUJOBS Project (www.neujobs.eu).

Munro, M. and P. Leather (2000), "Nest-building or investing in the future? Owner-occupiers' home improvement behaviour", *Policy and Politics*, Vol. 28, No. 4.

Littlewood, A. and M. Munro (1996), "Explaining disrepair: Examining owner occupiers' repair and maintenance behaviour", *Housing Studies*, Vol. 11, No. 4, pp. 503-525.

Rechovsky, D. and S. Newman (1991), "Home upkeep and housing quality of older homeowners", *Journal of Gerontology*, Vol. 46, No. 5.

Tuominen, P., K. Klobut, A. Tolman, A. Adjei and M. de Best-Waldhober (2012), "Energy savings potential in buildings and overcoming market barriers in member states of the European Union", *Energy and Buildings*, Vol. 51, pp. 48-55.

Notes

[1] ACE (2009); Itard et al. (2008).

[2] Janssen and Staniaszek (2012).

[3] See, inter alia, Littlewood and Munro (1996); Rechovsky and Newman (1991); Tuominen et al. (2012); and Munro and Leather (2000).

[4] Meijer et al. (2012); it must be noted, however, that many of the reviewed studies build on strong assumptions.

[5] Doling (2012).

[6] Ibid.

[7] Clapham et al. (2012)

[8] Horsewood and Dol (2013a).

[9] Horsewood and Dol (2013b).

[10] Dol and Horsewood (2013).

5. AGEING AND JOB GROWTH IN HEALTHCARE AND LONG-TERM CARE SERVICES

*ERIKA SCHULZ AND JOHANNES GEYER**

Health and social work are important sectors of the economy in all European countries, and have been highly dynamic in the past. In 2011, some 23 million persons were employed in health and social work in Europe, with approximately 5 million new jobs created between 2000 and 2011.[1] The healthcare workforce also increased during the economic crisis despite the overall trend of declining employment. In the future, however, the supply of the health and long-term care workforce will be affected by ageing and societal change. Demographic ageing is also likely to influence the demand for health and social work. Elderly people are more likely to be sick and to suffer from multiple diseases ('multi-morbidity'). Consequently, they have more frequent consultations with different types of doctors, they are more likely to be hospitalised, and on average they stay in hospitals for longer periods of time. Furthermore, in the oldest age groups functional impairments as well as mental illnesses are common, and these people depend on help and care from others. Thus, a significant growth in the demand for acute health as well as long-term care services is expected. Can the expected increase in demand be met by the labour supply?

* Erika Schulz and Johannes Geyer: German Institute for Economic Research (DIW), Berlin. This chapter is based on the contributors' own work for Germany and Denmark and the work of Stanisława Golinowska, Eva Kocot and Agnieszka Sowa (CASE) for Poland, Flavia Coda Moscarola (CeRP-CCA and University of Turin) for Italy, Marek Radvanský, Gabriela Dováľová, Ivan Lichner (Institute of Economic Research, Slovak Academy of Sciences) for Slovakia in Work Package 12 (Health and long-term care for an ageing population) of the NEUJOBS project.

The development of employment also depends on the institutional design of health and care systems, as well as public spending on health and long-term care services. Furthermore, demographic developments are being accompanied by changes in household composition and increasing female employment, with both trends expected to have different effects on curative healthcare and long-term care. Employment in long-term care depends strongly on the division of care tasks between members of the family and professional caregivers. Changes in household composition and family structures, as well as increasing female employment, will all have a greater impact on long-term care than on curative health care. We therefore distinguish between curative healthcare and long-term care activities.

Detailed analyses are carried out for five countries with different health and care systems: Denmark, Germany, Italy, Poland and Slovakia. To summarise the main focus of this chapter, our research question is: What is the impact of the demographic transitions and the framework conditions on the demand for and supply of health professionals and the long-term care workforce in these countries?

5.1 Health workforce: High shares of female, elderly and part-time employment

The share of health and social work in total employment shows marked differences across the countries studied. In the comprehensive welfare state of Denmark, one out of every five workers is engaged in health and social work. The sector's share amounts to 12% in Germany, while in Italy, Slovakia and Poland, the shares are between 6% and 7%, which are well below the EU average.[2]

The health and social work workforce is characterised by disproportionally high shares of female, elderly and part-time employment. On average in Europe, one out of every six female workers is engaged in health and social work. In 2011, the elderly health workforce (aged 55+) amounted to 3.9 million in Europe. Taking into account also the health workers aged 50-54 (3.2 million), over 6 million employees can be expected to exit the health and social-care market by 2025. The high share of the elderly in the health workforce is a challenge for all the countries studied. It is doubtful that the retiring employees will be replaced by graduates, trainees or workers from abroad entering the health

More than a quarter of health and care professionals will retire by 2025.

workforce. Additionally, all of the countries studied reported some kind of healthcare workforce shortage, leading to unmet needs and long waiting times. The expected higher share of retiring health professionals, in particular practising physicians, will worsen the situation.

Figure 5.1 Share of health workforce in total employment in 2000 and 2011

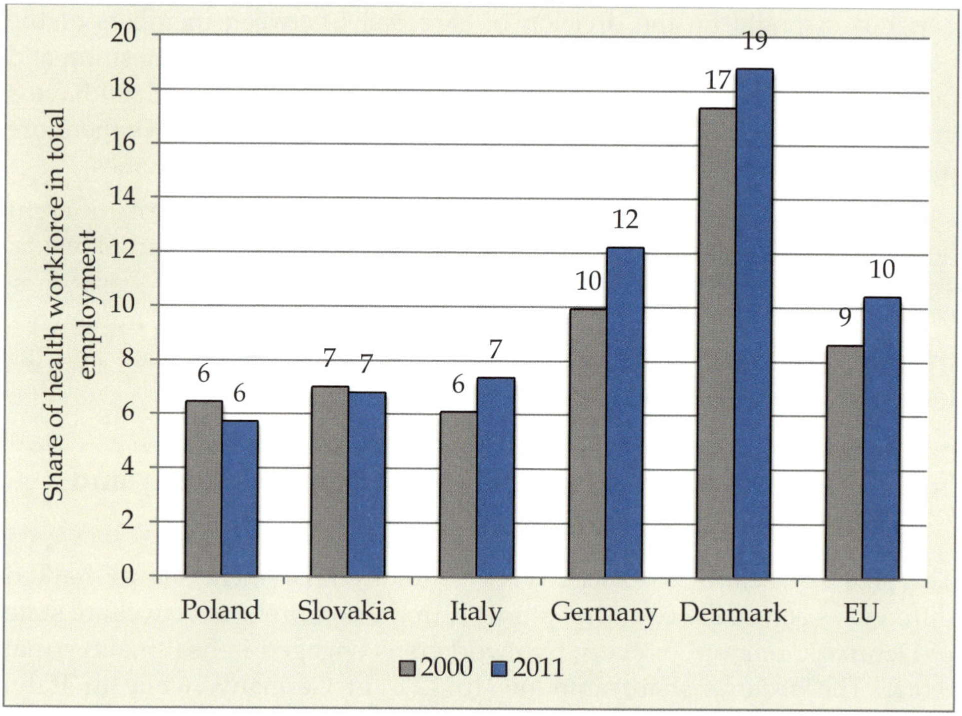

Data sources: Eurostat and LFS; calculations by DIW Berlin.

The 'human health and social work' sector consists of three sub-sectors: human health care, residential care and social work without accommodation. The majority of the health workforce is engaged in acute healthcare activities (13.2 million in Europe in 2011), while 4.5 million are engaged in residential care and 4.9 million in social work activities. In the countries studied, the share of the various sub-sectors is influenced by the level of publicly provided social care. Residential care and social work are uncommon in Poland and Italy: in both countries, less than 1% of total employment is engaged in these sub-sectors, which is less than half of the EU average. In contrast, Denmark is an example of a welfare state model that gives high priority to residential care and social work. Around 12% of total employment is concentrated in these activities and 'only' around 7% in human health. When comparing the situation across countries, we have to keep in mind national differences in the share of part-time employment. Part-time employment is uncommon in Slovakia (4%) and Poland (8%), while in Denmark and Germany the share of part-time employment is 25%. In healthcare activities, the share is even higher at 40% due to the high share of female employees. The share of part-time employment in Italy lies somewhere in-between.

Figure 5.2 Share of subsectors in human health and social work (sector Q), 2011

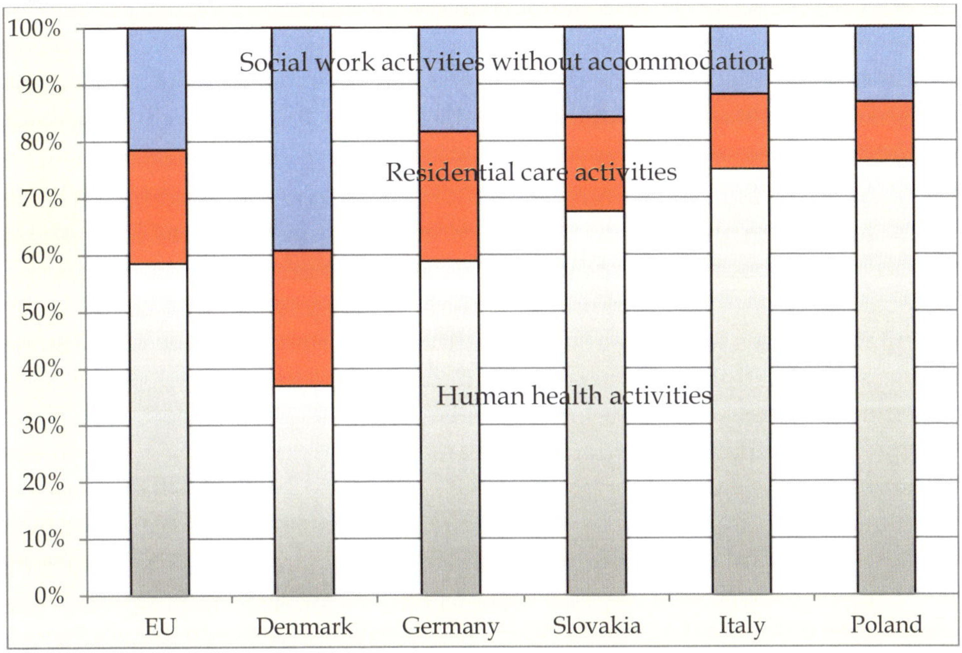

Data sources: Eurostat, LFS; calculations by DIW Berlin.

All of the studied countries provide universal coverage of defined sets of healthcare services financed either by taxes (Denmark and Italy) or mandatory public health insurance (Germany, Poland and Slovakia) with co-payments for some services. Thus, changes in the demand caused by demographic change have a direct influence on employment in the sub-sector of human health activities. This strict relationship does not exist in social work activities, in particular in long-term care services, due to a high share of privately provided and organised care. Thus, the impact of ageing and societal change on (formal) employment is analysed separately for human health and long-term care.

5.2 Healthcare services show a significant increase with age

Quantifying the effect of demographic change on employment in human healthcare is a methodological challenge. We apply two different methods in order to forecast demand and supply: a utilisation approach for the demand side, and a top-down approach for the supply side. The utilisation approach builds on age-specific utilisation rates of all kinds of medical activities, such as hospital stays and length of stay, contacts with general practitioners, specialists and dentists, use of therapeutic services and use of pharmaceuticals or medical aids. If we assume constant age-specific utilisation rates, changes in the size and age structure of the population lead to changes in the demand for health services and have a direct impact on the workforce needed to meet this demand.

We collected utilisation data for all of the countries studied for the main healthcare areas (i.e. hospital care, ambulatory care by general practitioners, specialists care and dental care). The utilisation data show the expected increase in demand with age for hospital activities and ambulatory healthcare services. In addition, we observe considerable variation across different treatments. A strong age-demand relationship can be observed for hospital treatments. The hospitalisation rate, as well as the average length of stay, increases with age with the exception of persons aged 95+.

There is a strong age-demand relationship in hospital services, but not in dental care.

For primary care, mostly provided by general practitioners, the relationship is not as strong as for hospital care. In the case of dental care, which is largely privately financed, the number of consultations per person increases up to the age of 60 and declines afterwards.

Figure 5.3 Hospital cases per 100 populations by age group, 2010

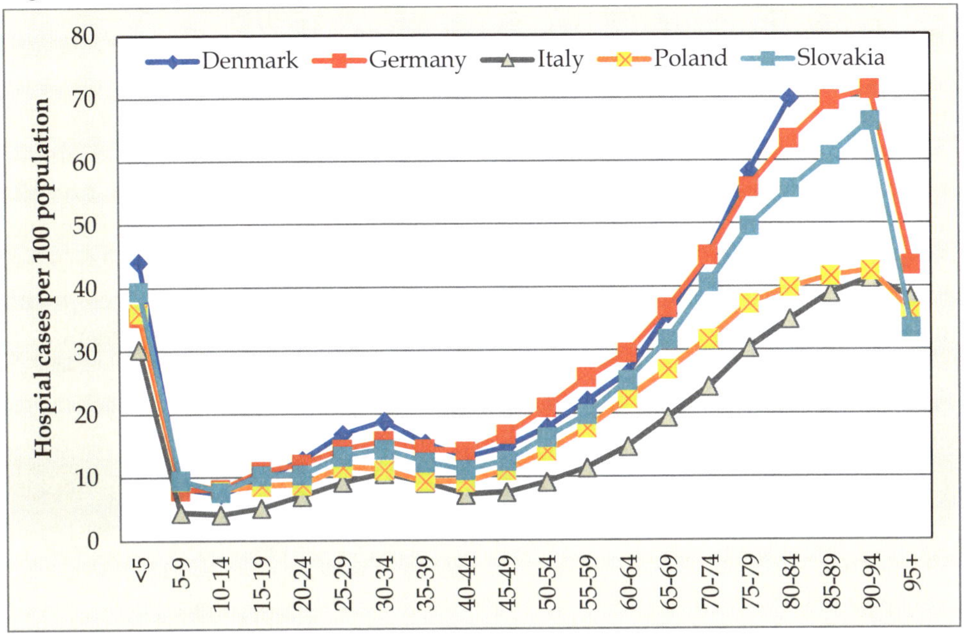

Data sources: Eurostat, hospital statistics; Statistics Denmark, calculations by DIW Berlin.

Figure 5.4 Length of hospital stays of inpatients, 2010

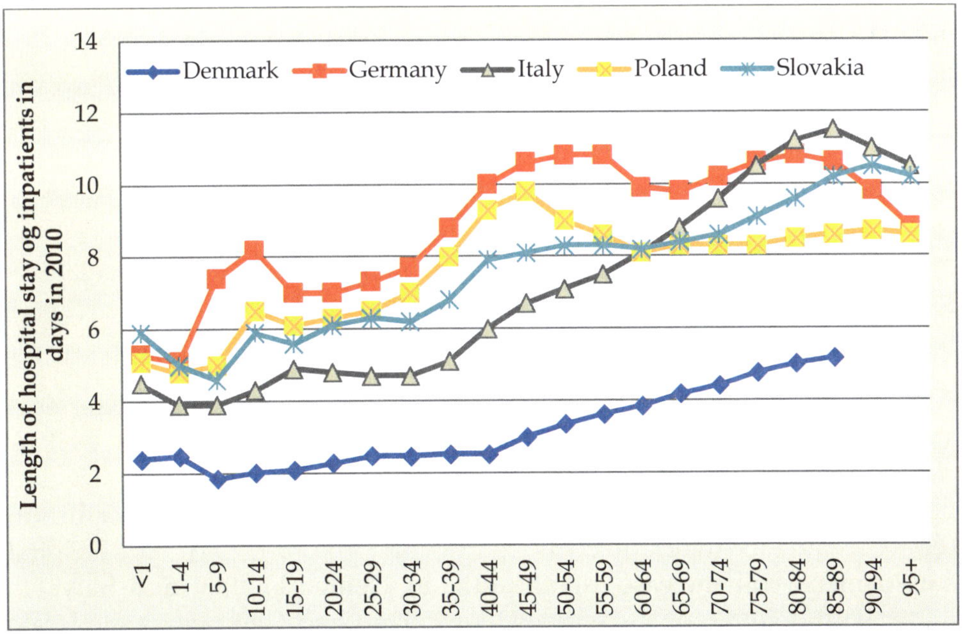

Data sources: Eurostat, hospital statistics and Statistics Denmark; calculations by DIW Berlin.

5.3 Changes in population are relevant to demand projections for the health workforce in 2025

Demographic projections are based on the 'tough' and 'friendly' scenarios described in the introductory Chapter 1 (see also Table 5.1 below). The friendly scenario assumes higher economic growth, higher employment, higher shares of highly educated people and higher population growth compared with the tough scenario. The differences in the projected size and the age structure of the population, as well as in economic development and employment in these alternative futures, will lead to differences in the projected employment in health and social care in European countries.

Table 5.1 Demographic changes and changes in health workforce demand between 2010 and 2025

	Demographic changes				Changes in the demand for health workforce in					
	Population size (%)		Share of 65+ (%-points)		Hospitals (%)		Offices of physicians and dentists (%)		Total (%)	
	Tough	Friendly	Tough	Friendly	Tough	Friendly	Tough	Friendly	Tough	Friendly
Denmark*	2.2	5.3	3.3	4.0	9.5	15.1	5.0	8.8	8.2	13.4
Germany	-8.0	-2.1	3.3	3.7	1.5	9.9	-4.2	1.8	-1.3	5.7
Italy**	1.4	8.0	2.9	3.1	9.1	16.7	1.5	7.8	8.5	15.8
Poland	-5.2	0.0	6.2	6.7	0.7	7.7	-1.7	3.7	-0.1	6.4
Slovakia***	-1.2	3.6	5.3	5.8	20.0	23.2	5.2	11.9	14.6	19.2

* Only GPs and dentists.

** Personnel of hospitals and specialists in ambulatories (no extraction of hospital staff possible); Offices of physicians only GP and paediatricians.

*** Including an increase of hospital employment of around 4,900 between 2010 and 2011.

Sources: Schulz (2013b); Schulz (2013c); Coda Moscarola (2013a); Golinowska et al. (2013a); Radvanský and Dováľová (2013).

The purely demographic effect on the demand for healthcare services and its workforce is shown using constant utilisation rates as well as constant ratios of treated persons to employees. Both population size and population ageing have a significant influence on the demand for health services and its workforce. In particular, the demand for hospital employment will increase significantly in Denmark, Italy and Slovakia under both demographic scenarios. For Poland and Germany, a moderate increase under the tough scenario and a significant increase under the friendly scenario can be observed. The ageing process also dominates this development in countries with a decline in population size (Germany in both scenarios; Poland and Slovakia in the tough scenario).

The increase in the ambulatory healthcare workforce is lower than the increase in hospital employment. In fact, due to the shrinking population in the tough scenario, a decline in the ambulatory health workforce is estimated for Germany and Poland. For ambulatory care, the ageing process is less important. In view of the development in total health workforce demand, the analysed countries can be classified into two groups: a group with a relatively strong increase under both demographic scenarios (Denmark, Italy and Slovakia), and a group with a decline in demand under the tough scenario and a moderate increase under the friendly scenario (Germany and Poland). Despite the demographic development, the total effect depends on the different divisions of healthcare tasks between hospitals and ambulatory facilities across the countries. The share of hospital employment in Slovakia, for example, is well above the EU average.

The crucial question is whether and how the increasing demand of the healthcare workforce can be accommodated.[3] The results of the tough scenario indicate that the demand for health services exceeds the health workforce supply in all countries except Poland, with the expected gap between demand and supply particularly large in Italy. The gaps are considerably lower under the friendly scenario in Denmark, Germany and Slovakia, but the situation in Italy is still expected to worsen.

The healthcare labour-market gap is expected to grow until 2025.

Figure 5.5 Changes in healthcare workforce demand and supply between 2010 and 2025 (%)

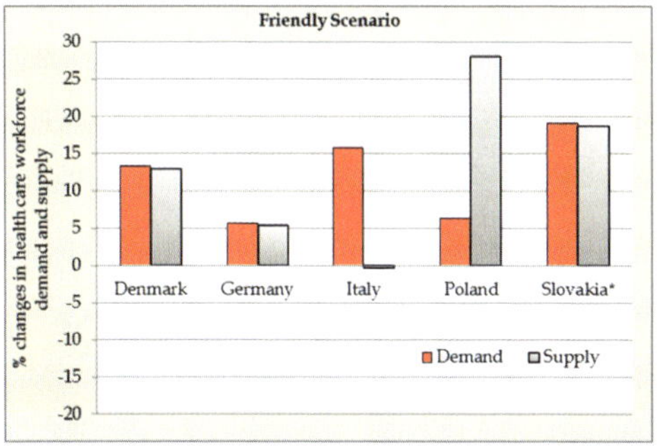

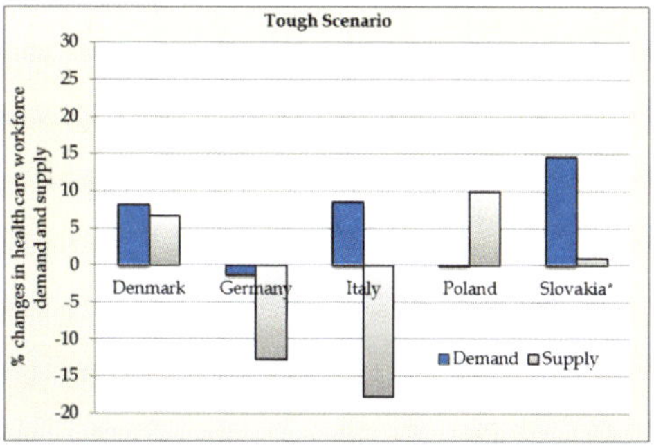

Source: Calculations by DIW Berlin based on the employment projections of the NEMESIS model and on the estimations of country-specific variations in the demand for health personnel by experts (Schulz et al., 2013).

5.4 The healthcare market is driven by a number of factors other than population

In addition to demographic change, the demand for the health workforce is influenced by a number of other factors. The healthcare market is highly regulated in all European countries. Policy interventions influencing demand and supply in this market are very common and are driven in particular by concerns about the sustainability of public finances. Other factors relevant to healthcare demand include changes in morbidity, technological innovations in medicine, changes in treatment methods, and changes in the organisation of care services. The health status of the population and the demand for healthcare services may also be influenced by the framework conditions of the scenarios discussed in Chapter 1. A transition away from fossil fuels towards solar and other low-carbon energy sources is expected to have an impact on climate change in terms of global warming and weather extremes. A reduction in the otherwise expected increases in heat waves, floods, droughts, storms and air pollution would have a positive influence on public health. Thus, under the friendly scenario (*ceteris paribus*), the demand for health services may be lower than under the tough scenario. Although it is not possible to quantify this effect, studies show that technological innovations in medicine in particular have a significant influence on health expenditure.[4] Furthermore, medical and pharmaceutical innovations allow the treatment of persons who could not be treated before, creating additional demand. Additionally, scientific progress may increase the possibility of detecting serious illnesses earlier and thus increase the chance of avoiding death. However, these effects could not be quantified either and cannot be taken into account.

Moreover, studies show that nearness to death has a greater influence on healthcare expenditure than age.[5] This can be partly traced back to the use of costly treatment methods in the last few months of life. Thus, the effect of nearness to death on demand is not as strong as for health expenditures. The increase in life expectancy may lead to a shift of health-service demand to older persons, but no changes in age-specific morbidity are taken into account.

5.5 Long-term elderly care is still predominantly provided by family members

In contrast to the workforce in healthcare, the long-term care workforce consists of both formal employees and informal caregivers. Traditionally, elderly care has been predominantly a task for the family in almost all European countries. In particular, spouses, daughters, daughters-in-law and other family members take over care tasks. However, the increase in female labour force participation, as well as the changes in household composition with more people living alone, reduces the ability of families to provide a large amount of care. The increase in the number of elderly, in particular the very oldest, intensified the discussion about adequate (publicly financed) provision of formal care. Today, some kind of formal long-term care (LTC) is available in the majority of European countries, either in nursing homes or at home through home-care services. Additionally, some countries provide cash benefits to support informal care by family members (Germany and Slovakia) or to partly compensate for extra costs due to disability (Italy). The amount and type of LTC services provided depend on the LTC system, which differs markedly across countries. In some countries no LTC system exists, and the care tasks are divided between social assistance and healthcare services (Poland and Slovakia). Additionally, in some countries no strict separation between LTC and assistance for disabled persons exists, meaning a clear assignment of care personnel is not possible. Both the amount of formal care services provided and the division of tasks influence the size and occupational structure of the LTC workforce.

In Denmark, all people in need can receive formal long-term care, whereas publicly financed long-term care services are virtually non-existent in Poland.

The number of workers engaged in LTC can only be estimated. According to the Labour Force Survey (LFS), across the five studied countries around 0.7 million were employed in nursing homes in 2010 and 0.5 million in social work activities without accommodation for the elderly and disabled. The majority of employees are nurses, nursing assistants or personal care workers (social-care workers). This is only a raw indicator of employment in services for the elderly, because not all persons engaged in social work activities for the elderly are employed in LTC activities, and other social work activities can utilise LTC personnel as well. Based on information from national statistics from 2010-11, it is estimated that around 1.5 million employees were engaged in LTC activities in the five studied countries: 952,000 in Germany, 334,000 in Italy, 140,000 in Denmark, 72,000 in Poland and 25,000 in Slovakia.

Table 5.2 Dependent people and informal and formal care

		Share of formal care recipients		Share of persons relying on			
	Number of dependent persons	At home	In institutions	Informal, private financed or no care	Informal care		No care or private financed help
	2010	2010	2010	2010	2006		2010
	In 1,000s	In %	In %	In %	In %		In %
Denmark[a]	371	34.6	11.9	(53.5)	5.0		(48.5)
Germany	7847	21.4	9.6	69.0	41.5		27.5
Italy	3143	19.0	12.3	68.7	128.4	**	0.0
Poland	2490	0.1 *	3.5	96.4	48.8		47.6
Slovakia	475	17.6	7.0	75.4	12.0	***	63.4
Total	14326	17.4	9.1	73.5	59.9		26.7

[a] Formal care recipients are persons receiving elderly care and care for the handicapped, while the dependent include also young persons, thus formal care is underestimated.

* 2006; ** 2003; *** 2010.

Sources: Eurostat, EU SILC; OECD Health Data; calculations by DIW Berlin.

Apart from in Slovakia, information on the number of informal caregivers is rare. According to the data collected by the OECD, which are based on national surveys, the number of informal caregivers amounts to 8.6 million in the five countries studied: 4 million in Italy, 3.3 million in Germany, 1.2 million in Poland, 57,000 in Slovakia and 19,000 in Denmark. These estimates have to be interpreted with caution because the data sources are different and not fully comparable. For example, in Italy the number of informal caregivers comprises all types of help and personal care provided by the family, while in Germany only the main caregiver is accounted for.

The data are used to show the importance of formal and informal care by comparing the number of recipients of formal and informal care with the total number of people in need of care. Based on the EU SILC (Statistics on Income and Living Conditions) survey, we classified "people in need of care" as persons reporting severe impairments to activities they usually do due to long-standing illnesses (of more than six months). The share of dependent people increases sharply with age (from age 55 onwards). In total, 14.3 million people were in need of care in the five countries in 2010. A comparison of dependent persons and people receiving formal care shows that the majority either rely on informal or privately financed care, or receive no care. Dependent people receiving no care may cope with their situation by themselves using new technologies, privately financed helpers, and/or measures to adapt their homes to their needs. But they may also receive help and care from their partner, which is usually not considered 'informal help and care' and instead is taken as a matter of course. Thus, receiving 'no care' does not necessarily mean that there is no active help within the household.

5.6 The number of individuals 'in need of care' will significantly grow up to 2025

What are the effects of population ageing and societal changes on the formal LTC workforce? Answering this question requires estimations of the change in the number of dependent people, changes in the potential for informal caregiving and the availability of formal-care services. Our forecasting model takes into account changes in the number of dependent people and the potential of available informal care. We assume no changes in LTC systems or available care services.

As the risk of multi-morbidity, impairments to daily living and mental illness increases strongly with age, the ageing process dominates the development of dependent people in the steady-state scenario. The number of dependent people is expected to increase significantly, although the trend shows remarkable variation across the countries studied.

Figure 5.6 Changes in dependent persons between 2010 and 2025 (%)

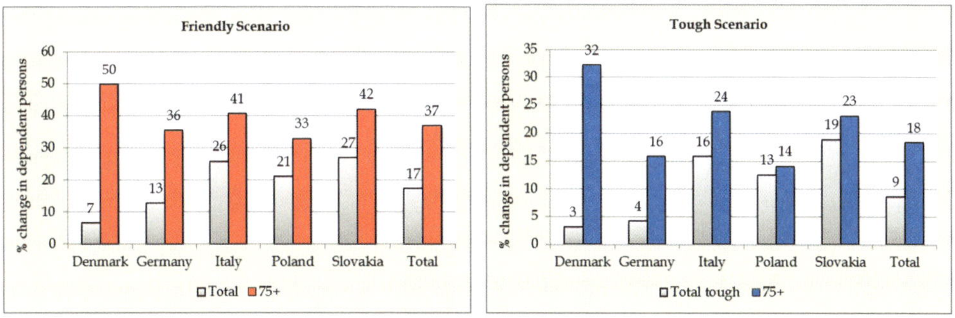

Data sources: Huismann et al. (2013) and EU SILC; calculations by DIW Berlin.

Growth is lowest in Denmark and highest in Slovakia. In total, the number of dependent people is expected to increase by 1.24 million under the tough scenario and by 2.5 million under the friendly scenario. In all countries the changes are markedly higher among the oldest people. In the tough (friendly) scenario the increase in dependent people aged 75+ ranges from 14% (33%) in Poland to 32% (50%) in Denmark. The driving factor is the increase in life expectancy for both males and females.

The relationship between changes in life expectancy and morbidity (poor health status due to acute healthcare problems or long-standing illnesses) has been extensively discussed in the last few decades. Three theories have been developed - the compression of morbidity, the expansion of morbidity and the dynamic equilibrium - but no consensus has been reached. Additionally, changes in morbidity do not directly influence functional impairments and therefore the 'need for care'. Mental illnesses are the exception, but there is no indication that new medical treatments will lead to a decline in their prevalence or incidence in the near future. Therefore no changes in age-specific need for care are assumed.

5.7 Increase in partner care expected

The future number of informal caregivers will be influenced by two trends: first, changes in living arrangements with more singles in the middle-age groups and an increase in the very oldest living together due to the increase in life expectancy; and second, the increase in female labour-force participation reducing the possibilities for providing intensive informal care to elderly relatives.

Informal care is mostly provided by members of the family living within or outside the household of the dependent. Informal caregiving is more likely within the household (mostly partner care) than outside the household (mostly caregiving by children). Thus, the expected changes in living arrangements reduce the potential of informal caregivers. However, our analysis based on the Survey of Health, Ageing and Retirement in Europe (also known as SHARE data) shows that the number of informal caregivers aged 50+ increases significantly in all of the studied countries under both demographic scenarios.

The increase in the number of people in need of care is six times higher in Slovakia than in Denmark.

Figure 5.7 Changes in informal caregivers between 2010 and 2025 (%)

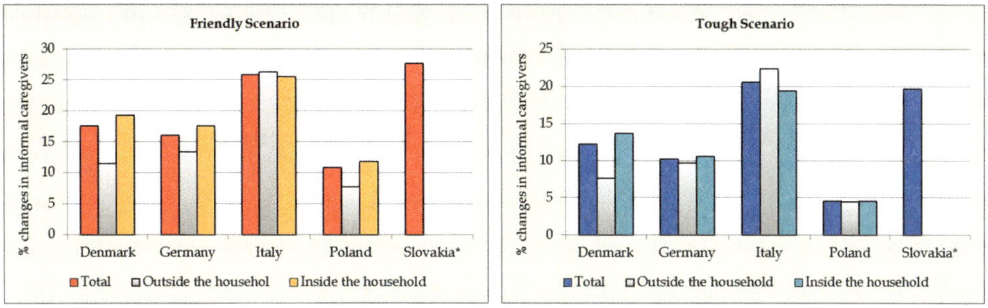

Data sources: Huismann et al. (2013); SHARE wave 1, 2 and 4, weighted and pooled data; Radvanský and Lichner (2013) (data for Slovakia); calculations by DIW Berlin.

A large group of informal caregivers is made up of working-age females (aged 40-69). As caregiving is often a physically and mentally demanding full-time job, the impact of caregiving on the labour-force participation of women has dominated the political debate on this issue over the last two decades. Empirical studies show that the impact of the need for caregiving on labour-force participation depends on various factors: the intensity of caregiving, the availability of LTC services, measures supporting informal carers to combine care tasks with formal employment and the situation in the labour market. In Slovakia, Denmark and Poland, no effect of caregiving on labour-force participation can be observed. In Denmark this is due to the generous social assistance system, while in Poland and Slovakia it is due to poorly developed formal care services. In Germany, the effect depends mainly on the intensity of the caregiving needed. Due to data restrictions, this could not be taken into account. Italy is the only country where caregiving has a negative effect on labour-force participation.[6]

5.8 The gap in the formal long-term care market will widen up to 2025

Depending on the LTC system, people in need of care receive a mix of informal and formal care services. The change in the number of formal-care recipients is calculated using constant age-specific utilisation rates for home care, nursing home care and cash benefits. Under the tough scenario, the number of residents in nursing homes and the recipients of home-care services will increase by 260,000 each. Under the friendly scenario, the increase in the number of formal care recipients is even higher: 513,000 in institutional care and 488,000 in home care. The increase is greater in institutional care than in home care in Denmark and Germany, while home care grows more in Poland. A high proportion of care recipients receive cash benefits for self-organised informal care in Germany, and care allowances directed to persons caring for them in Slovakia. The number of recipients of cash benefits increases to a lesser extent than the number of recipients of benefits in kind. In Italy, most severely disabled people receive a universal cash benefit to cope with care expenditures; around 498,000 people received this type of benefit in 2010.[7]

The growth in life expectancy leads to more couples growing old together, so the probability of caring by partners increases.

Figure 5.8 Change in recipients of formal long-term care in kind and in cash between 2010 and 2025 (%)

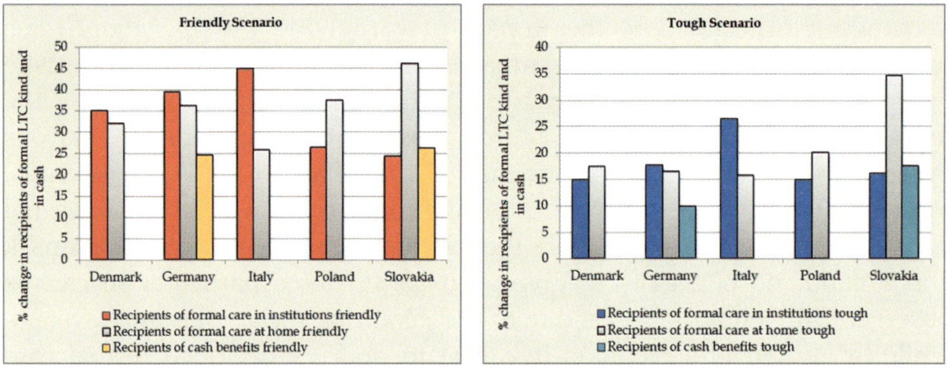

Data sources: Schulz (2013d), Coda Moscarola (2013b), Golinowska et al. (2013b) and Radvanský and Lichner (2013); calculations by DIW Berlin.

The growing number of formal-care recipients requires additional staff to carry out the necessary tasks. The number of personnel needed can be calculated using constant ratios of recipients to staff employed in institutional care and home care. The underlying assumption is that the current number of staff engaged in nursing care activities is adequate, i.e. no shortage of staff exists. In Denmark, an additional 24,000 (under the tough scenario) or 45,000 (friendly) personnel are required to meet the increasing demand; the majority of staff required are social and health workers or assistants. In Germany, around 165,000 (tough) or 366,000 (friendly) personnel are required; the majority are geriatric nurses, nurses and nursing assistants. In Poland, 11,000 (tough) or 20,000 (friendly) additional personnel are required, and in Slovakia the number is 6,000 (tough) or 8,000 (friendly). In Italy, the demand for residential-care personnel is expected to increase by 53,000 (tough) or 86,000 (friendly). In

Italy, currently 800,000 additional privately financed caregivers are employed, supported by the universal cash benefit for the disabled. However, a great proportion of them are employed illegally.[8]

Although an increase in the workforce supply in residential care and social work is expected in Denmark, Poland, Slovakia and (under the friendly scenario) Germany, the gap in the nursing and care market will widen. In Italy, a decline in the care workforce under both scenarios is expected, while the demand for the formal workforce is estimated to increase in line with the development of dependent people by around 19% (tough) or 31% (friendly). The demand side for the care workforce is also more dynamic than the supply side in the other countries studied.

Table 5.3 Changes in the demand and supply of nursing and caring personnel between 2010 and 2025 (%)

	Tough scenario		Friendly scenario	
	Demand*	Supply**	Demand*	Supply**
Denmark	17.1%	6.6%	32.6%	12.9%
Germany	17.3%	-2.7%	38.5%	20.9%
Italy***	18.7%	-17.7%	31.2%	-0.3%
Poland	15.8%	9.9%	28.1%	28.1%
Slovakia	21.8%	0.9%	30.6%	18.8%

* Demand for formal long-term care workforce based on national statistics.

** Results of the NEMESIS model for the sector non-market services; Germany for residential care and social work.

*** Change in dependent people as a proxy for formal labour demand.

Sources: Boitier et al. (2013); Schulz (2013d); Coda Moscarola (2013b); Golinowska et al. (2013b); Radvanský and Lichner (2013); Schulz and Geyer (2013); calculations by DIW Berlin.

Although an increase in the workforce supply in residential care and social work is expected (except in Italy), the gap in the nursing and care market will widen. The situation will worsen in particular in Italy. These results have to be interpreted with caution because the supply side is based on the results of the NEMESIS model that provides estimates of changes in employment in the broad 'non-market services' (Denmark, Italy, Poland and Slovakia) and 'residential care and social work' (Germany) sectors (Boitier et al., 2013). The changes in nursing and caring activities may be higher than the average change. Nevertheless, the huge difference between the estimated demand and supply indicates the expected imbalances in the care market.

5.9 Finding a balance between family and formal care is a major challenge

What can be done to reduce the gap between demand and supply in the long-term care markets?

Three areas of activity to meet the future care demand are discussed in public policy circles:

a) Measures to increase the potential of informal care

Informal caregivers are expected to remain the main care workforce in the future. Several strategies are discussed to support informal caregivers and to encourage more people to take over informal care or to increase their caregiving engagement, including care leave, financial support to family carers, training, counselling, flexible working time arrangements for carers, ICT to reduce the caregiving burden and support from professional caregivers.

b) Recruitment of long-term care workers from abroad

Measures to support the recruitment of foreign qualified nurses and carers include simplified recognition of vocational training certificates from abroad, free language courses, help with finding affordable housing, help with administration tasks and equal wages.

c) Measures to increase the domestic long-term care workforce

Employees in long-term care facilities experience unfavourable working conditions, such as working night-time shifts, high time pressures, low competences, low salaries and a low image of nursing professions.[9] The improvement of working conditions is a high priority for the recruitment and retention strategies of nursing homes and home-care services. Relevant measures include an increase in wages, an increase in flexible working-time arrangements, an increase in the standing of nursing and caring professions, changes in the requirements for vocational training (substitution of formal training by training on the job), an increase in competences and the reorganisation of caring tasks and a reduction in formal documentation tasks.

The future development of the formal-care workforce depends not least on the financial resources of the communities that are responsible for social care provision and national and regional politics with regards to LTC. To cope with the ageing population, politicians assign a high priority to measures supporting family caregivers and measures to provide formal care that is supplementary or complementary to family care.

Bibliography

Boitier, B., N. Lancesseur and P. Zagamé (2013), "Global scenarios for European socio-ecological transition", NEUJOBS Working Paper D9.2, NEUJOBS Project (www.neujobs.eu).

Breyer, F. and V. Ulrich (2000), "Gesundheitsausgaben, Alter und medizinischer Fortschritt: eine Regressionsanalyse", *Jahrbücher für Nationalökonomie und Statistik*, Vol. 220, pp. 1-17.

Coda Moscarola, F. (2013a), "Health care workforce in Italy", NEUJOBS Working Paper D12.1, Supplement D, NEUJOBS Project (www.neujobs.eu).

Coda Moscarola, F. (2013b), "Long-term care workforce in Italy. Country report", NEUJOBS Working Paper D12.2, Supplement C, NEUJOBS Project (www.neujobs.eu).

Colombo, F., A. Llena-Nozal, J. Mercier and F. Tjadens (2011), "Help Wanted? Providing and Paying for Long-Term Care", OECD Health Policy Studies, OECD Publishing, Paris.

European Commission (2012), *EU Employment and Social Situation. Quarterly Review*, Special Supplement on Health and Social Services, European Commission, Brussels, December.

Golinowska, S., A. Sowa and E. Kocot (2013a), "Impact of ageing on curative health care workforce. Country Report Poland", NEUJOBS Working Paper D12.1, Supplement E, NEUJOBS Project (www.neujobs.eu).

Golinowska, S., E. Kocot and A. Sowa (2013b), "Employment in long-term care. Report of Poland", NEUJOBS Working Paper D12.2, Supplement D, NEUJOBS Project (www.neujobs.eu).

Huisman, C., J. de Beer, R. van der Erf, N. van der Gaag and D. Kupiszewska (2013), "Demographic scenarios 2010 - 2030", NEUJOBS Working Paper D10.1, NEUJOBS Project (www.neujobs.eu).

Radvanský, M. and G. Dováľová (2013), "Impact of ageing on curative health care workforce. Country report Slovakia", NEUJOBS Working Paper D12.1, Supplement F, NEUJOBS Project (www.neujobs.eu).

Radvanský, M. and I. Lichner (2013), "Impact of ageing on long-term care demand and supply in Slovakia. Country report", NEUJOBS Working Paper D12.2, Supplement E, NEUJOBS Project (www.neujobs.eu).

Schulz, E. (2013a), "Employment in health and long-term care in European countries", NEUJOBS Working Paper D12.1, Supplement A, NEUJOBS Project (www.neujobs.eu).

_____ (2013b), "Impact of ageing on curative health care workforce. Country report Denmark", NEUJOBS Working Paper D12.1, Supplement B, NEUJOBS Project (www.neujobs.eu).

_____ (2013c), "Impact of ageing on curative health care workforce. Country report Germany", NEUJOBS Working Paper D12.1, Supplement C, NEUJOBS Project (www.neujobs.eu).

_____ (2013d), "Ageing, care need and long-term care workforce in Germany. Country report", NEUJOBS Working Paper D12.2, Supplement B, NEUJOBS Project (www.neujobs.eu).

Schulz, E. and J. Geyer (2013), "Societal change, care need and long-term care workforce in selected European countries", NEUJOBS Working Paper D12.2, NEUJOBS Project (www.neujobs.eu).

Schulz, E., F. Coda Moscarola, S. Golinowska, M. Radvanský and J. Geyer (2013), "Impact of ageing on curative health care workforce in selected EU countries", NEUJOBS Working Paper D12.1, NEUJOBS Project (www.neujobs.eu).

Zweifel, P., S. Felder and M. Meier (1999), "Aging of Population and Health Care Expenditure: a Red Herring?", *Health Economics*, Vol. 8, pp. 485-496.

Notes

[1] European Commission (2012).

[2] "EU" always means EU27.

[3] To answer this question, the estimated changes in workforce demand are compared to the projections of future changes in employment differentiated by sectors under the friendly and tough scenarios (Boitier et al., 2013.).

[4] See, for example, Breyer and Ulrich (2000).

[5] See, for example, Zweifel et al. (1999).

[6] This is taken into account by the national expert in calculating the changes in informal caregivers.

[7] Coda Moscarola (2013b).

[8] Coda Moscarola (2013b).

[9] Colombo et al. (2011).

6. TWO FACES OF AGEING: OLDER WORKERS AND OLDER CONSUMERS

*ANNA RUZIK-SIERDZIŃSKA AND MAREK RADVANSKÝ**

Due to lower fertility and longer life expectancy, today a larger share of the population than ever before is over 50 years of age. Demographic projections by Eurostat show that the share of people between the ages of 50 and 74 of the population aged 20-74 will increase in the EU27 countries from the current 40% to 47% by 2050. As a result, older people represent an increasing share of employment. This is not only a fact but also a necessity: the predicted shrinking of the European labour force requires workers to be productive and active for a longer.[1] Another, less discussed consequence of ageing is that it might change the composition of household consumption in Europe, but it is unclear yet in what ways.

The first part of this chapter is dedicated to possibilities for labour market adaptation to the ageing process, especially possibilities for workers to stay economically active and productive for longer. It would appear to be easier for older people to work longer when they are relatively healthy and live longer, but there is no strong link between life expectancy and working life. Recent public system pension reforms have reduced expected replacement rates at lower ages and increased retirement ages. Will such changes be enough to induce people to work longer and make employers want to retain them? The answer is not obvious.

---

* Anna Ruzik-Sierdzińska: CASE – Center for Social and Economic Research and Warsaw School of Economics; Marek Radvanský: Institute of Economic Research, Slovak Academy of Sciences. This chapter was compiled on the basis of research conducted within NEUJOBS Work Package Nos. 12 and 17 by a broad team of experts.

Working longer is also important for the level of future pensions. Old-age income should be high enough (or 'adequate') to prevent poverty and allow for a satisfactory level of consumption by future retirees. Pensioners in developed countries are relatively well protected against poverty today. The reduction of old-age poverty in OECD countries to 12.8% in 2010 (lower than for the younger population) is an achievement.[2] Recent or planned changes to pension systems usually include a stronger link between the level of old-age benefits and contributions paid or age of retirement. This makes some groups more vulnerable to the risk of poverty in future, such as women with shorter average tenure than men (see also Chapter 7 of this volume).

The second part of this chapter is dedicated to the influence of ageing on the structure of consumption and its effect on employment in specific economic sectors. Changes in both household consumption and the structure of consumption should be the driving forces behind what is often referred to as the 'silver economy'. This term refers to the set of economic activities linked to the production of goods and services targeted at the elderly. This segment of the economy is expected to grow significantly because of the ageing of the population. The aim of this section is to provide relevant information on the nature of the expected growth based on changes in private consumption and its possible effects on European labour markets.

6.1 Transition from work to retirement varies between countries

The future size and quality of the European labour force are important to economic growth in the region. Countries differ in terms of elderly activities and only part of life is spent in labour market activity (see Figure 6.1). Earlier or later retirement is related to various social, health and economic factors, including social security systems and labour market institutions. As demographic ageing is expected to continue, it is important to know more about all of these factors in order to answer important questions: What efficient policy measures could avoid early retirement, which increases the costs of the pension system and the risk of poverty at old age? What can be done in the short term and in the long term? Are the 'recipes' the same for all European countries?

Figure 6.1 Duration of working life and life expectancy in European countries, 2012

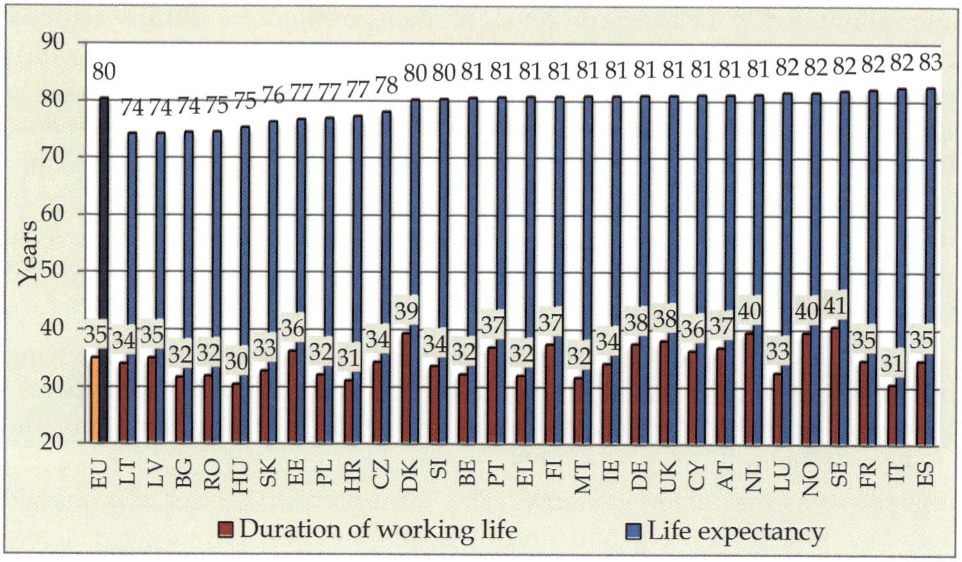

Source: Eurostat.

When we look at employment rates at 50+ years of age and the average employment length in a life cycle, European countries can be divided into four groups.[3] In the group with high rates of employment at 50+ and a long working life ('high-long' countries) we find Norway, Sweden, Finland, the Netherlands, Denmark, Germany, Latvia, Estonia, Iceland and the UK. The countries where employment after 50 is low and average working careers are short ('low-short') are Belgium, Luxembourg, Italy, Hungary, Slovenia and Poland. The two other groups are 'high-short' (with Austria, France, Czech Republic, Slovakia and Bulgaria) and 'low-long' (Ireland, Cyprus, Portugal, Spain, Greece, Lithuania, Romania). Differences in retirement preferences of workers across countries are driven mostly by differences in labour market institutions and social security systems. Whereas the impact of health and disability on retirement is similar in all countries examined, institutional factors - such as benefit systems, taxes, labour market legislation, education and the availability of training or active labour market policies - create different (dis)incentives to work in different countries.[4]

Health or disability are significant to retirement in all countries; other factors have different effects depending on the country.

Recent research demonstrates that around 79% of men and 81% of women receiving pensions in 2006 were working just before retirement, 5.4% of men and 4.8% of women were unemployed, and 8.7% of men and 7.6% women retired from a state of long-term sickness or disability.[5] The share of those who retire directly from work increases with age. In the youngest age group (aged 50 to 54), almost 19% declared that they retired from a status other than work, unemployment or disability. This implies that there are fewer and fewer disincentives to work until old age provided by the social security systems and labour market institutions in European countries. But what are the other determinants of the transition from work to retirement?

The sector of employment surely plays a role. Working in a 'green job' decreases the likelihood of wanting to stay employed longer in countries that have high employment rates at older ages but short average professional careers. This could be explained by the fact that 'green jobs' are usually physically demanding. Moving from physically demanding to intellectually demanding work environments could lead people to remain active in the labour market for longer in the future. This would not necessarily require a change in the structure of the economy, but rather the introduction of some improvements in existing sectors. For example, it has also been found that workers in agriculture plan to retire earlier in central and eastern Europe, which may reflect different working conditions. Also those employed in social or personal services plan to retire later in rich western Europe.[6]

Respondents' opinions on what would make retirees work longer (i.e. postpone their decision to stop working) show that flexible working time would be an advantage, and slightly less important would be better safety at the workplace. Only 5.6% of men and 5.5% of women think that more opportunities to update their skills would delay their retirement. The share of people saying that they would work longer with some prerequisites is higher among early retirees (see Table 6.1).

Table 6.1 Contributing factors to staying in work longer (persons not working and with an individual retirement pension)

	More flexible working time	More opportunities to update skills	Better health / safety at workplace
Sex			
Men	10.5%	5.6%	10.9%
Women	10.1%	5.5%	9.6%
Age			
50-54	20.3%	13.8%	20.3%
55-59	13.9%	7.9%	13.8%
60-64	10.2%	5.1%	9.6%
65-69	7.7%	3.9%	7.8%
Total - N	11 119	6 035	10 979

Note: Percentages of persons in the study group who answered "yes", i.e. they assume that the respective factor would have contributed to the person staying in work for longer.

Source: Riedel and Hofer (2013); calculations based on Ad Hoc Module of LFS 2006.

These findings allow certain policy conclusions. As health status and disability are important in all countries, public support should be used to address the social and physical health issues of older persons and to promote prevention and healthy lifestyles at younger ages. Activities promoting health and preventive activities (e.g. screening for the most prevalent chronic diseases after 50 years of age) could therefore be beneficial in terms of longer economic activity.

6.2 The labour market and other activities are not substitutes in countries with high employment of older workers

What do workers do after the end of their working life? Different types of activities at older ages can be substitutes for paid work, but some are chosen more often by older people in countries with higher labour-force participation at older ages. On average, older adults in Europe are rather active in non-labour market activities outside the household, despite the decline in societal cohesion and the increasing fragmentation of society. Izabela Styczyńska et al. analysed older people's engagement in social activities through declared participation in leisure activities, changes in participation in religious services and voting behaviour.[7]

Leisure activities can be those shared with other people or solitary activities such as watching television or listening to the radio. Activities performed at home, such as watching television and listening to the radio, were the most popular way of spending leisure time for older people in Europe. The least commonly reported activity in this group is use of the internet.

Research found that social activity can be treated as a substitute for labour market activity in low-employment clusters, but not in high-employment clusters. This shows that labour market inactivity in low-employment countries does not necessarily lead to social exclusion but can be replaced by other types of social engagement, and people who engage in more social activities have a weaker preference for paid work at an older age.

In countries where the employment rate at older ages is high, older people's level of engagement in meeting with friends is also higher. Furthermore, higher economic activity is found in countries where people claim to be happiest.

Participation in religious services and meetings is another way in which people engage with their communities. This was measured as either active participation in religious services or the declaration of belonging to a particular religion. The majority of people indicate that they are associated with a particular religion. However, attendance of religious services is much less common. In clusters of countries with low employment rates at older ages, attendance of religious services is higher but decreases with time in all countries, confirming the hypothesis that the elderly are also participating in the ongoing secularisation of society.[8]

Engagement of older people in social life is higher in countries with high employment rates at 50+.

The type of welfare regime could provide us with a framework for thinking about the relationship between the socio-ecological transition (SET) and elderly activity and wellbeing. Nordic countries have extensive institutional support for the elderly or families with children, while in southern European countries the majority of social services are provided and financed by family members. Thus, a one-size-fits-all policy addressed at increasing the participation of the elderly in social and economic lives might not be efficient due to various constraints on decision-making. These findings support the policy recommendations of the World Health Organization (WHO), which emphasises the need to "increase the number of people participating actively as they age in the social, cultural, economic and political aspects of society in paid and unpaid roles and in domestic, family and community life" in order to improve their quality of life and wellbeing.[9]

6.3 Productivity does not have to decrease with age

Does productivity increase or decrease with age? The answer to this question is not as easy as intuition might suggest, and in fact the relationship between age and productivity is still not clear. Some studies underline that a small decline in physical and mental abilities from age 50 is gradual and heterogenic (i.e. differs between people).[10] Other functions remain unchanged or improve with age, and deterioration in abilities can also be moderated by lifestyle factors. Another issue is whether wages are a good approximation of productivity (as assumed in the classical model of the labour market) or whether they exceed productivity at older age.

Assuming that earnings can approximate productivity (at least in certain occupations), are age-earnings profiles observed in the data linked to individual and employment characteristics, lifelong learning and labour market institutions? Researchers tried to answer this question by analysing how individual productivity changes with age in different countries and whether lifelong learning can contribute to higher labour productivity in the future.[11] They found that age-earning profiles are partially explained by the structure of the workforce (age, education) and the sector/occupation of employment. The dynamics of earnings after the age of 50 differ less across educational and occupational groups than for younger employees. Under the assumption that wages are a good approximation of productivity, different structures of economies mean that the effect of ageing on productivity will not be homogenous across countries.

A decrease in the employment rate after fulfilling requirements for retirement can hardly be attributed to falling personal productivity or earnings ability.

Table 6.2 Projected age of maximum monthly earnings (expected turning point of the age-earning profile) in Poland, France and Spain

			Type of profession		Sector of employment		
	2002	**2006**	**ISCO 1-4**	**ISCO 5-9**	**Industry and manufacturing**	**Market services**	**Non-market services**
Poland	62	59	68	46	56	48	90
France	60	62	63	50	59	60	113
Spain	58	60	63	64	65	57	55

Note: Based on estimated age-earning profiles.

Source: Ruzik-Sierdzinska et al. (2013); calculations based on the Structure of Earnings Survey.

The example above shows that countries can have similar age-earning profiles but when employees are divided into groups, the picture becomes more interesting. In more intellectually demanding occupations (ISCO 1-4) wages increase until retirement, while in more manual occupations (ISCO 5-9) they start decreasing even as early as at 46 years of age. This creates an incentive for people engaged in non-manual tasks to work for longer, thus driving the earnings profile up. At the same time, lower-paid individuals leave the labour market prematurely – a phenomenon that is stronger in countries with younger eligibility for retirement and higher replacement rates. However, sudden falls in employment rates when people become eligible for retirement benefits do not imply a loss of ability to perform work-related tasks. The retirement age thus seems to artificially shorten the working life of individuals.

Furthermore, ageing-related declines in productivity could be delayed or prevented by investments in adult training and learning for firms and workers. The estimation of the impact of participation in lifelong learning (LLL) on the earnings of employees aged 50+ shows a possible increase in wages, even as high as 6.5%. Estimated increases are higher in continental and southern countries than in northern countries. In line with previous studies, there is a negative correlation between the incidence of and returns to training for older workers. Furthermore, participation in training (in the previous month or year) is higher among females than males, declines with age and increases with the level of educational attainment.[12]

The impact of ageing on productivity could be mitigated with adult training and lifelong learning.

Age-earning profiles in some occupations and countries depend on the tenure at an employer. Preliminary results of the study using the SHARELIFE dataset point out to a bipolar distribution of tenure in life.[13] Some employees may work for about 20 years at one employer and others for about 40 years; some change jobs less often, some more often. In countries where people retire at higher ages, there are more frequent changes and shorter tenures at one firm. If this result is confirmed by other studies, effective policies should be focused on moving people from one group to another and identifying an effective instrument for this move.

Figure 6.2 Average duration of a job among people with a minimum of 30 years of work experience

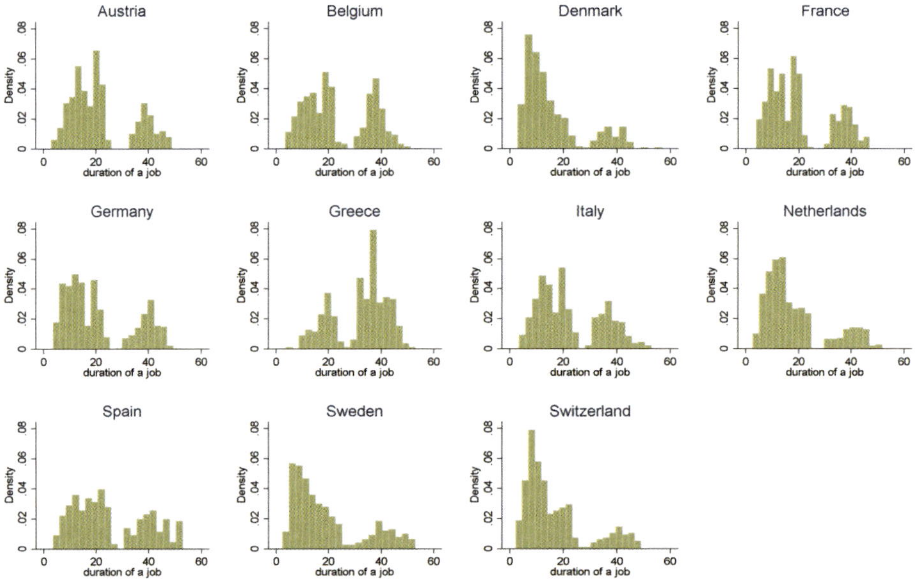

Source: Calculations by Lis and Potoczna in Ruzik-Sierdzińska et al. (2013), based on SHARELIFE data.

Complex but successful policy measures have been applied in countries with high employment rates among people aged 50+. Some examples of these include the introduction of incentives to postpone retirement by easing the wage loss associated with job changes (between sectors with no seniority-based compensation system) and support for lifelong learning. Thus, having comprehensive and appropriate policies in place is necessary to cope with the future ageing of the workforce.

6.4 Employers and working environment play an important role in retirement decisions

A discussion of longer working lives cannot be considered complete without raising the questions of how organisations deal with the phenomenon and which human resource policies are best designed for and applied to older workers. The factors that determine human resource practices in a company include: i) the organisation's characteristics; ii) job requirements within the organisation; and iii) management restrictions in dealing with older workers.[14]

In addition to the industry in which organisations operate, one of the important organisational characteristics is the number of older employees working within an organisation. A study shows that the higher the share of older workers, the more likely the company is to actively accommodate the needs of older workers.[15] Second, job requirements depend on the importance of firm-specific versus general knowledge for the organisation's competitiveness. Older workers will have an advantage when firm-specific knowledge is important. As a result, the company will try to invest in these workers and create disincentives for early retirement. Finally, the ability of management to enhance the productivity of older workers might be constrained by institutional factors, such as the strength of unions.

It also explains that firms organise their personnel policies in relation to older workers according to three strategies:[16]

- a focus on exit through retirement;
- accommodation, i.e. actions and measures to compensate for the possible decline in physical and cognitive capacities with ageing; and
- development, i.e. measures to increase the productive capacity of older workers.

Employers have a bias towards using exit strategies, possibly particularly during recession times, with large differences across countries. Only 20% of employers in six countries analysed (Denmark, Germany, Italy, the Netherlands, Poland and Sweden) use at least one measure from each of the three age-based strategies. Therefore, the majority of European employers do not engage in human resource strategies that promote active ageing in the labour market. But the higher the proportion of older workers in organisations, the more likely those organisations are to employ

Promoting longer working lives can be a natural strategy for organisations when the workforce is older and smaller in number.

strategies of exit, development or accommodation. The same has been found in organisations using more seniority-based compensation, as they have a higher level of labour union involvement and require more training. Public-sector organisations are more age conscious in their HR strategies than private sector firms. It was not possible to examine changes over time on the cross-sectional database, but some previous studies show that employers' behaviour and attitudes are gradually improving.

A focus should be placed on improving employers' attitudes and HR policies by promoting the concept of 'active ageing', following the example of organisations that already today have a high percentage of older workers and therefore have elaborated various strategies of age management. However, employers usually tend to opt for exit strategies, such as using the possibility of early retirement. This is especially easy when labour market institutions and social security systems do not prevent such behaviour. Choosing exit strategies can be a hangover from earlier times when social security systems were often treated as tools for HR management, especially under unfavourable economic conditions.

The business cycle matters for employment policies. In times of economic decline, publicly co-financed investments for training older workers could be more important than forcing employers not to use exit strategies. Observations of past behaviour of firms suggest that promoting longer working lives can be a natural strategy for organisations when the workforce is older and smaller in number.

6.5 Future elderly activity depends on the policies and attitudes of employers and potential workers

The socio-ecological transition is changing the traditional patterns of employment. Part-time work and fixed-term contracts are becoming more common as labour market flexibility increases.[17] This could affect the market activity of the elderly in different ways. Nordic countries, with their highly developed social protection systems, provide more stability for workers. Labour market rigidity, which is higher in other groups of countries, could make the labour market situation of the elderly less favourable. Prolonging labour market activity depends on various demand and supply factors, some of which can be influenced by policy measures, e.g. incentives in the social security system, health of the older population, LLL for older workers, safety at work, promotion of flexible solutions in the organisation of work, support for families with care duties. Others, such as preferences for leisure, are more difficult to change, at least in the short run.

Future elderly activity has been investigated with regards to two aspects.[18] First, there are policies of employers that are age-management friendly (indicated as 'proper') or anti-active ageing ('wrong'). These policies can be supported to some extent by public active labour market policy programmes. The second aspect is a change in productivity - either an acceleration in growth that enhances longer activity, or a deceleration in growth. Productivity growth will depend on the development of lifelong learning as well as the health status of older workers. Four possible scenarios are discussed below on the basis of these two variables.

It is reasonable to assume that in the shorter term, i.e. until 2025, age management could have a larger impact. By 2050, changes in productivity could be more important.

Table 6.3 Possible scenarios of the labour force development dependent on two factors

	Proper age management	Wrong age management
Productivity increase	'Maximum labour force with high productivity' (S1)	'With the productivity increase of the knowledge-based economy, wrong age management not so damaging for economic growth' (S2)
Productivity decrease	'Less competitive economies, even with high labour-force participation rates' (S3)	'Decrease in productivity combined with smallest labour force' (S4)

Scenario S1 combines the maximum labour force with high productivity. Scenario S4 indicates that a decrease in productivity combined with employer policies enhancing early retirement would result in the smallest labour force. Scenarios S2 and S3 depend on the future structure of the economy, i.e. the sectors in which labour demand will be created. In a knowledge-based economy with a productivity increase, the wrong (or a lack of) age management (S2) would not be so

Ageing provides an opportunity to enhance the competitiveness of the European economy through special products targeted at the older population.

damaging for economic growth, but it would cause lower labour-force participation rates at older ages. In flexible labour markets with a safety net that does not cause an inactivity trap, wrong age-management is also less distortive. A productivity decrease with proper age-management (S3) can lead to less competitive economies, even with high labour-force participation rates. It is difficult to say which scenario is the most probable. European countries differ; therefore various elements of active ageing policy measures (such as an increase in LLL participation or the promotion of age-management) should be presented in the presence of different country-specific institutions and preferences for leisure at older ages.

6.6 Ageing as an opportunity for the European economy

Besides the labour supply presented in the previous section, ageing and the related working life transition also influence people's behaviour as consumers. Changes in demand and in the structure of consumption due to changes in the structure and number of older people in European economies should be the driving forces of what is often referred to as the 'silver economy'. This term refers to a set of economic activities linked with the production of goods and services targeted at the elderly population. The European Commission is also continuously exploring this idea. For example, its 2009 ageing report emphasised possible positive effects of ageing on the private sector: *"Ageing societies bring new opportunities to innovative firms through the demand for new or adapted goods and services"*.[19]

> *Future development of the labour force will depend not only on demography but also on employers' attitudes, social and labour market policies and lifelong learning.*

Ageing is currently considered a significant social and economic issue in Europe. The effects of ageing on consumption structures will lead to structural economic challenges. An increase in the demand for some specific goods and services can be considered an opportunity for some sectors or even for some small countries. On the other hand, some sectors will have to adapt to a decrease in demand due to behavioural changes. The main concept of the 'silver economy' is that supplying goods and services for the growing sector of elderly consumers has the potential to stimulate economic growth and create new jobs. In this chapter we will refer to 'silver demand', which is related to the consumption of households with a reference person over 60 years of age.

The complexity of the 'silver economy' lies in the fact that the elderly do not have identical consumption habits across the various EU member states. Among the ageing populations, there are many economic, social and cultural factors that influence consumption patterns. Generally, we can expect an increase in 'silver demand' in all member states that will differ only in volume and structure. It is assumed that both public and private expenditures will have significant effects on the structure of the economy. The most significant increase in demand is expected in the mostly publicly financed sector of health and social services, which is explored in Chapter 5. In this chapter, only the future effects of private consumption are considered.

6.7 The increasing significance of 'silver demand'

The aggregate demand of households divided by age groups is determined by several factors, with the most important being the number of households and their wealth. Wealth is represented by average income in the relevant age group and levels of savings. However, whether older people finance their consumption by public and private transfer or by accumulated assets, in the aggregate view consumption by the older population can be expected to rise in the aggregate, thanks not only to the second demographic dividend theory[20] (and the implications for savings and capital accumulation broadly described in the economic literature), but also simply because the number of retirees will increase rapidly over time. (Any eventual drop in their purchasing power in the future will likely be easily offset by unprecedented rises in their number.) The most recent empirical studies therefore focus not only on the macroeconomic effects of their rising share in the total population and on production and consumption shifts, but also on consumption by older people themselves. Expressed another way, demand will be mostly affected by the structure of their consumption and changes in their consumption patterns.

Silver demand will grow by more than 20% by 2030, mostly due to an increase in the number of elderly over time.

According to forecasts, population ageing will have a significant impact on the age structure of Europe's households (see Figure 6.3).[21] The number of households with a head of household (or 'reference person') aged over 60 in 2030 will significantly increase in both the friendly and tough scenarios. The number of households with a reference person aged 45-59 years reaches its peak in 2020 and will then gradually reduce to the level of 2006. Conversely, in the two youngest groups there will be either stagnation or a decline in the number of households. The situation across member states may vary slightly.

Figure 6.3 Estimated number of EU households by age of the reference person (millions)*

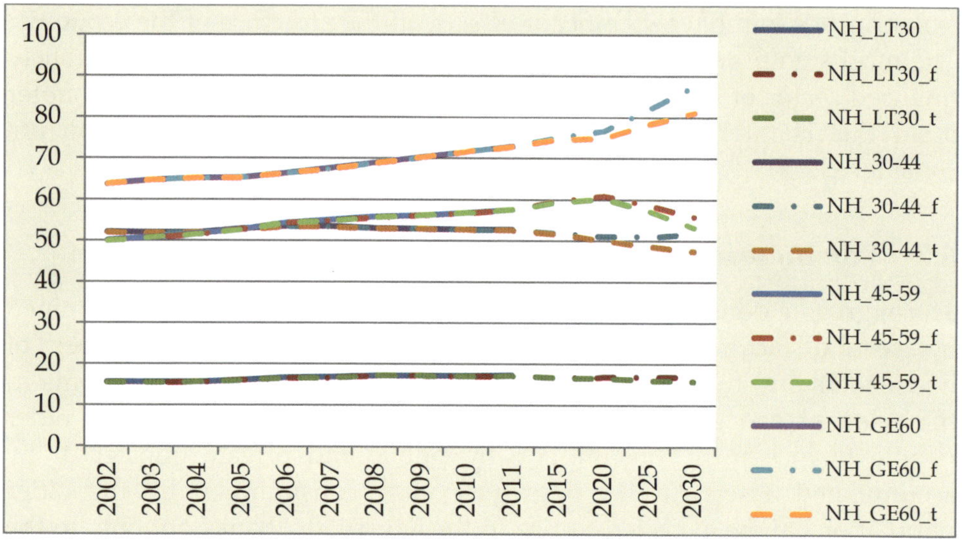

* Except Denmark, Finland, Sweden and Slovenia, where data availability of HBS was limited.

Sources: Eurostat; Štefánik et al. (2013).

In 2010, demand from silver households across European countries comprised roughly 28% of total household consumption.[22] Considering the fact that silver households make up almost 36% of the total number of households, we can see that lower incomes in retirement lead to a decreasing ability to consume. The spending structure varies with the different ages and levels of wealth in each country. In Slovakia, 'silver demand' represents a relatively low share of total demand, standing at just under 25%. In contrast, a much higher share of over 32% can be observed in Germany, which is already facing an ageing population. According to the results of estimations, we can expect an increased share for 'silver demand' in the future.

In the EU27, the share of households with a reference person aged over 60 will increase from almost 36% in 2010 to more than 43% in 2030 (growth of over 20%). Similarly, in the case of total household consumption, an increase in the share of 60+ households to 32% in 2025 and

35% in 2030 is expected. The highest share is expected in Germany (38% in 2025 and around 42% in 2030). The growing demand of these households will be significantly responsible for an increase in demand within the sectors with expected positive growth.

6.8 The increasing share of older households will change the consumption structure

Young households differ from older ones in their consumption structure, but there are also significant differences among older households. The increase in relative mean spending on housing is much higher in the case of the 80+ group than for the 65-79 group. The highest proportion of single households can also be expected in this group.[23] Expenditure on transport (as a share of the total) of 80+ households is half that of households whose reference person is in the age group 50-64, whereas health expenditure grows with the age of the reference person, and spending on food remains at nearly the same level.

When looking at international differences in the consumption patterns of households, a cluster analysis allows us to group the countries into three clusters based on similarities in the structure of consumption.[24] In the first cluster, high-income European countries belonging to the original EU15 are joined by some of the more successful new member states, along with Norway and Croatia. The second cluster groups together low-income countries with new EU member states, joined by the former Republic of Macedonia. The third (Mediterranean) cluster covers some of the countries of southern Europe that differ from the countries in the first cluster, namely Malta, Cyprus, Greece, Portugal, Spain and Turkey.

The sectors with the highest growth potential are those producing/providing food and beverages, housing and utilities, restaurants and hotel services and, above all, privately financed health, social and long-term care. Therefore, similar additional effects can also be expected in publicly financed services, as the total demand in this sector is significantly covered by health and social insurance.[25] Luxury goods and services such as restaurants, recreation and culture or alcohol and tobacco are more often demanded and consumed in countries with higher average incomes (mostly western Europe). In

The structure of silver demand is quite strictly divided between western and central-eastern Europe, due to significant wealth differences.

countries with lower average incomes, represented mainly by the new EU member states, the elderly spend a larger share on services and products that are important for day-to-day living (food and housing).

Figure 6.4 Clusters of countries based on the structure of consumption of households with reference person aged 60+

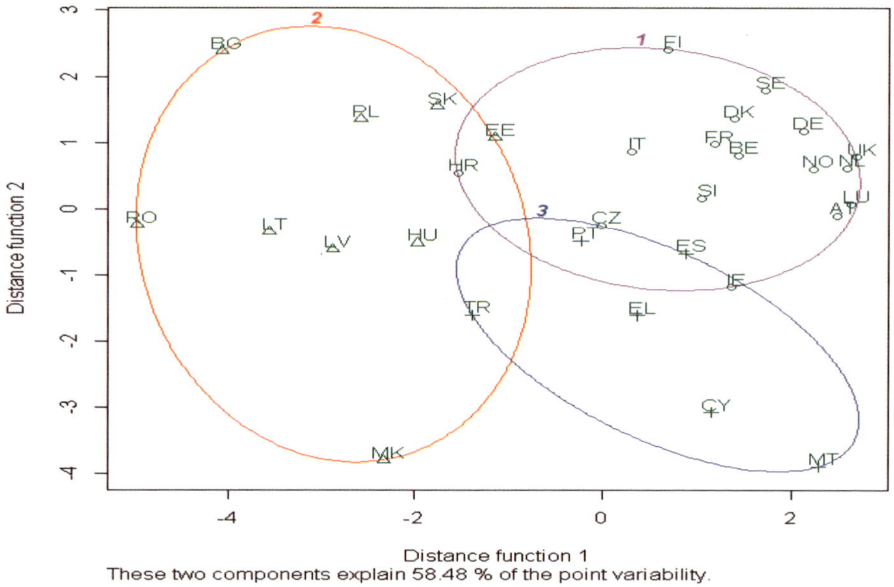

Note: Distance function 1. These two components explain 58.48% of the point variability.
Source: Štefánik et al. (2013), based on Eurostat data.

The structure of consumption is affected by a rise in the living standards of the EU population as a whole, or by the ageing of stronger, higher-income age groups leaving the labour market. Both could distort the structure of consumption towards more luxury goods, as they would have a positive effect on the income of the elderly. Thus, the core of silver demand is currently concentrated in high-income countries and its future development in central and eastern Europe will depend mostly on the speed of convergence across the EU.

Demand for each product group will be affected differently depending on income flexibility, the welfare of households in each individual country, the rate of convergence and several other factors. Consumption of younger cohorts tends to decrease. There are, of course, products and services for which demand will decrease more significantly, such as transport, clothing and footwear, and will thus face a higher proportional demand from younger age cohorts.

Table 6.4 Shares of total consumption of households in European countries (based on friendly demographic projections) (%)

	2005		2010		2015		2020		2025		2030	
	60-	**60+**	**60-**	**60+**	**60-**	**60+**	**60-**	**60+**	**60-**	**60+**	**60-**	**60+**
Food	9.74	4.35	9.53	4.72	9.50	4.83	9.45	4.95	9.11	5.39	8.74	5.82
Alcohol and tobacco	1.72	0.55	1.74	0.55	1.72	0.56	1.69	0.58	1.61	0.63	1.54	0.68
Clothing	4.47	1.21	4.42	1.17	4.38	1.20	4.37	1.23	4.23	1.34	4.8	1.45
Housing and utilities	18.99	9.28	19.00	9.80	18.85	10.1	18.56	10.22	17.61	11.14	16.62	12.3
Furnishing	4.16	1.60	4.5	1.59	4.2	1.62	3.98	1.66	3.85	1.81	3.74	1.96
Health	1.92	1.26	1.74	1.37	1.74	1.40	1.76	1.44	1.80	1.57	1.90	1.70
Transport	9.98	2.65	9.71	2.68	9.63	2.73	9.59	2.79	9.30	3.6	9.5	3.31
Communi-cations	2.27	0.67	2.35	0.70	2.30	0.71	2.23	0.72	2.6	0.79	1.88	0.84
Recreation and culture	6.71	2.36	6.69	2.31	6.61	2.34	6.51	2.39	6.22	2.62	5.95	2.82
Education*	NA	NA	NA	NA	NA	NA	NA	NA	NA	NA	NA	NA
Restaurants and hotels	4.61	1.21	4.55	1.17	4.55	1.20	4.57	1.23	4.47	1.34	4.36	1.46
Miscella-neous	6.88	2.48	6.68	2.46	6.58	2.53	6.50	2.60	6.30	2.82	6.13	3.4
Total	**72.34**	**27.66**	**71.37**	**28.63**	**70.77**	**29.23**	**70.09**	**29.91**	**67.39**	**32.61**	**64.77**	**35.23**

* The information on private expenditures on education were not reliable in the HBS.

Source: Authors' calculations based on HBS; Štefánik et al. (2013).

From a country perspective, German silver consumers tend to spend a significant part of their income on health care (mainly as co-payments), recreation and culture. This is determined by high income. The expected development of silver demand in Italy is fairly similar to that in Germany. Additionally, the elderly in Italy will spend a relatively high share of their expenditure on luxury products. In Slovakia, based on cultural and social behaviour, demand will mostly target goods and services for day-to-day living and health care. The demand of silver customers in Finland will target day-to-day necessities, as well as other more luxurious types of products and services.

6.9 The different impacts of ageing on job creation under the 'friendly' and 'tough' scenarios

In both scenarios, the highest expected increase in the consumption of younger people is related to restaurant and hotel services. We can explain this fact by an expected higher standard of living in the EU that could result in increased demand for these types of services. In both scenarios, the highest increase in total private demand is expected to target health-care services for two reasons. The first is the fact that there will be more elderly citizens demanding care services. There will also be a large group of aware younger-age cohorts demanding preventive health care. In most of the selected products and services, the additional demand from both types of households by age is quite similar, and it needs to be borne in mind that as the base of the elderly is smaller, it is more dynamic. There are, of course, some exceptions - e.g. education, clothing and transport - for which a higher proportion is related to younger-age cohorts. With respect to demographic and economic changes in total demand for selected product groups, an increase of 19-38% will be seen in the case of the friendly scenario and 11-27% under the tough scenario (Figure 6.5).

The net effect of the silver economy will lead to loss of 1.9 million jobs in the 'tough' scenario and a gain of 3.9 million in the 'friendly' one.

Structural shifts in demand will result in a change in the structure of labour demand. Productivity is expected to increase during the reference period by 21.7% under the tough scenario and 22.2% under the friendly one. The changes discussed above concerning demand could affect labour demand in different ways. For example, we can look at the expected changes in employment in sectors producing food, beverages and tobacco in the friendly scenario. In this scenario, the additional demand of both groups of households by age in 2025 is equal to around 15% of total demand in 2010. Due to higher productivity, and the assumption that employees producing products for younger customers at the beginning of the reference period will be producing this type of product over the whole period, a loss of approximately 100,000 jobs can be expected. Conversely, the increased demand of the elderly will generate an expansion in labour demand of around 1.1 million new jobs. In such a case, employees who are superfluous to the production of goods for younger households will effectively be employed in production for the elderly. The additional demand of elderly households will create approximately 4.4 million new job opportunities according to the friendly scenario.

Figure 6.5 Additional EU27 demand by product/services group and by age of household under the 'friendly' (F) and 'tough' (T) scenarios, 2010-2025 (%)

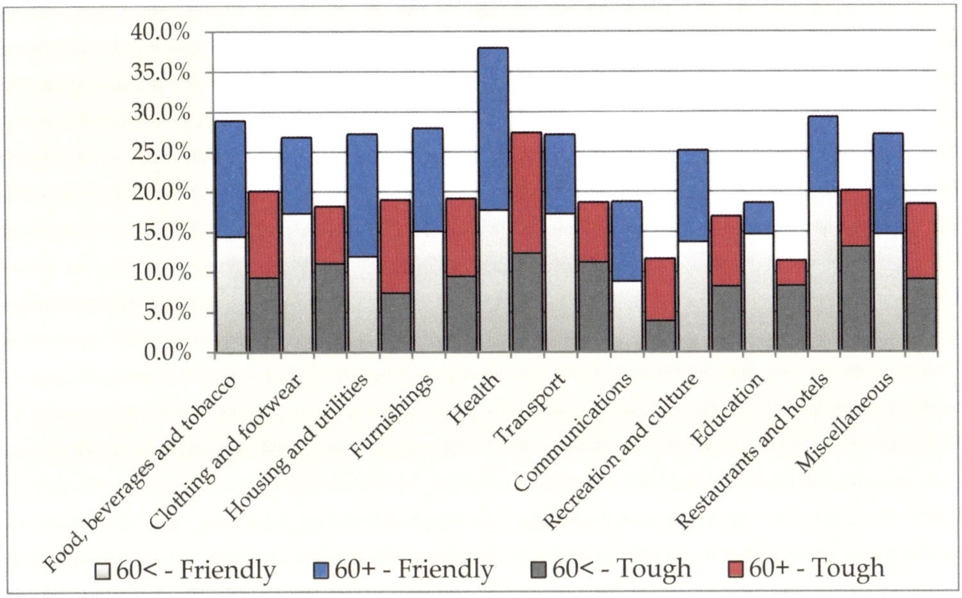

Source: Authors' calculations; Štefánik et al. (2013).

Figure 6.6 Expansion of EU27 labour demand generated by demographic transition by age of reference person under 'friendly' (F) and 'tough' (T) scenarios, 2010-2025 (thousands of jobs created)

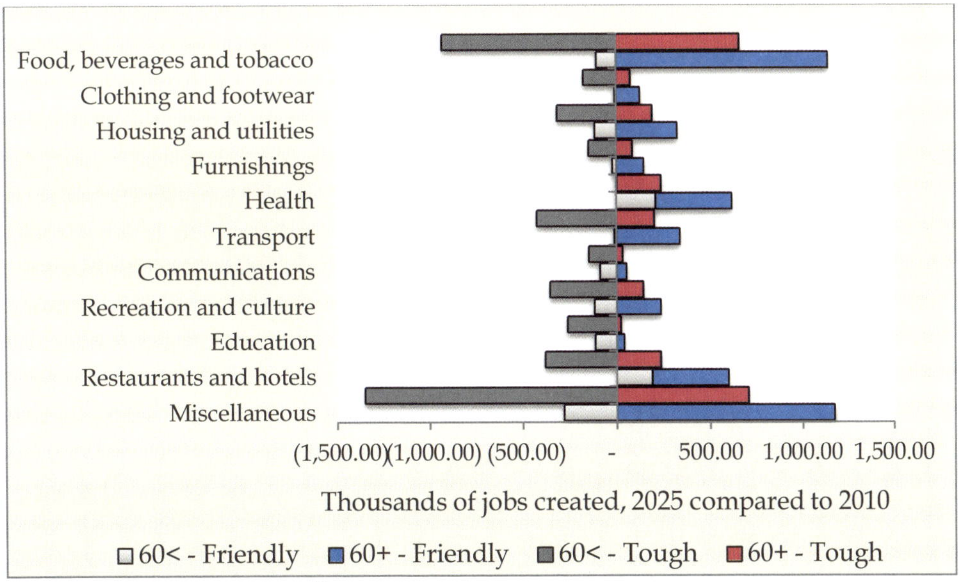

Source: Authors' calculations; Štefánik et al. (2013).

Across countries there are two contrasting ageing effects on total employment: the effects of decreasing demand of households under 60 and the positive effects of older ones. Taking a more detailed country perspective, the negative effects of younger households on the total workforce ranges between -3.5% (friendly scenario) and -5.3% (tough) in Germany and between -0.1% and 0.6% in Slovakia from 2010 to 2025. Additional employment caused by growing silver demand is equal to 0.0-0.6 % of the total workforce in Germany, 1.1-2.2% in Slovakia, 0.5-1.6% in Italy, 0.8–1.3% in Finland, and 1.2–2.0% in the EU27 as a whole. The total impact of changed consumption on employment varies from 0.5-2.0% of additional employment in Slovakia to job losses of between 2.9% and 5.3% in Germany.

In Europe as a whole, the gross effect of the increased demand of the elderly will generate as many as 2.6 to 4.4 million new jobs during 2010-2025. In contrast, changes in the demand of younger households, along with productivity gains, will result in job losses of approximately 0.5-4.5 million. The total net effects of changed consumption on employment under the presented assumptions will lead to a loss of 1.9 million jobs in the tough scenario, and the creation of 3.9 million additional jobs in the friendly scenario. This decrease under the tough scenario should be considered as an important change and, in the light of EU employment targets, appropriate reform measures should be directed at the labour market in order to address it.

6.10 The elderly as workers and consumers: Two sides of the same coin

Population ageing in European countries is an inevitable process, and one that is generally perceived as negative. We have shown that this process has its specific characteristics and is influencing the economy and the labour market. Particular circumstances and the policies anticipating this process could even boost employment and innovation within EU member states, or at least diminish the negative effects of ageing.

From an employment point of view, the majority of countries are taking measures to increase the retirement age (through changes in pension schemes, etc.). As was shown in the first part of this chapter, this approach requires more than just a simple adjustment of social security schemes related to older workers and retirees. Preventing skill obsolescence at older ages requires more investment in lifelong learning. Attitudes of employers are usually an important determinant for the demand for older workers, and improved safety-at-work measures and support for families with care duties can influence the activity of certain groups of employees. Keeping the elderly in the labour market has a positive effect - not only by decreasing the burden on the pension systems but also by improving the standard of living and demand of the elderly.

At the same time, changes in the volume and structure of consumption caused by the growing share of the elderly population may boost some sectors, while we will observe a decrease in aggregate demand in others. These 'silver economy' effects should lead to innovation in providing specific 'silver goods and services', which could even boost the EU's export potential within the global economy.

Based on the findings briefly described in this chapter, we can recommend the following policies that view the ageing process as an opportunity for further sustainable growth under the current processes of the socio-ecological transformation:

- promote healthy ageing and prevention of disabilities;
- adjust employment laws and policies to the specific needs of the elderly;
- promote the single market in the cross-border use of health and social services, especially relating to long-term care; and
- support the innovation processes related to prospective 'silver sectors'.

Bibliography

Beblavý, M., I. Maselli and M. Veselková (2014), *Let's get to work: The Future of Labour in Europe, Vol. 1*, Centre for European Policy Studies, Brussels.

Bloom, D.E., D. Canning and J. Sevilla (2002), *The Demographic Dividend: A New Perspective on the Economic Consequences of Population Change*, Santa Monica, CA: RAND.

Boitier, N., N. Lancesseur and P. Zagamé (2013), "Global scenarios for socio-ecological transition", NEUJOBS Working Paper No. 9.2 (www.neujobs.eu).

European Commission (2009) "Dealing with the impact of an ageing population in the EU", COM(2009) 180 final, European Commission, Brussels.

European Commission (2006) "The demographic future of Europe - from challenge to opportunity", COM(2006) 571 final, European Commission, Brussels.

European Commission (2003), "Household Budget Surveys in the EU. Methodology and recommendations for harmonisation - 2003", Luxembourg: Office for Official Publications of the European Communities.

Fischer-Kowalsky, M., W. Haas, D. Wiedenhofer, U. Weisz, I. Pallua, N. Possanner and A. Behrens (2012), "Socio-Ecological Transitions: Definition, Dynamics and Related Global Scenarios", NEUJOBS Working Paper No. 1.2 (www.neujobs.eu).

Lalonde, M. (1974), "A New Perspective on the Health of Canadians", Working Document, Government of Canada, Ottawa.

Lührmann, M. (2005), "Population Aging and the Demand for Goods and Service", Discussion Paper No. 95-05, Mannheim Research Institute for the Economics of Ageing, University of Mannheim.

Mason, A. and R. Lee (2007), "Transfers, Capital, and Consumption over the Demographic Transition", in R. Clark, N. Ogawa and A. Mason (eds), *Population Aging, Intergenerational Transfers and the Macroeconomy*, Cheltenham, UK: Edward Elgar, pp. 128-162.

OECD (2013), *Pensions at a Glance 2013: OECD and G20 Indicators*, Paris: OECD Publishing (http://dx.doi.org/10.1787/pension_glance-2013-en).

Riedel, M. and H. Hofer (2013), "Determinants of the transition from work into retirement", NEUJOBS Working Paper No. 17.1 (www.neujobs.eu).

Ruzik-Sierdzińska, A., M. Lis, M. Potoczna, M. Belloni and C. Villosio (2013), "Age and Productivity. Human Capital Accumulation and Depreciation", NEUJOBS Working Paper No 17.2 (www.neujobs.eu).

Ruzik-Sierdzinska, A. (2014), "Future Scenarios for the Development of the Labour Force", NEUJOBS Policy Brief No. 17.5 (www.neujobs.eu).

Styczyńska, I., A.-J. Riekhoff, M. Lis and A. Kamińska (2013), "The impact of institutional and socio-ecological drivers on activity at older ages", NEUJOBS Working Paper No 17.3 (www.neujobs.eu).

Štefánik, M., T. Domonkos, P. Horvát, V. Hvozdíková, I. Lichner, T. Miklošovič, V. Páleník and M. Radvanský (2013) "Modelling Economic Potential of Silver Economy", NEUJOBS Working Paper No. 12.3 (www.neujobs.eu).

Van Dalen, H.P, K. Henkens and M. Wang (2014), "Recharging the Older Worker: Human Resource Strategies of European Employers", NEUJOBS Working Paper No 17.4 (www.neujobs.eu).

WHO (2002), *Active Ageing: A Policy Framework*, World Health Organization, Geneva.

Notes

[1] A chapter is dedicated to this issue in the companion volume to this present work (see Beblavý et al. (2014).

[2] OECD (2013), p. 164.

[3] Styczyńska et al. (2013)

[4] Riedel and Hofer (2013).

[5] The conclusions of Riedel and Hofer (2013) are based on an analysis of data from ad hoc module 2006 (AHM2006) of the European Labour Force Survey (LFS) in the EU27 countries.

[6] Ibid.

[7] Styczyńska et al.

[8] Ibid.

[9] WHO (2002).

[10] See, for example, OECD (2006) cited by van Dalen et al. (2014)

[11] Ruzik-Sierdzinska et al. (2013).

[12] Ruzik-Sierdzińska et al. (2013)

[13] SHARELIFE is a retrospective part of panel Survey of Health, Ageing and Retirement in Europe; see Ruzik-Sierdzińska et al. (2013).

[14] For more detailed background description, see van Dalen et al. (2014)

[15] van Dalen et al. (2014).

[16] Ibid.

[17] Fischer-Kowalski et al. (2012)

[18] Ruzik-Sierdzińska (2014).

[19] European Commission (2009).

[20] This concept was introduced by Mason and Lee (2007), who examined the relationship between economic development and demographic transition. In the first stages of economic development, economies benefit from concentration of the population in the working age. Such gains, however, appear to be transitory: as economies mature, fertility declines and life expectancy rises, and the population ages. Nevertheless, transitory gains can be transformed into sustainable gains through the creation of human, and especially physical capital. The 'second demographic dividend' thus refers to a period of more rapid economic growth and a permanently higher level of per capita income and consumption.

[21] For a detailed overview of the data and methodology, see Štefánik et al. (2013).

[22] Results are based on information about the structure of consumption from the European Household Budget Surveys (HBS). The limitations of cross-country comparisons are explained in European Commission (2003).

[23] See, for example, Štefánik et al. (2013).

[24] The relative mean expenditure of households with reference persons older than 60, on 12 COICOP 1-digit items entered the cluster analysis. For a detailed description of the data and the methodology, see Štefánik et al. (2013).

[25] The chapter is covering only private consumption effects.

7. WOMEN AS WORKERS – IN THE MIDDLE OF A MARATHON

*IGA MAGDA AND AGNIESZKA KAMIŃSKA**

Is it possible to further improve the position of women on the European labour market? What will be the drivers for and obstacles to increasing female employment in the next decade? The socio-ecological transition, and above all its demographic component, will inevitably reshape the structure of labour markets: according to Eurostat forecasts, the European Union's working age population will shrink by a considerable 8 million people by 2025 and its median age will increase considerably. Labour shortages are likely to hinder GDP growth and increase wage and inflationary pressures, threatening the sustainability of welfare states. Thus, policies that help to fill the gaps in labour supply are of great importance, and increasing women's labour market participation appears to be the most important of these.

Women already have more and more incentives to be active on the labour market, and these incentives will be reinforced in the future. Female labour market entrants are increasingly well educated, which makes them more likely to find employment and to remain on the labour market (or to return to it after childbirth). The labour shortages in the coming decades will increase wage pressures, changing women's preferences from unpaid home duties to a working income, drawing more of them into paid employment.

Nevertheless, problems and obstacles remain and despite a considerable improvement over the past two decades, the labour potential of women is far from being fully utilised – their employment and participation rates remain below the levels observed for men (10.6 and 12

* Iga Magda: Vice President of the Board, Institute for Structural Research, Warsaw; Agnieszka Kamińska: Institute for Structural Research, Warsaw.

percentage points lower, respectively). Increasing these figures remains a challenge, as only well-coordinated, complex actions targeting various aspects and determinants of women's labour market attachment will be effective. This chapter summarises the main components of the necessary policy mix, describing the challenges and potential best solutions in the fields of education, maternity, retirement, lifelong learning, care choices, flexible employment contracts and wages.

7.1 Women's labour market participation could still grow

Over the last two decades, the European Union has experienced a significant improvement in women's labour market participation.[1,2] This is the result of both long-term trends evident across developed countries and changes made to institutional frameworks in specific countries. Recent evidence from the global economic downturn has shown that the employment of women is more resilient to recessions than that of men, partially because of gender sectoral segregation (i.e. the male domination of the crisis-hit construction and manufacturing sectors, and the female domination of the services sector, which was spared the worst effects of the crisis). The fact that since the 1990s, women have contributed to the lion's share of employment improvements highlights their growing role in labour markets. However, there is still significant potential for further action, since the gender employment gap – i.e. the difference between the employment rates of men and of women – is greater than 10 percentage points in half of European countries.[3]

The gender employment gap is still greater than 10 percentage points in half of the EU member states.

Changes in female employment and participation rates display strong age-specific patterns. Women of older age groups (45-64 years) have experienced the most notable employment improvements, and significant positive employment changes were also observed among prime-aged women.[4] On the other hand, employment rates among younger women (under 25 years of age) have decreased in most European countries, mainly due to increasing enrolment of women in tertiary education.[5]

Most improvements in female employment in the last two decades were driven by changes in the intensity of employment, i.e. increases in the amount that women of various socio-demographic groups are involved in the labour market. A positive contribution was also made by a shift in educational composition among the female population – well-educated women have higher employment rates,[6] so the increasing share of women graduating from tertiary education positively influenced total employment rates. This educational shift played a relatively greater role in central and eastern Europe (CEE) than in western European countries.[7] Demographic changes observed over the 1990s and 2000s did impact the relative position of women in different age groups, but did not matter for the overall changes in employment levels. However, this will change considerably over the coming years.

7.2 School-to-work transitions need to be made easier

In the last two decades, the number of young people enrolling in tertiary education has increased considerably. Recent data show that two thirds of young women enter university, compared with 52% of young men.[8] Thus, young women entering the labour market are now much better educated than both their male counterparts and women of older cohorts. The rising human capital levels of women positively affect both their own career prospects and macro-level growth rates.

However, in many countries students tend not to combine education with work, so the expansion of tertiary education has led to an increase in the average age of people entering the labour market and to lower employment rates for younger age groups (see Figure 7.2 and Figure 7.2). At one extreme, there is a group of elitist educational systems (e.g. South Korea) where employers strongly value diplomas from the best universities and students have little incentive to combine study and work, which delays graduation and adversely affects employment.[9] At the other extreme is a group of Nordic countries where young people demonstrate high levels of mobility between employment and education, moving between the two many times before completing tertiary education.[10] In the latter countries, the age at which tertiary education is commenced and completed is considerably higher than in the former countries. Yet, school-to-work transitions are easier in countries where studying is frequently combined with work, so this educational model should be supported by public policies.

School-to-work transitions are easier in countries where study is frequently combined with work

Figure 7.1 Economic activity rate among 15-24 year olds in the OECD and EU15, by sex, 1985-2011 (%)

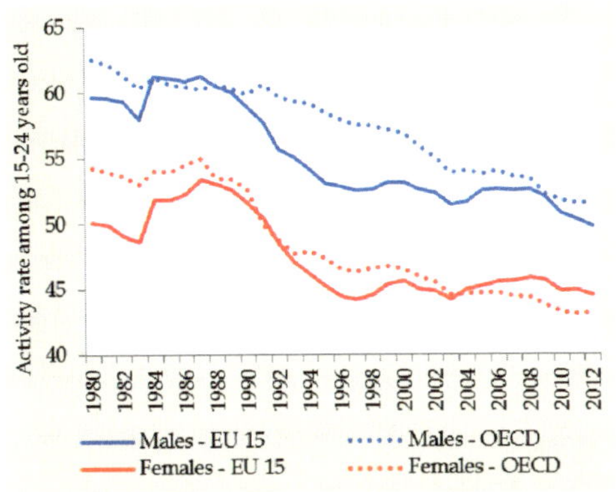

Source: Chłoń-Domińczak et al. (2013).

Figure 7.2 Leaving education and combining school and work in OECD countries, 2008

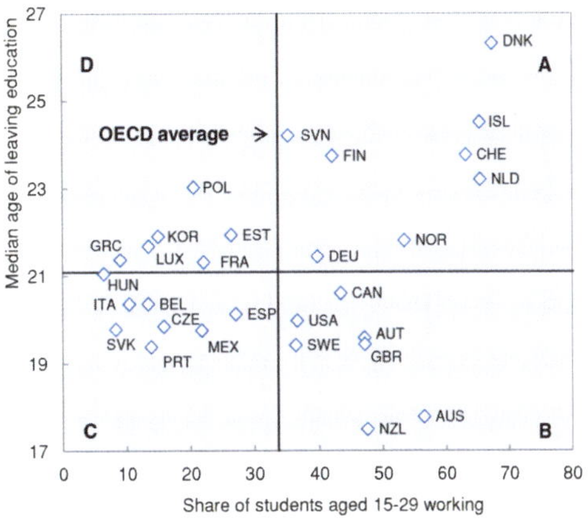

Source: Chłoń-Domińczak et al. (2013), based on OECD (2010).

The Great Recession of 2008-09 aggravated the problem of joblessness among young people.[11] Weak economic conditions after the recession have resulted in fewer job opportunities, making the transition from education to employment much harder. Young people find it more difficult to get a job, as they lack work experience. Although women have higher educational aspirations than men, they are less likely to be in either employment or education (see Figure 7.3). The traditional explanation for this is the responsibility of being young mothers.[12] In 2013, about a third of inactive non-studying women aged 15-24 in the EU were not looking for a job due to their care responsibilities.[13] However, a large share of NEETs is also made up of young persons who do not face family obstacles but cannot find a job.

Finding a first job is harder for women despite being, on average, more educated than men.[14] Generally, men and women in the EU only have similar levels of transition to a first job in the first few months after completing education. Later, the genders diverge and men are slightly more likely to find their first job than women. As mentioned, a plausible reason for this gender gap could be care responsibilities often resulting in difficulties in achieving a work-life balance. Compared with other women and with fathers, mothers are less likely to have made a rapid transition to their first job.[15] However, maternity is only one potential explanation for the gender differences in school-to-work transitions; studies suggest that women encounter other difficulties in entering and re-entering the labour market.[16]

Figure 7.3 Percentage of 15-24 year-olds in neither employment nor education (NEET), by gender (2011)

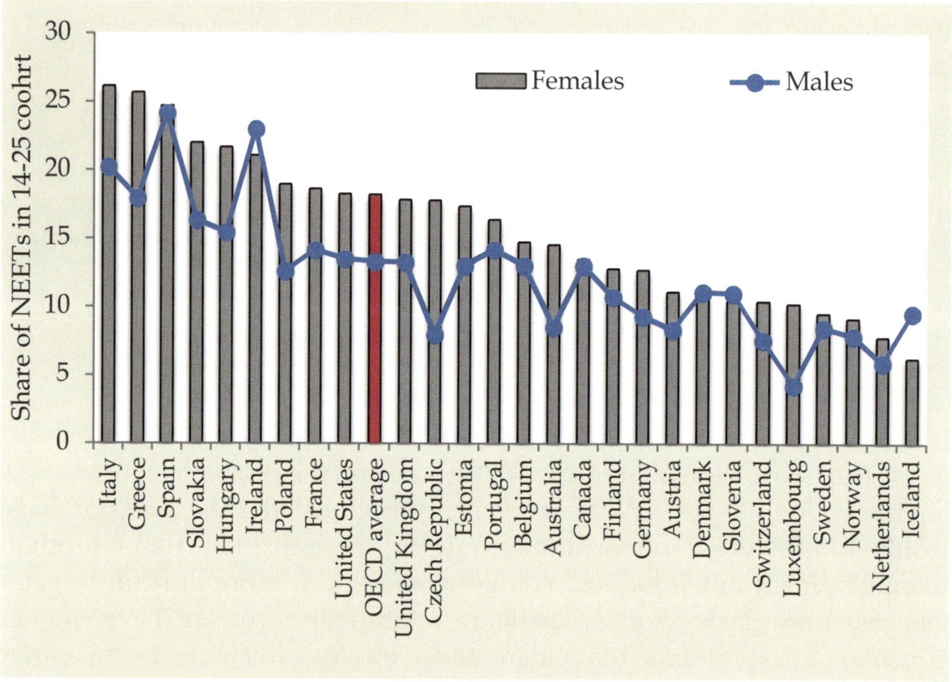

Source: Chłoń-Domińczak et al. (2013) on the basis of OECD (2013).

The problem of NEETs is a major policy challenge, since long periods spent outside of employment and education have an adverse effect on young peoples' future career paths. Work experience gained during studies is a key factor in helping to smooth the transition between education and employment and in increasing young workers' - in particular, women's - labour force participation rates. This can be achieved in two complementary ways. The first solution is apprenticeship programmes. Universities should ensure that these programmes equip students with further knowledge and skills valued by employers. For some students, apprenticeships provide a real job opportunity, as employers offer positions to the best apprentices.[17] More demanding is the second solution to gain work experience - combining tertiary education with employment. Labour market institutions are essential in ensuring a work-education balance. Students are usually unable to work full-time jobs, and so would benefit from the promotion of part-time employment and flexible working hours arrangements.

Access to public employment services should be extended to all young people, not only to those who are unemployed.[18] Assistance measures such as job counselling might also be beneficial to those who are not currently seeking employment. Finally, policies targeting NEETs must be more diversified, because there are different reasons behind joblessness among this group (such as parenthood, a lack of skills or the decision to take a 'gap year'). Policies aimed at increasing their skills (i.e. training programmes) and subsidising employment to provide them with work experience may be preferable. However, any considerable decrease in NEET rates will be caused by more vigorous economic growth fuelling labour demand.

7.3 Combining work with maternity requires further support

Maternity and childcare often require women to take a break from their professional lives, so employment rates among mothers are lower than those among other women. Young mothers in particular often withdraw from the labour market, as they are unable to combine employment with family responsibilities.[19] The proportion of mothers leaving the labour market due to maternity varies across the EU (see Figure 7.4). The figure is lowest in the Nordic countries, where the employment rate among mothers is almost the same as the employment rate among childless women. In contrast, in most of the new member states there is a considerable difference between labour market outcomes for women with and without (small) children.

Figure 7.4 Employment rates among all women aged 25-54 and those with a child aged below 15 among EU countries, 2011

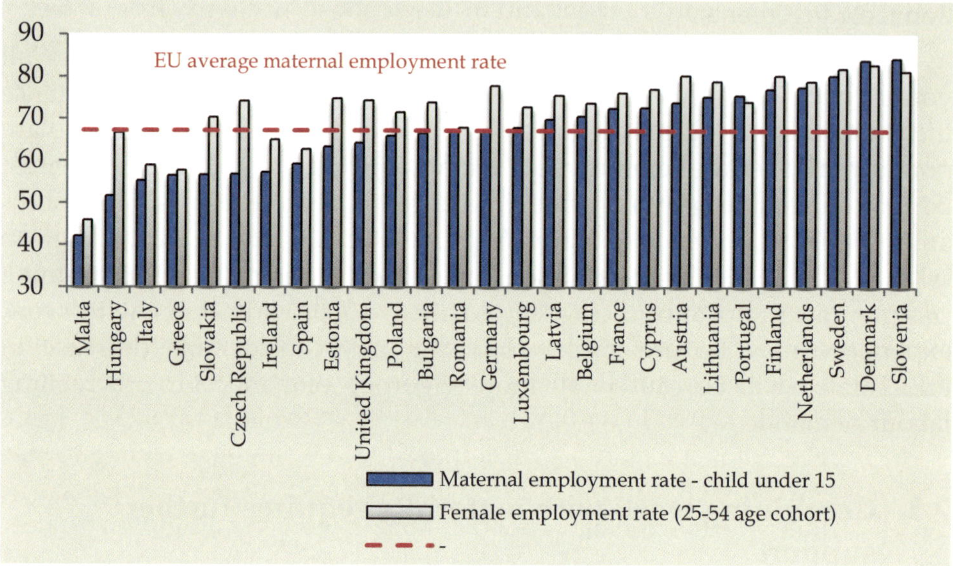

Source: Own calculations based on Eurostat and OECD data.

The development of public childcare services is a crucial factor shaping mothers' behaviour in the labour market.[20] Countries that offer the highest availability of pre-school child services (e.g. the Nordic countries and France) tend to have higher employment rates among young mothers. These services should not only be widely accessible, but also affordable. This is of particular importance for low-skilled and low-income women, whose labour market attachment is the weakest and who are most likely to fall into an inactivity trap.

Access to affordable, good quality public childcare services is a crucial factor shaping mothers' behaviour in the labour market

Flexible workplace arrangements, such as flexible working hours, are another means of helping parents cope with childcare. These seem to play a particularly important role when other policies ensuring a family-work balance are not sufficiently developed.[21] However, flexible contracts are a double-edged sword. On the one hand, higher flexibility tends to be associated with a lower degree of employment protection, and as such allows more jobs to be created. On the other hand, discriminatory practices or too little employment protection may discourage mothers from entering the labour market.[22]

The duration of parental leave should be assessed carefully. If it is too short and the child still needs special care, women might not be able to return to full-time employment and instead choose inactivity, from which it is usually more difficult to return.[23] On the other hand, if parental leave is too long this will lead to skill deterioration and a decrease in women's chances to return to the labour market. A transitory period of reduced working hours and the retention of some maternity benefit may be a good way for parents to gradually return to regular employment.

A more equal distribution of childcare and home responsibilities across genders is as important for women's employment prospects. This also includes caring duties related to the elderly, which we describe in more detail in Section 7.7. The fact that women are disproportionately burdened with caring obligations strongly diminishes their employment prospects, as they are likely to remain away from the labour market. At the same time, employers are more incentivised to discriminate against then as they assume women will have a higher propensity to have longer career breaks. Thus, effective policies aimed at raising women's employment need to encourage fathers to take an increased role in childcare duties, which will lift the burden from mothers. Making paternity leave obligatory, or designating a part of parental leave for men only, is an example of a policy practice in this area.

Another maternity-related policy is ensuring that old-age pension system arrangements reward periods of inactivity due to childcare. This is necessary, yet these provisions should not discourage women from longer activity in the labour market. An example of a bad policy in this area is the provision of early retirement for mothers. Yet, as D'Addio concludes, pension systems, however well designed, will not be able to compensate on a large scale for inequalities on the labour market between men and women, or between parents and childless individuals.[24] They form only a part of the overall policy response in a broader context of income redistribution and reduction of poverty among the elderly.

7.4 Retirement policies have a major impact on women's employment at older age

The increase in employment among older women has been responsible for most of the employment progress in Europe over the last two decades.[25] However, employment rates among women aged 55 or above are still significantly lower than those for prime-age women. There is thus room for further improvement, and bearing in mind Europe's ageing population and solvency issues surrounding public pension systems, this poses another major policy challenge.

The number of years spent by women on the labour market varies widely across European countries (see Figure 7.5). Women in Sweden and Denmark are active on the labour market for more than 35 years on average, whereas in southern European countries such as Italy and Greece, the number of expected years in employment for women is under 25. Southern Europe's poor performance in this respect is due more to women's complete withdrawal from the labour force than to longer career breaks related to education and childbearing. Lengthening women's labour market activity would strongly boost these countries' total employment rates, helping to alleviate the gaps caused by population ageing.

Figure 7.5 Average expected years in employment for women, 2002, 2006 and 2011

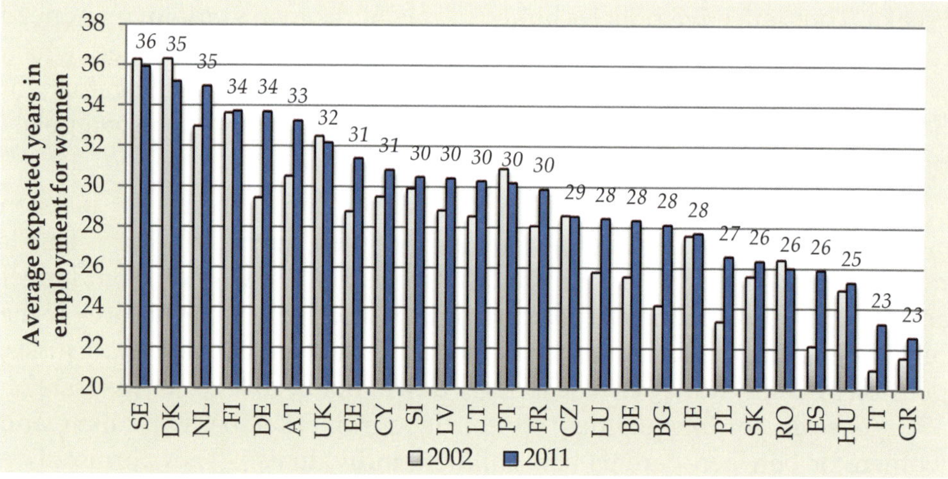

Source: Chłoń-Domińczak et al. (2013).

Many European countries have made attempts to harmonise their statutory retirement ages for men and women.[26] By 2040, the number of countries with different pensionable ages for men and women is expected to have fallen from 12 to 3 (see Figure 7.6).[27] At the same time, the legal retirement age for women is expected to increase in 19 EU member states. Evidence from countries that have already increased the retirement age for women suggests that this has a crucial impact on retirement decisions, postponing women's withdrawal from the labour market. Hence, a further increase in total employment rates among women – stemming from the rising labour market participation rates among those aged 55-64 alone – is to be expected.

Figure 7.6 Average pensionable age in OECD countries by gender, 1950-2050

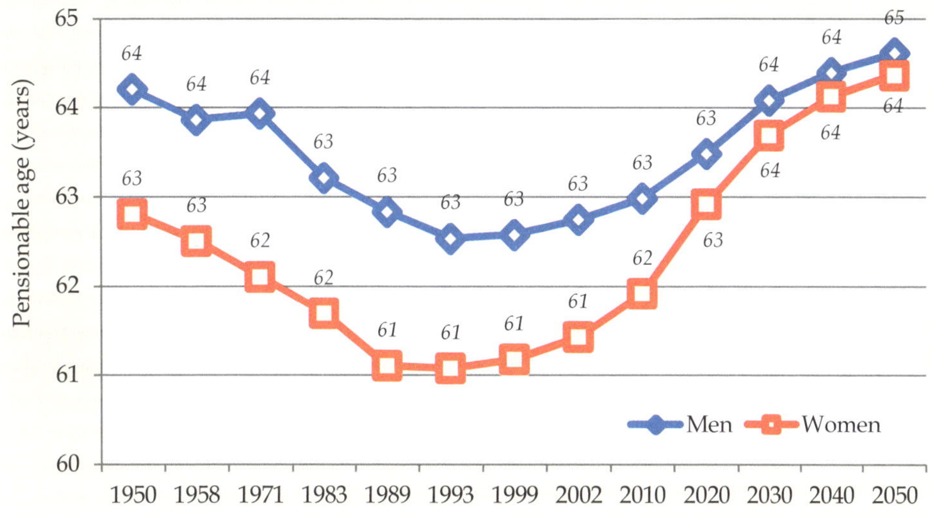

Source: Chłoń-Domińczak et al. (2013) on the basis of Chomik and Whitehouse (2010).

Figure 7.7 Pensionable age in EU countries by gender, 2011 and 2040

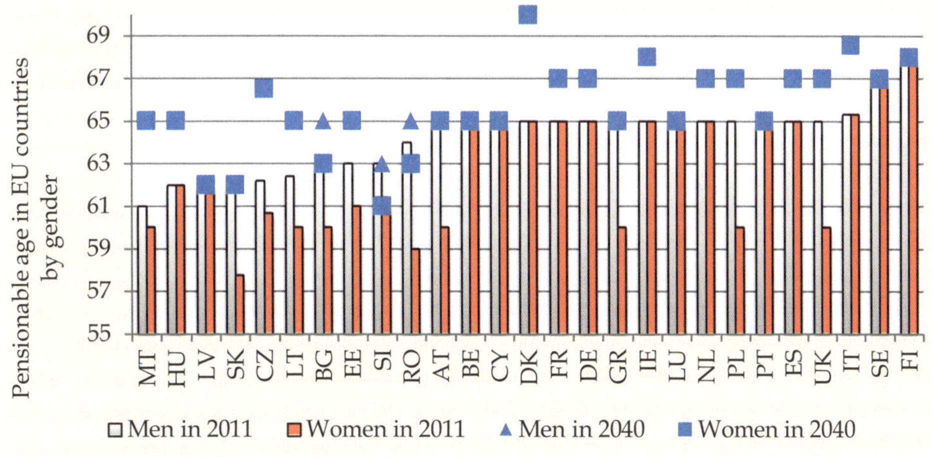

Source: Chłoń-Domińczak (2013) on the basis of a Polish Ministry of Finance mimeo.

The replacement rates provided by pension systems are another important factor determining retirement decisions. Higher replacement rates discourage continued employment, especially for people on low incomes. Current pension system reforms that introduce a closer link between lifetime contributions and pension benefits will negatively impact women, since they accumulate less contributions and experience longer periods out of employment than men.[28] However, this change will postpone the decision of women to withdraw from the labour market and thus increase employment rates, in particular among older women.

Current pension system reforms, introducing a closer link between lifetime contributions and pension benefits, will negatively impact women.

Finally, the aforementioned compensation for maternity and parental leaves within pension systems is another element that may impact women's decisions on when to retire.[29] A strong link between contributions and pensions will lower benefits paid to parents (mainly mothers), encouraging (or forcing) them to stay on the labour market for longer. On the other hand, generous maternity pension compensations may lead to excessively long periods out of labour market, which decrease the chances of returning to the labour market and future earnings (due to less work experience), again translating into lower pension benefits. Early retirement schemes offered to mothers are also likely to act against them, due to the lower pensions they would receive. Summing up, there are no easy solutions for incorporating maternity and parental breaks into pension systems in order to balance the family and pension policy goals. However, the increasing participation of women in higher education is likely to at least partially solve this problem by providing a strong incentive to stay on the labour market longer in order to reap the benefits of the investment in human capital.

7.5 Lifelong learning improves employability

Another crucial factor for increasing women's employment rates (in particular, by helping to extend their working lives) is their participation in various forms of education at later stages in the lifecycle, which would help them to update skills, compensate for their skill loss during periods outside the labour market and adapt them to the changing labour market demand. There is a large strand of the literature on how the development of workers' skills through lifelong learning (LLL) is essential to extending the length of time spent on the labour market and increasing employment levels.[30] Better-qualified workers stay in employment longer as their skills, knowledge and experience are more highly valued by employers. From a macroeconomic perspective, better human capital positively affects a country's competitiveness and growth rates.

Participation rates among adults in formal, informal (i.e. unorganised, associated for instance with leisure or learning from family members) and non-formal education (carried out within an organised framework) vary significantly across EU countries, and the challenges related to improvements in this area are different for men and women.[31] The key factors determining adults' participation in lifelong learning activities are age (a higher age implies lower participation), educational attainment (well-educated individuals tend to participate much more frequently in LLL activities), the economic sector (people working in agriculture and industry invest little in gaining new qualifications), and labour market status (being employed increases the chances of participating in LLL activities).

Gender differences play a minor role in determining overall LLL participation rates. Men and women take part in job-related training at similar rates in the majority of EU countries, with the exception of Denmark and Sweden. However, women are less likely to participate in formal education than men, while they outnumber men in non-formal training.[32] Moreover, training participation is higher in the more female-dominated sectors. That said, due to less continuous employment and to career breaks related to maternity, women experience a shorter average time spent in education, hence the need for stronger support for LLL activities for women.[33]

Moreover, women and men differ when it comes to their reasons for not participating in training. Women are much more likely to opt out of further education due to family reasons.[34] When interpreting this result, we should remember that answers are subjective and can be country-specific In the Netherlands, the high share of respondents may stem from the high value assigned to family, including family responsibilities and childcare. The largest relative gender differences are observed in Sweden and Portugal. However, recent research suggests that the presence of children in a household does not create a difference in the intensity of formal education among men and women in adult life, though it does lower female participation in non-formal learning.[35]

Women and men differ in their reasons for not participating in training

Figure 7.8 Obstacles to participation in education related to family responsibilities by country

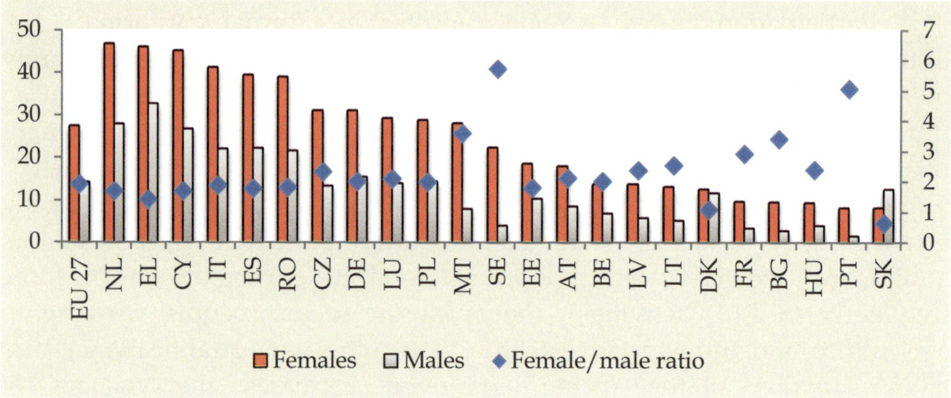

Source: Chłoń-Domińczak and Lis (2013).

As family obligations prevent women from obtaining more qualifications, an improvement in their LLL participation can be achieved by policies that remove obstacles to the balance between education and family life. Such policies (again) include greater access to affordable childcare and flexible working hours. A more equal distribution of family obligations between partners would also play a positive role.

Well-educated individuals are more likely to engage in LLL compared with those with lower educational attainment.[36] This means that the differences in human capital levels across socio-economic groups increase with age. To prevent rising human capital inequalities, it is crucial to pay particular attention to low-skilled women with low labour market attachment, as they are least likely to invest in improving their qualifications. Moreover, the design of sector-level policies should be differentiated to reflect variation in sectoral LLL participation, which is much higher in knowledge-intensive services. These differences also contribute to lifetime educational inequalities.

Furthermore, women might benefit from the recognition of informal learning. For instance, they are much more likely to adopt skills related to caring for children or the elderly.[37] Their care competences could be formally recognised (with some additional training, if needed). Increasing demand for people with care skills is expected due to population ageing, and formal qualifications could be successfully put to use in the labour market.

The policy solutions should also involve counselling by public employment services and helping women to plan their educational choices to reduce the mismatch between skills learnt and skills demanded by the labour market. This will translate not only into higher probabilities of finding a job, but also longer average duration and better quality of jobs, further increasing female employment rates.

7.6 Gender pay gaps remain a challenge, in particular among older workers

Gender pay gaps exist in all European countries, and on average women earn less than men with similar endowments employed in similar workplaces.[38] Average pay gaps hide a large degree of variation in female wage penalties (i.e. the difference in women's wages with respect to those of men with similar characteristics working in similar workplaces) depending on age and level of pay. Similar observations relate to the economic returns to flexible employment forms (i.e. fixed-term contracts and part-time jobs), which exhibit significant variation in wage premia and penalties depending on age and earning level.[39] Moreover, the ongoing structural changes in the labour market (mainly the demographic impact increasing the employment of older cohorts and increasing use of new, flexible forms of employment, as well as higher wage differentials) are modifying the existing shape and structure of female/male wage differentials.[40]

The ongoing structural changes in the labour market are modifying the existing shape and structure of female/male wage differentials.

The size of gender pay gaps varies significantly across countries. They are fairly low in the Netherlands and Norway, and are higher by a factor of more than three in the Czech Republic, Poland, Portugal and Slovakia, where, *ceteris paribus,* female prime-age workers earn approximately 25-30% less than their male colleagues. The size of the gender wage gap differs with age, but with no uniform pattern across Europe. In the majority of countries, the wage gap grows with age, with the peak at around 40-49 years, and tends to decrease at the age when female labour market participation declines (see Figure 7.9). However, the evidence on low pay gaps between labour market entrants does not hold for all European countries, particularly parts of central and eastern Europe where, early on in their careers, women already earn less than 'comparable' men.[41] This is mostly due to relatively higher pay gaps among top earners than among low-paid young women. It suggests that better-educated women in these countries experience more difficulties in effective education-to-employment transition and are more likely to face a glass ceiling.

Figure 7.9 Gender pay gaps tend to increase with age, but not everywhere (median earnings, 2006)

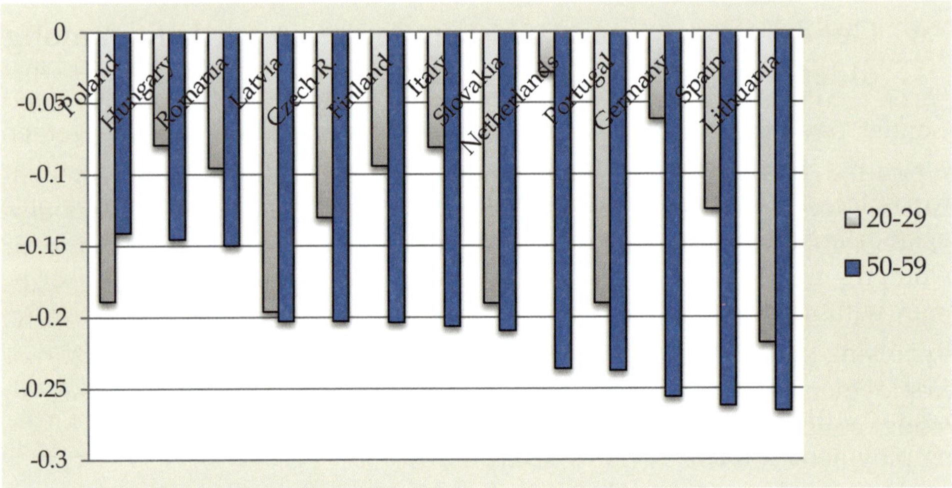

Source: Own calculations based on Eurostat data.

Forms of flexible employment appear to be a mixed blessing from a wage perspective. Women working on fixed-term contracts earn less than those working on a regular basis, all else being equal. The notable exceptions are Latvia, France and Greece, where fixed-term contracts are associated with higher earnings. Moreover, the decrease of the permanent job premium with age is confirmed for only a few (western European) countries,[42] while in contrast to that in Poland or Hungary there is a clear rise in temporary contract wage penalties with age. Fixed-term contracts also pay clearly less than permanent jobs in CEE countries. Looking at other aspects of job flexibility, in all EU countries except Portugal and Hungary, women working on a part-time basis tend to earn less per hour than 'similar' women working full-time. At the same time, part-time work is relatively more beneficial for well-educated women with higher incomes, i.e. the hourly wage of top female earners is higher for part-time than for full-time workers.[43] Finally, part-time work pays less for older women in particular; the gap is much lower among young female workers. The ongoing demographic changes are likely to further change the observed total wage gap. In particular, the increasing share of women employed at the age of 50 and above will probably lead to deepening their gender pay gaps, especially in those countries where their participation rates are low at the moment and where women are likely to self-select to better paid employment.

Reducing gender pay gaps is no easy task, partly because one cannot really know how much is due to discrimination. However, policies helping women to combine work and family life (e.g. childcare services) can be recommended since they decrease the so-called 'motherhood penalty'. Countries with well-developed policies supporting mothers tend to have lower gender pay gaps. Another crucial factor is fathers' increased involvement in caring obligations and household duties, which needs to be supported both by legal changes (e.g. more parental leave targeted at fathers) and promotional campaigns. Collective wage-bargaining may also play an important role in determining the position of low- and high-paid individuals. Decentralised bargaining schemes, where pay-setting takes place mainly at the firm level, support lower wage differences. Finally, equalising employment protection levels under different types of employment contract reduces labour market dualism and is likely to reduce contract-based wage gaps.

7.7 Unbalanced division of caring duties impedes women's employment growth

The increase in female employment in the EU has triggered an expansion of dual-income households, but this does not automatically imply a more balanced division of paid and unpaid labour between women and men.[44] Alongside gender equality policies, particular welfare and care regimes affect female employment differently and shape the gender division of paid work and care by households. In addition, gender equality and care policy choices may have significant demographic consequences through their impact on the decision to have children.

Care policies are represented by five models that broadly (though not precisely) reflect the classification of welfare regime typology.[45] The two major policy components in the field of care are (and probably will continue to be) formal, institutional, publicly provided care on the one hand, and market-oriented, publicly funded but privately provided cash-for-care schemes on the other. Research shows that the gender gaps in labour market participation correlate significantly and positively with the provision of formal care, whereas they correlate significantly and negatively with the provision of informal care.[46] Moreover, there is an almost linear relationship between the relative political empowerment of women and the expansion of formal care provision.

From a policy perspective, short-term cash-for-care schemes seem to provide a cheaper and more flexible alternative to formal and institutional care.[47] However, this market-oriented policy can only ensure the desired positive aspects (freedom of choice, good quality of care and decent employment for care workers) together with decreasing gender inequalities if it ensures quality control, standard basic employment guarantees and a well-established legal and institutional framework to prevent discrimination.

In those countries where gender equality policies are weakly developed and/or informality plays a dominant role in social relations, the expansion of dual-earner households without the dual-carer family model may reinforce existing gender inequalities within households due to uneven care responsibilities and by imposing multitasking on women.[48] The importance of comprehensive gender equality policies (the political empowerment of women and addressing work-life balance issues, including the transfer of care and domestic duties to men) is therefore obvious in shaping public perception and ensuring a supportive environment for dual-carer policy measures, which are necessary to boost female employment.

Comprehensive gender equality policies ensure a supportive environment for dual-carer policy measures and boost female employment.

Finally, one of the proposed policy solutions to the problem of the increasing burden of caring duties related to ageing is the massive influx of migrant female care workers (who are often employed in the informal economy under substandard employment conditions), but this obviously generates new forms of gender inequality. The paid employment opportunities for women who are supported by cheap and flexible care workers may improve; however, the (mainly migrant and female) care workers are at particular risk from the negative consequences of inequality. Thus, specific policies must be developed not only to guarantee the quality of privately provided services, but also the employment standards of the care providers themselves. A legal and institutional framework to prevent discrimination against and unfair treatment of care workers is one of the fundamental conditions of a fair market environment in the field of care.

7.8 Higher female participation rates can be encouraged by a coordinated, complex set of policies

The previous two decades saw further significant changes in the position of women on the European labour markets. Women constitute an increasing share of the total workforce, and this trend will continue in the future. Despite more incentives to enter and remain on the labour market - such as higher educational attainments raising the probability of being employed (and the alternative costs of staying inactive) or future wage growth driven by labour shortages - obstacles to higher female participation rates remain. These require a coordinated, complex set of policies targeting various factors influencing women's employment determinants and barriers, at both the micro and macro levels.

The most important recommendation for the policy mix is for the institutional setting to help to reconcile jobs with family life. Here, flexible employment arrangements and better access to childcare facilities will play a crucial role in increasing women's attachment to the labour market from a life-cycle perspective, as a quicker return to employment after a period of raising a child increases labour market opportunities and also employment chances at an older age. More involvement of men in family life will also be of considerable importance for women's greater employment and must be supported by legal changes. Flexible job provisions would be helpful, *inter alia,* for women who aim to increase or update their qualifications. Another area of policies affecting female employment concerns the redesign of pension systems so as to lower disincentives to withdraw from the labour market (at older age, but also during child-related career breaks) without penalising maternity leave.

Most of the policy recommendations proposed and discussed are not new solutions - in fact, they are at the top of the labour market and social policy agendas in Europe - and as such require no new funding. For instance, European countries are already undertaking several steps to smooth labour market entry for young people or to improve childcare access as part of the Europe 2020 strategy agenda. However, what is required is constant fine-tuning and revision of the policy solutions in response to changing needs and labour market settings, as well as local (national and regional) circumstances. No one-size-fits-all set of policies is possible, and this is not only because of diversity of labour market institutions across EU countries. The structure of labour demand also matters from an international, but also a regional, perspective. To give an example, policies aimed at helping women return to the labour market after childbearing rely heavily on the participation of employers, but here the solutions must be different in a country/region dominated by large employers, who will be more likely to cooperate and appreciate long-term targets of helping in retaining women's labour market attachment, from the solutions in a country/region where work opportunities are created mostly by small and medium-sized entrepreneurs, for whom softer and more flexible solutions will be required so as not to create disincentives to hire women at all.

Bibliography

Baran, J., A. Bartha, A. Chłoń-Domińczak, O. Fedyuk, A. Kamińska and P. Lewandowski, M. Lis, I. Magda, M. Potoczna and V. Zentai (2014), "Women on the European Labour Market", NEUJOBS Policy Brief No. 16.5.

Bartha, A., O. Fedyuk and V. Zentai (2014), "Gender Equality and Care Choices in the Light of Population Ageing", NEUJOBS Working Paper No. 16.4.

Blanchard, O. and A. Landier (2002), "The perverse effects of partial labour market reform :fixed-term contracts in France", *The Economic Journal*, Vol. 112, No. 480, pp. F214–F244.

Blanden, J., F. Buscha, P. Sturgis and P. Urwin (2010), "Measuring the returns to lifelong learning", Centre for Economics of Education, LSE.

Chevalier, A. (2004), "Motivation, Expectations and the Gender Pay Gap for UK Graduates", IZA Discussion Paper No. 1101.

Chłoń-Domińczak, A. (2013), "Female Transition to Retirement", NEUJOBS Working Paper No. D16.2B.

Chłoń-Domińczak, A. and M. Lis (2013), "Does gender matter for lifelong learning activity?", NEUJOBS Working Paper No. D16.2A.

Chłoń-Domińczak, A., A. Kamińska and I. Magda (2013), "Women as a potential of the European labour force", NEUJOBS Position Paper No. 16.2 C.

Chomik, R. and E. Whitehouse, E. (2010), "Trends in Pension Eligibility Ages and Life 1950-2050", OECD Social, Employment and Migration Working Papers, OECD, Paris.

D'Addio, A.C. (2013), "Pension Entitlements of Women with Children: The Role of Credis within Pension Systems in OECD and EU Countries", in R. Holzmann, E. Palmer and D. Robalino (eds), *Nonfinancial Defined Contribution Pension Schemes in a Changing Pension World. Volume 2: Gender, Politics and Financial Stability*, Washington, D.C.: World Bank, pp. 75–110.

Greve, B. (2012), "Reconciliation of Work and Family Life in Four Different Welfare States", NEUJOBS Working Paper No. D 5.5.

Holzmann, R., E. Palmer and D. Robalino (eds) (2012), *Nonfinancial Defined Contribution Pension Schemes in a Changing Pension World, Volume 2: Gender, Politics and Financial Stability*, Washington, D.C.: World Bank.

Hoobler, J., S. Wayne and G. Lemmon (2009), "Bosses' Perceptions of Family-Work Conflict and Women's Promotability: Glass Ceiling Effects", *Academy of Management Journal,* Vol. 52, No. 5, pp. 939–957.

Jenkins, A. (2004), "Women, Lifelong Learning and Employment", Discussion Paper No. 39, Centre for Economics of Education, LSE.

Lewandowski, P., I. Magda, J. Baran, O. Fedyuk and A. Bartha (2013), "Gender Dimension of the Labour Markets over the Past Two Decades", NEUJOBS Working Paper No. D16.1.

Magda, I. and M. Potoczna (2014), "Does Flexible Employment Pay? European Evidence on the Wage", NEUJOBS Working Paper No. 16.3.

Magda, I., J. Perek- Białas and A. Ruzik-Sierdzińska (2014), *Kształcenie i dokształcanie się z perspektywy aktywności zawodowej,* Educational Research Institute, Warsaw.

Matysiak, A. and D. Vignoli (2011), "Different women's employment and fertility behaviours in similar institutional settings: Evidence from Italy and Poland", Working Paper No. 15/2011, Institute of Statistics and Demography, Warsaw School of Economics.

Mills, M. and I. Mooi-Reci (2012), "The Gendered Consequences of Unemployment Insurance Reforms", *Social Forces,* Vol. 91, No. 2, pp. 583-608.

Mills, M. and P. Präg (2014), *Gender inequalities in the school-to-work transition in Europe,* Santa Monica, CA and Cambridge, UK: RAND Corporation.

Neumark, D. (2009), "Alternative Labor Market Policies to Increase Economic Self-Sufficiency: Mandating Higher Wages, Subsidizing Employment and Raising Productivity", NBER Working Paper No. 14807.

OECD (2010), *Off to a Good Start? Jobs for Youth,* Paris: OECD.

_____ (2011), *Doing Better for Families,* Paris: OECD.

_____ (2012a), *Better Skills, Better Jobs, Better Lives: A Strategić Approach do Skills Policies,* Paris: OECD.

_____ (2012b), *Education Indicators in Focus 2012/01,* Paris: OECD, January.

_____ (2012c), *Closing the gender gap,* Paris: OECD.

_____ (2013), *Education at a Glance 2013,* Paris: OECD.

Ok, W. and P. Tergeist (2003), "Improving Workers' Skills: Analytical Evidence and the Role of the Social Partners", OECD Social, Employment and Migration Working Papers, Paris.

Quintini, G. (2011), "Over-Qualified or Under- Skilled. A review of existing literature", OECD Social, Employment and Migration Working Papers, Paris.

Young Women's Trust (2014), *NEETs and Gender. Preliminary study for 'Scarred for Life?' an inquiry led by Young Women's Trust,* London: Young Women's Trust.

Notes

[1] Chłoń-Domińczak et al. (2013).

[2] Lewandowski et al.(2013).

[3] Chłoń-Domińczak et al. (2013).

[4] Chłoń-Domińczak (2013).

[5] Chłoń-Domińczak et al. (2013).

[6] OECD (2012b).

[7] Lewandowski et al.(2013).

[8] Chłoń-Domińczak et al. (2013).

[9] OECD (2010).

[10] OECD (2010).

[11] Baran et al. (2014)

[12] Young Women's Trust (2014).

[13] Own calculation based on Eurostat data.

[14] Mills and Präg (2014).

[15] Mills and Präg (2014).

[16] Mills and Präg (2014); Mills and Mooi-Reci (2012); Hoobler et al. (2009)

[17] Neumark (2009); OECD (2010).

[18] Baran et al. (2014).

[19] Matysiak and Vignol (2011).

[20] OECD (2011).

[21] Greve (2012).

[22] Magda and Potoczna (2014).

[23] OECD (2011).

[24] D'Addio (2013).

[25] Lewandowski et al.(2013).

[26] Chłoń-Domińczak (2013).

[27] Chomik and Whitehouse (2010).

[28] Holzmann et al. (2012).

[29] D'Addio (2013).

[30] Ok and Tergeist (2003); Jenkins (2004); Blanden et al. (2010); OECD (2012a); Chłoń-Domińczak and Lis (2013).

---

[31] Chłoń-Domińczak and Lis (2013).

[32] Chłoń-Domińczak and Lis (2013).

[33] Quintini (2011); Chłoń-Domińczak and Lis (2013).

[34] Chłoń-Domińczak and Lis (2013).

[35] Magda et al. (2014).

[36] Ok and Tergeist (2003).

[37] Chłoń-Domińczak and Lis (2013).

[38] OECD (2012c).

[39] Magda and Potoczna (2014).

[40] Lewandowski et al. (2013).

[41] Chevalier (2004).

[42] Blanchard and Landier (2002).

[43] Magda and Potoczna (2014).

[44] Bartha et al. (2014b).

[45] The liberal model, the Nordic model and three types of the Bismarckian model (Western European continental, Southern European and post-socialist), Bartha et al. (2014b).

[46] Bartha et al. (2014b).

[47] Bartha et al. (2014b).

[48] Bartha et al. (2014b).

8. A COMMON LABOUR IMMIGRATION POLICY FOR THE EU? RETHINKING 'ATTRACTIVENESS' AND SOCIO-ECONOMIC INCLUSION

*SERGIO CARRERA, ELSPETH GUILD AND KATHARINA EISELE**

Societies and policy-makers in Europe will face key labour market challenges in the years to come relating to economic recovery, ageing populations and shrinking workforces. The negative impact of the reduction in the size of the labour force could be mitigated by increased immigration. However, even under the assumptions of the 'friendly' scenario described in the introductory chapter (high fertility, extended life expectancy and increased immigration), the majority of EU countries will face a short-term decline in their working-age population. Immigration will not be able to fully compensate for a decline in the working age population, but it can bring about immediate population growth.[1]

The importance of immigration in combating demographic challenges has been recognised by the European Commission, which has stated that "some of the additional and specific skills needed in the future could be found only outside the EU".[2] The EU has attempted to actively develop an 'attractive' labour immigration policy with the objective of

* Sergio Carrera: Senior Research Fellow and Head of the Justice and Home Affairs research unit, CEPS; Elspeth Guild: Jean Monnet Professor ad personam of European Migration Law at Radboud University Nijmegen and Queen Mary, University of London, Associate Senior Research Fellow at CEPS and partner at Kingsley Napley; Katharina Eisele: Researcher in the Justice and Home Affairs research unit of CEPS.

encouraging foreign highly skilled workers to come to the EU.[3] In this chapter, we examine the determinants and challenges of the current EU framework for immigration law and policy. The key aspects and debates surrounding the attractiveness and selectiveness of labour migration policies include the discussion about the trade-off between migrant rights and openness to immigration, considerations on a revamped EU guest worker model, as well as debates on the importance of skill recognition in the EU. Our comparative approach enables us to draw lessons from other international experiences, such as those of the United States and Canada.

8.1 Immigration policies to attract highly skilled workers are high on the EU agenda

Labour immigration policies that attract foreign professionals to the EU have been high on the agenda of policy-makers. The Europe 2020 strategy identifies the need to attract highly qualified third-country nationals in a context of growing global competition. Top priority has been given to third-country workers labelled as 'highly qualified' to fill the perceived needs of EU member states' labour markets.[4] In policy discourses, however, the EU seems somehow a less advantageous or appealing destination in comparison to other countries.[5] The European Commission stated in 2007 that:

> The attractiveness of the EU compared to such countries [as the United States and Canada] suffers from the fact that at present highly qualified migrants must face 27 different admission systems, do not have the possibility of easily moving from one country to another for work, and in several cases lengthy and cumbersome procedures make them opt for non-EU countries granting more favourable conditions for entry and stay.[6]

Thus, the US and Canadian labour migration systems are often cited as successful models to follow in an alleged race for the brightest minds. The priority of an EU labour immigration policy is of relevance for the wider development of a common EU migration policy.

The European Commission has confirmed this attractiveness and 'competition for talent' policy paradigm in its Communication titled "An Open and Secure Europe – Making it Happen" of May 2014. The Communication underlined that "Europe must attract new talent and compete on the global scale" and that:

> Demographic changes, in particular the shrinking of the working population in Europe, coupled with significant skill shortages in certain sectors [...] hinder the EU's productivity and thus its economic recovery. Increasing global competition for skills and talents affects labour markets in many Member States and will be a decisive factor for Europe's economic prosperity in the decade ahead.[7]

The European Council Conclusions of 26-27 June 2014[8] adopted the new Strategic Guidelines for the Area of Freedom, Security and Justice (AFSJ) for the period 2015-20.[9] The Guidelines consider it a key priority to develop rules maximising the opportunities for legal immigration to make the EU an attractive destination for 'talents and skills'. As the Stockholm Programme,[10] the third EU multi-annual programme covering EU policies on AFSJ, comes to an end in 2014, the development of a European immigration policy is in a crucial phase.

8.2 Key challenges of the EU's labour immigration policy

Since the Tampere Conclusions and the entry into force of the Amsterdam Treaty in 1999, the EU has tried to build an AFSJ. While important European laws and agreements have been adopted over this 15-year period, the current policy picture is one in which a common EU labour immigration policy is still very much lacking. Indeed, the legislative framework that has been developed so far reveals a number of deficiencies or unfinished elements affecting its normative and political configurations. We have identified four such features of the current EU labour immigration policy.

First, EU immigration policy is affected by fragmentation and dispersion dynamics, which lead to legal complexity and uncertainty. This is partly the result of the Council's failure to reach agreement on the Commission's 2001 proposal for a directive intended to (horizontally) regulate the entry and residence conditions for all third-country nationals exercising paid and self-employed activities.[11] The Commission subsequently presented the Policy Plan on Legal Migration that established the basis for a hierarchical, differentiated and fragmented EU legal framework on labour immigration granting variable sets of rights, standards and conditions for entry/residence to different migrant worker groups and countries of origin.[12] The rationale behind this fragmented policy approach was driven by the attractiveness and selective policy paradigm, i.e. to 'attract' third-country nationals who were by then deemed to be 'needed' in the EU, in particular 'highly skilled' and 'seasonal' workers.

Nine years later, the package of sectoral legislative initiatives has been adopted including: a Directive on a common application procedure for a single (work and residence) permit and a common set of rights for legally residing third-country nationals;[13] the EU Blue Card Directive;[14] the Seasonal Employment Directive;[15] the Intra-corporate Transferees and Unremunerated Trainees Directive;[16] and the re-casting proposal of the Researchers' and Students' Directive.[17] Alongside these Directives, international agreements and mobility partnerships between the EU and third countries stipulate rules and standards, some of which foresee employment- or education-related provisions. These instruments provide the basis for a highly fragmented EU framework for immigration law and policy.

A second feature characterising the first generation of EU labour immigration policies is discrimination in respect of categories of workers resulting from the above-mentioned Policy Plan.[18] Indeed, when the Commission proposed to adopt a sector-by-sector approach, actors such as the European Economic and Social Committee (EESC), the EU body representing civil society and social partners, expressed concerns about the consequences for workers.[19] This critical issue has also been emphasised by others - Cholewinski stresses that the internationally recognised principle of non-discrimination was challenged in the EU through the implementation of the 'sectoral policy approach'.[20] Indeed, extra-Union labour immigration policy heralds the allocation of different rights to third-country workers depending on their perceived value to the EU labour markets.[21]

A third feature affecting the current normative shapes of the EU's immigration policy is the multi-layered nature and multiplicity of legal statuses for third-country workers across the EU. Groenendijk identifies a practice of dual or multiple migratory statuses and the tendency for member states to continue issuing national residence and work permits rather than the permits provided for in EU migration law[22] such as the EU Blue Card Directive, which has led to a competing and complex multi-level system of statuses and schemes for 'highly qualified third country nationals'.[23] The Blue Card Directive has established minimum standards providing "for a common floor, not a common ceiling".[24] The possibility given to member states to retain their national migratory schemes for highly qualified immigrants has not been conducive to a genuine European scheme and even raises questions over the added value of the Blue Card system.

A final characteristic of the EU's immigration policy is the barriers for third-country nationals to access rights under EU immigration law. EU immigration law already provides a supranational set of rights concerning various aspects, including access to long-term permanent residence, family reunification or highly qualified employment. However, it has been pointed out "it is not rights enshrined in the law what matters but rather access to them".[25]

The issue of 'attractiveness' of immigration policies is closely related to the question of why people decide to migrate (or not) from one country to another. Yet, research suggests looking beyond push/pull theories that have been shaped by scholars such as Ravenstein and Lee.[26] With his paper "The Laws of Migration", Ravenstein attempted to explain migratory movements within and between countries.[27] These laws state, inter alia, that economic factors are the main causes of migration,[28] and Ravenstein's theory formed the basis for the 'push/pull factor theory', which was developed by Lee in 1966.[29] Different migration theories have been proposed to explain why international migration begins and why it perpetuates across time and space.[30] However, as Massey et al. emphasised in 1998, "at present, there is no single theory widely accepted by social scientists to account for the emergence and perpetuation of international migration throughout the world, only a fragmented set of theories that have developed largely in isolation from one another, sometimes but not always segmented by disciplinary boundaries".[31] Thus, the strength of the overall economy and labour market conditions may very well induce people to go to a certain destination country, but they relate to only one pull factor that cannot explain migratory movements in their entirety; otherwise, no professionals would be left in the southern hemisphere.

No single theory has been widely accepted to account for the emergence and perpetuation of international migration.

8.3 'Rights versus numbers': Is a trade-off in immigration policy possible?

The relationship between rights and the degree of openness in immigration policies has received considerable attention and debate in scholarly and policy venues. Does the granting of rights play a role in the attractiveness of migration policies? Bestowing rights and non-discrimination on third-country nationals is crucial for their socio-economic inclusion and integration into the receiving societies.[32] The legally binding EU Charter of Fundamental Rights is inclusive as it applies to a large extent to everyone, not just nationals of EU member states but also third-country nationals.[33] Is there a trade-off between the openness of migration policies and the granting of rights?

Ruhs argues that one of the main reasons why states often hesitate to ratify international migrants' rights instruments lies in the ways in which these instruments affect their sovereignty/national interests when granting or restricting migrant rights. In his view, it is important to focus on the 'costs and benefits' that the granting of specific rights to third-country workers implies for receiving countries. Ruhs' starting premise is that migrants' rights perform an instrumental role as determinants in international labour migration. His main argument is that there are 'trade-offs' in high-income countries between 'openness' to admitting migrant workers and rights granted to them after admission.[34]

The equation between 'equality of rights' and 'restrictive immigration policy' has been subject to extensive discussion.[35] It has been emphasised that there is no evidence in immigration policy debates of a linkage between openness and rights in the UK: "The recent British experience suggests that increased numbers are a more important constraint upon – or driver of – changes to rights' regimes than the openness of policy *per se*."[36] Indeed, increased numbers of one category of migrant (e.g. migrants from the European Economic Area, or EEA) can lead to effects in the policy sphere upon other unrelated groups (non-EEA).[37]

Some of these rights are actually minimum labour standards foreseen in International Labour Organization (ILO) instruments. Indeed, one of the more problematic aspects inherent to the 'more openness, less rights' logic is that it may challenge the set of international labour standards developed by organisations such as the ILO. The current emphasis on temporariness and rights trade-offs can be highly problematic from the perspective of ensuring the protection of migrant workers' rights and labour standards.[38] In Cholewinski's opinion, the trade-off framing is inappropriate as it locks individuals into a 'zero sum game' (rights versus numbers). It also leads to a 'race to the bottom' and frames third-country workers as commodities, with economic 'utility' at its core.

Ruhs advocates "the liberalisation of international labour migration, especially of lower-skilled workers, through temporary migration programmes that protect a universal set of core rights […] by restricting a few specific rights that create net costs for receiving countries", which he denominates as a "core rights approach". The question arises of the extent to which such costs are based on objective evidence. Are these real costs or perceived costs? How do these costs, as well as the practice of granting different sets of rights to different groups of migrants, influence social cohesion?

Tentative answers to these questions are offered by Acosta Arcarazo, who highlights experiences from South American countries on the 'rights versus numbers' rhetoric and comes to the following conclusion: in Argentina, Spain and Portugal, migration has been mostly affected by the economic opportunities in certain labour market sectors rather than by any specific legal framework restricting third-country nationals' rights and benefits.[39] It is, in his view, far from clear whether it is rights or job availability that matters the most. The degree of restrictiveness of an immigration policy does not seem to be the most decisive factor in determining immigration or emigration, but it may lead to social exclusion, harsher living conditions and unnecessary obstacles to human mobility.

8.4 Matching demand and supply: A redesigned EU 'guest worker' model?

A main dilemma raised by the trade-off discussions relates to the degree of temporariness that the emerging EU labour immigration policy implicitly promotes, in the form of a revamped 'guest-worker' model. One of the main challenges facing the current and next generation of EU immigration policy-makers is to not repeat the past mistakes of the failed guest-worker programmes. Indeed, the adoption of the EU Directives on seasonal employment and intra-corporate transferees show a worrying trend towards 'temporariness' that resembles too closely the failed guest-worker programmes of Germany and Switzerland.[40] The former Swiss model of employment of the 1960s and 1970s, for example, allowed Italian workers to be employed for nine months a year for many subsequent years without ever obtaining a more stable and secure residence status.[41] Thus, it can be concluded that such temporary migration policies might well be at odds with the social inclusion of immigrant workers into the receiving societies, as they are primarily based on exclusion and expulsion after a certain period of time in the receiving country.[42]

The academic literature underlines the importance of taking due account of 'historical experiences' and of 'lessons learnt' from previous policies. A growing body of literature points to the inherent 'policy failure', 'fallacy' or 'policy gap' between the publicly stated goal and objectives of states' migration control policies and the actual outcomes that can be observed regarding the social phenomenon of cross-border human mobility for employment-related purposes.[43] This gap may become even greater when a supranational migration policy actor, such as the EU, is at stake.

With a view to future EU policy-making, it is therefore essential to consider the fact that more often than not, migration control policies have achieved precisely the opposite effects to what was originally intended by national policy-makers. Castles highlights the well-known example of the German guest-worker recruitment policy between 1955 and 1973, which was intended to recruit workers temporarily but resulted in permanent settlement, family reunion and the emergence of diverse societies in Germany.[44] Is the emerging EU immigration policy likewise prone to failure? As Castles points out, "migration policies may fail if they are based on a short-term view of the migratory process [...] it is necessary to analyse the migratory process as a long-term social process with its own dynamics", as a 'societal process' which cannot be enshrined in law in liberal democratic regimes.[45] 'Short-termism' (a short-term perspective) in policy-making tends to be a commonly shared trend in this area.

Preferential treatment of certain migrants based on a 'narrowly defined measured demand for skills' is a self-defeating policy option.

From an economic viewpoint, Kahanec shows how 'skills-based selective frameworks' in which preferential treatment is given to certain migrants based on a "narrowly defined measured demand for skills" is a self-defeating policy option.[46] This is also the case from the perspective of financial costs. In his view, the "identification of skill needs and regular adjustment, fine tuning and monitoring of the system involve significant pecuniary and non-pecuniary costs". Moreover, the criteria for 'selection' are based on "a small set of observable characteristics that only proxy the true determinants of migrants' employability and labour market potential".[47]

International experiences reveal similar deficiencies. "Although the US legal framework is predicated on non-citizens obtaining their immigrant visas overseas at a US consulate, [...] only a miniscule number of individuals coming to the United States as permanent labour migrants are overseas when they seek permanent resident status. Rather, almost everyone who satisfies the employment-based immigrant categories is already working in the United States."[48] Labour migration to the United States is mainly employer-led and a large majority of non-US citizens enter the country as 'temporary visitors' or 'non-immigrants'. Fullerton points out that temporary foreign workers have a weaker legal status in terms of bargaining power and labour mobility, including limited options to change employer, in comparison to those migrants benefiting from permanent pathways.[49] This demonstrates the vulnerability of cost/benefit and selective migratory schemes.

A similar move towards a system said to combine the US and Australian models has been identified in Canada, where the system increasingly functions as a points-based system geared towards specific skills (a points-based selection model) and mainly focuses on temporary admission of foreign workers. When examining the so-called 'Canadian Experience Class', Gabriel highlights that the system focuses purely on the interest of the state and that the economy renders vulnerable those temporary workers in "low-skilled occupations offering no path to permanent residence" and leads to irregularity of their stay, thus "subjecting Canada to similar problems to those European countries experienced with their guest workers".[50]

8.5 Recognition of skills and qualifications plays a key role in attractiveness

The opportunities that countries grant to skilled individuals to make full use of their qualifications and competences constitutes a central determining factor fostering attractiveness, competitiveness and growth. Thus, efficient systems for the recognition of foreign-acquired diplomas, skills and work experience represent a key instrument to realise this potential. In practice, however, obtaining recognition of one's qualifications and diplomas, and lengthy administrative recognition procedures, continue to present major obstacles to international mobility and the inclusion of third-country workers in domestic and international labour markets.

The assumption that the US and Canada provide more attractive migratory schemes in comparison to the EU has been contested.

The EU is no exception in this respect. The lower returns to foreign education and work experience, combined with limited mastery of the host country's language, help explain higher over-qualification rates for immigrants relative to native-born workers.[51] Kahanec therefore argues not only that Europe is losing in the global competition for skilled migrant workers, but also that migrants to Europe tend to downgrade to jobs below their level of qualification.[52] Amongst the various options available in respect to migration policy frameworks, one that might be of more relevance is the identification of skills in shortage in a given labour market. In Kahanec's view, however, a key challenge of such a policy is to identify skills shortages in a way that is not 'political' and takes due account of market failures.

Securing skills recognition remains very limited in practice. A key issue is that there is no commonly shared definition of what constitutes a 'skill', or one that clarifies what is a 'high', 'medium' or 'low' skill or talent.[53] The definitions are too often poorly and artificially framed in terms of 'occupational skills' or 'educational attainment', or even in terms of the receiving country's 'needs'.[54] These challenges have also been addressed by Kahanec, who poses the following questions: How can a particular worker be assigned to a specific skill group? How can the fact that 'needs' for specific skills are time-dependent and vary over the short, medium and long term be addressed? What may be needed today may not be needed tomorrow. Kahanec believes that time-dependency and politicisation are the two main obstacles challenging the effectiveness of skills recognition and skills matching.[55]

The experience of Canada is illuminating. Gabriel highlights the uncertainties over whether 'labour needs' can be effectively determined by the state. She points out that admission to a country does not guarantee immigrants a job commensurate with their experience and skills. In her view, points-based systems face a common challenge consisting of the difficulty in differentiating between qualifications of varying quality and utility. Gabriel criticises the selective approach (to match demand and supply) in Canadian migration policy on the basis of "immigrant skill underutilisation" and a main policy focus on "short-term economic gain".[56]

The lack of skills recognition forces migrants to Europe to downgrade to jobs below their level of qualification.

Indeed, discussions on skills and labour market needs are too often hampered by a narrative that categorises skills as 'low' and 'high' and assumes the viability of these categories in domestic and supranational contexts.[57] 'Medium' skills are often ignored. Yet, as has been demonstrated in several EU member states and as is also the case with the EU Blue Card, the labelling of an individual as a 'highly skilled' third-country national does not necessarily relate to the specific 'skills', qualifications or experience of the person involved, but rather to first, the 'utility' of the worker in a labour market sector that is considered to be facing 'gaps', and second, the actual salary level that the worker will receive in the receiving country.

So when official discourses refer to a 'mismatch' or lack of 'supply' and 'demand', it is not entirely clear what they are referring to. Moreover, an interesting development is that the 'temporary' or 'guest-worker' migration management models are now redefining the target group of 'good' immigrants they want to attract. Increasing numbers of states are shifting their policies on 'attractiveness' and 'permanent settlement', or even granting nationality to 'investors' and 'entrepreneurs' with golden visa programmes and/or citizenship-for-sale schemes.[58]

8.6 Dilemmas of labour migration policies persist

There are a number of dilemmas and challenges associated with labour migration policies in different supranational and international settings, and key questions arise that call for further research.

First, policies are 'attractive' in comparison to where? The rhetoric of attractiveness presupposes that other 'developed' world economies such as the United States or Canada seem to be in conscious competition with the EU over a certain kind of desired foreign labour force, the so-called 'talented', 'highly qualified' or 'brightest' workers. This competition is used to justify differential treatment in relation to the desirable labour migrant. Yet, is there such a 'person'? It is also often assumed that these countries may constitute 'good examples', 'lessons learnt' or even 'models' for the EU to follow in its ongoing internal deliberations on the way forward. This holds true for certain elements but the US and Canadian immigration systems face similar dilemmas and are not as 'attractive' as they are often portrayed in the EU policy discourse. For example, the downside of the employer-driven US system is that this system translates into less protection offered to immigrants *vis-à-vis* employers. The admission procedures under the US immigration scheme are not as straightforward or quick as assumed; this is one element that the US bill pending in the House of Representatives entitled "Border Security, Economic Opportunity, and Immigration Modernization Act 2013" aims to remedy.[59] Also, geographical mobility in the US cannot easily be compared with intra-EU mobility due to a number of reasons, including structural, linguistic and cultural differences.[60]

Second, policies are attractive to whom? It must also be borne in mind that the 'attractiveness' of migration policies is in the eye of the beholder; by focusing on the 'attractiveness' of the policies to a foreign labour force purely from an economic perspective – i.e. in terms of the 'needs' of the receiving state – the 'attractiveness' of policies from a migrant worker's viewpoint is relegated to a secondary policy concern. For migrant workers, 'attractiveness' may well concern issues related to security of residence, non-discrimination, access to fundamental social rights and compliance with international labour standards.[61] This aspect is closely connected to the next point.

Third, how can an immigration policy be made 'attractive'? Among the factors here, reference is often made to an improved set of rights and benefits conferred on foreign workers and other incentives such as the easing of administrative procedures (fast-track), unrestricted access to the labour market, the provision of information/employer sponsorship, and so on. While some of the rights and benefits are indeed non-negotiable core components of international and European instruments by which EU member states are bound, there is little evidence of their effects on emigration. It is also difficult to argue that there is a direct correlation between the granting of rights and openness. An underlying problem is that any trade-off framework legitimises inequality of treatment on the basis of dubious grounds related to 'quotas', 'skills' or 'needs', which are often hugely politicised and based on short-term considerations.

Fourth, what kind of foreign worker is it hoped will be 'attracted' by an immigration policy? The paradigm of attractiveness often refers to a recruitment logic focusing on those individuals considered to be the 'brightest' available. The starting principle here is a utilitarian and economics-oriented approach that justifies inequality of treatment amongst workers. But who are those highly skilled and talented individuals? Which criteria are used to categorise a worker in a specific skill group? It is often assumed that exact methodologies exist to identify and match relevant 'skills' and 'needs' in national labour markets. The argument appears to assume that achieving a perfect match between skills of immigrants and national labour market needs and priorities is feasible, but this assumption has been challenged in this chapter.

8.7 Future EU migration policy must overcome fragmentation and legal uncertainty

In the next generation of EU labour immigration policy, action must be taken to overcome fragmentation, legal uncertainty, discrimination and competing multi-layered migratory statuses. This action can take different forms. One view suggests that the European Commission under President Jean-Claude Juncker should present new legislative initiatives. For example, Peers advocates the introduction of an EU immigration code (or code on legal immigration) as previously proposed by the Commission.[62] This code should establish a more ambitious level of harmonisation than currently exists by, first, raising existing EU standards, and second, creating a simplified and more consistent set of common regulations.[63] A non-legally binding corpus or compendium of existing EU rules and statuses could be a first step in that direction. Any proposal for codification should be firmly anchored in a rights-based and non-discriminatory approach.[64]

Any EU proposal to codify the existing fragmented instruments, statuses and rules should be firmly anchored in a rights-based and non-discriminatory approach.

Another priority should be to remove both formal and informal obstacles to the recognition of qualifications and diplomas, as they constitute barriers to international mobility and to the inclusion of third-country workers in labour markets. Measures that improve the use of foreign-acquired skills include: disseminating information on recognition procedures and their outcomes; facilitating early and timely recognition; implementing procedures for recognising professional credentials acquired abroad and allowing early labour market access; and, finally, negotiating mutual recognition agreements between receiving and sending countries.[65]

An alternative approach emphasises improved monitoring and enforcement of existing EU migration standards. The European Commission under President Juncker should focus on making better use of infringement proceedings where necessary. Here, common EU guidelines aimed at national practitioners and civil society organisations to better ensure implementation by relevant regional and local administrations and litigation before the relevant courts are vital. Broadening the dialogue with and inputs from social partners (employers' associations and trade unions) and civil society organisations is equally important. Finally, strategic partnerships with relevant actors - such as the Council of Europe, the United Nations and the ILO - could prove to be useful in this area. As the

Commission has underlined, significant efforts are still required to improve the implementation of internationally agreed frameworks and to better enforce the protection of human rights of migrants.[66] The EU should therefore promote international human rights and labour standards, in particular with respect to those immigration policy dimensions now falling within the scope of EU law.

Bibliography

Acosta Arcarazo, D. (2014), "Rethinking Attractiveness: The Case of South America", in S. Carrera, E. Guild and K. Eisele (eds), *Rethinking the Attractiveness of EU Labour Immigration Policies: Comparative perspectives on the EU, the US, Canada and beyond*, Centre for European Policy Studies, Brussels.

Alboim, N. and K. Cohl (2012), *Shaping the Future: Canada's Rapidly Changing Immigration Policies*, Toronto: Maytree.

Beblavý, M., I. Maselli and M. Veselková, I. (2014), *Let's get to Work! The Future of Labour in Europe, Vol. 1*, Centre for European Policy Studies, Brussels.

Bigo, D. and E. Guild (2005), *Controlling Frontiers: Free Movement into and within Europe*, Aldershot: Ashgate.

Carrera, S. (2014), "How Much does EU Citizenship Cost? The Maltese Citizenship for sale Affair: A Breakthrough for sincere cooperation in citizenship of the Union", CEPS Paper in Liberty and Security in Europe No. 64, Centre for European Policy Studies, Brussels.

Carrera, S. and E. Guild (2014), "The European Council's Guidelines for the Area of Freedom, Security and Justice 2020: Subverting the 'Lisbonisation' of Justice and Home Affairs?", CEPS Essay No. 13, Centre for European Policy Studies, Brussels.

Carrera, S., A. Faure, E. Guild and D. Kostakopoulou (2011), "Labour Immigration Policy in the EU: A Renewed Agenda for Europe 2020", CEPS Policy Brief No. 240, Centre for European Policy Studies, Brussels.

Castles, S. (2004), "Why migration policies fail", *Ethnic and Racial Studies*, Vol. 27, No. 2, pp. 205-227.

_____ (2006), "Guestworkers in Europe: A Resurrection?", *International Migration Review*, Vol. 40, No. 4, pp. 741-766.

Cholewinski, R. (2014), "Labour Migration, Temporariness, and Rights", in S. Carrera, E. Guild and K. Eisele (eds), *Rethinking the Attractiveness of EU Labour Immigration Policies: Comparative perspectives on the EU, the US, Canada and beyond*, Centre for European Policy Studies, Brussels.

Cornelius, W., P.L. Martin and J.F. Hollifield (1994), *Controlling Immigration: A Global Perspective*, Stanford, CA: Stanford University Press.

Council of the European Union (2010), "The Stockholm Programme: An open and secure Europe serving and protecting citizens", Official Journal C 115, Brussels.

Czaika, M. and H. de Haas (2013), "The Effectiveness of Immigration Policies", *Population and Development Review,* Vol. 39, No. 3, pp. 487-508.

De Somer, M. (2012), "Trends and Gaps in the Academic Literature on EU Labour Migration Policies", NEUJOBS State of the Art Report No. 5, NEUJOBS Project (www.neujobs.eu).

Desiderio, M.V. (2014), "Qualifications and Skills", in S. Carrera, E. Guild and K. Eisele (eds), *Rethinking the Attractiveness of EU Labour Immigration Policies: Comparative perspectives on the EU, the US, Canada and beyond,* Centre for European Policy Studies, Brussels.

Docquier, F., C. Ozden and G. Peri (2014), "The Labour Market Effects of Immigration and Emigration in OECD Countries", *The Economic Journal,* Vol. 124, No. 579, pp. 1106-1145.

Eisele, K. (2013), "Why come here if I can go there? Assessing the 'Attractiveness' of the EU's Blue Card Directive for 'Highly Qualified' Immigrants", NEUJOBS Working Paper No. D18.2, NEUJOBS Project (www.neujobs.eu).

_____ (2014), "The US Labour Immigration Scheme – All about being attractive? EU Perceptions and Stakeholders' Perspectives Reviewed", NEUJOBS Working Paper No. 18.3, NEUJOBS Project (www.neujobs.eu).

European Commission (2001), "Proposal for a Council Directive on the conditions of entry and residence for the purpose of paid employment and self-employment activities", COM(2001) 386, Brussels.

_____ (2005), "Communication on a Policy Plan on Legal Migration", COM(2005) 669, Brussels.

______ (2006), "Withdrawal of Commission proposals following screening for their general relevance, their impact on competitiveness and other aspects", 2006/C 64/03, OJ C64/3, Brussels.

_____ (2007a), "Communication on applying the global approach to migration to the eastern and south-eastern regions neighbouring the European Union", COM(2007) 247, Brussels.

_____ (2007b), "Explanatory Memorandum to the Proposal for a Council Directive on the conditions of entry and residence of third-country nationals for the purposes of highly qualified employment", COM(2007) 637, Brussels.

_____ (2010), "Communication on the Europe 2020 Strategy", COM(2010) 2020, Brussels.

_____ (2011), "The Global Approach to Migration and Mobility", COM(2011) 743 final, Brussels.

_____ (2013a), "Proposal for a Directive of the European Parliament and of the Council on the conditions of entry and residence of third-country nationals for the purposes of research, studies, pupil exchange, remunerated and unremunerated training, voluntary service and au pairing (recast)", COM(2013) 151, Brussels.

_____ (2013b), "Communication on Maximizing the Development Impact of Migration", COM(2013) 292, Brussels.

_____ (2014), "Communication on an open and secure Europe: making it happen", COM(2014) 154, Brussels.

European Council (2014), "Conclusions of 26 and 27 June 2014", EUCO 79/14, Brussels.

European Economic and Social Committee (2004), "Opinion of the European Economic and Social Committee on the Green Paper on an EU approach to managing economic migration", COM(2004) 811 final, 2005/C 286/05, Brussels.

Fullerton, M. (2014), "An Overview of Labour Migration Policies in the United States", in S. Carrera, E. Guild and K. Eisele (eds), *Rethinking the Attractiveness of EU Labour Immigration Policies: Comparative perspectives on the EU, the US, Canada and beyond*, Centre for European Policy Studies, Brussels.

Gabriel, C. (2011), "'Advantage Canada' and the Contradictions of (Im)migration Control", in E. Guild and S. Mantu (eds), *Constructing and Imagining Labour Migration: Perspectives of Controls from Five Continents*, Ashgate: Farnham, pp. 137-155.

_____ (2014), "Labour Migration in Canada: A Matter of 'Supply' and 'Demand', in S. Carrera, E. Guild and K. Eisele (eds), *Rethinking the Attractiveness of EU Labour Immigration Policies: Comparative perspectives on the EU, the US, Canada and beyond*, Centre for European Policy Studies, Brussels.

Groenendijk, K. (2014), "Which Way Forward with Migration and Employment in the EU?", in S. Carrera, E. Guild and K. Eisele (eds), *Rethinking the Attractiveness of EU Labour Immigration Policies: Comparative perspectives on the EU, the US, Canada and beyond*, Centre for European Policy Studies, Brussels.

Groenewold, G. and J. de Beer (2014), "Economic and Demographic Change in the EU: Implications for Immigration and Integration Policies", NEUJOBS Policy Brief D18.5, NEUJOBS Project (www.neujobs.eu).

Guild, E. (2011), "Equivocal Claims? Ambivalent Controls? Labour Migration Regimes in the European Union", in E. Guild and S. Mantu (eds), *Constructing and Imagining Labour Migration: Perspectives of Controls from Five Continents*, Ashgate: Farnham, pp. 207-228.

Guild, E. and S. Mantu (2011), *Constructing and Imagining Labour Migration: Perspectives of Controls from Five Continents*, Ashgate: Farnham.

Guild, E., S. Carrera and K. Eisele (2013), *Social Benefits and Migration: A Contested Relationship and Policy Challenge in the EU*, Centre for European Policy Studies, Brussels.

Hun Kim, S. and W. Ma (2011), *The Korean Diaspora and Christian Mission*, Oxford: Regnum Books International.

Kahanec, M. (2014), "Labour Market Needs and Migration Policy Options: Towards More Dynamic Labour Markets", in S. Carrera, E. Guild and K. Eisele (eds), *Rethinking the Attractiveness of EU Labour Immigration Policies: Comparative perspectives on the EU, the US, Canada and beyond*, Centre for European Policy Studies, Brussels.

Kureková, L., C. Haita and M. Beblavý (2013), "Being and Becoming Low-Skilled: A Comprehensive Approach to Studying Low-Skillness", NEUJOBS Working Paper No. 4.3.1, NEUJOBS Project (www.neujobs.eu).

Lee, E. (1966), "A Theory of Migration", *Demography*, Vol. 3, No. 1, pp. 47-57.

Massey, D., J. Arango, G. Hugo, A. Kouaouci, A. Pellegrino and J.E. Taylor (1993), "Theories of International Migration: A Review and Appraisal", *Population and Development Review*, Vol. 19, No. 3, pp. 431-466.

_____ (1998), *Worlds in Motion: Understanding International Migration at the End of the Millennium*, Oxford: Clarendon Press.

Peers, S. (2014), "An EU Immigration Code: Towards a Common Immigration Policy", in S. Carrera, E. Guild and K. Eisele (eds), *Rethinking the Attractiveness of EU Labour Immigration Policies: Comparative perspectives on the EU, the US, Canada and beyond*, Centre for European Policy Studies, Brussels.

Popova, N. (2014), "Challenges in Skills Identification, Anticipation and Monitoring", in S. Carrera, E. Guild and K. Eisele (eds), *Rethinking the Attractiveness of EU Labour Immigration Policies: Comparative perspectives on the EU, the US, Canada and beyond*, Centre for European Policy Studies, Brussels.

Ravenstein, E.G. (1885), "The Laws of Migration", *Journal of Statistical Society of London*, Vol. 48, No. 2, pp. 176-235.

_____ (1889), "The Laws of Migration", *Journal of the Royal Statistical Society*, Vol. 52, No. 2, pp. 241-305.

Ruhs, M. (2014), "Rethinking Migrant Rights", in S. Carrera, E. Guild and K. Eisele (eds), *Rethinking the Attractiveness of EU Labour Immigration Policies: Comparative perspectives on the EU, the US, Canada and beyond*, Centre for European Policy Studies, Brussels.

Ruhs, M. and P. Martin (2008), "Numbers vs. Rights: Trade-Offs and Guest Worker Programmes", *International Migration Review*, Vol. 42, No. 1, pp. 249-265.

Ryan, B. (2014), "Are there Trade-Offs between Openness, Numbers and Rights in Britain's Immigration Policy?", in S. Carrera, E. Guild and K. Eisele (eds), *Rethinking the Attractiveness of EU Labour Immigration Policies: Comparative perspectives on the EU, the US, Canada and beyond*, Centre for European Policy Studies, Brussels.

Shachar, A. (2006), "The Race for Talent: Highly Skilled Migrants and Competitive Immigration Regimes", Research Paper No. 883739, University of Toronto Legal Studies Series.

Shachar, A. and R. Hirschl (2014), "On Citizenship, States and Markets", *Journal of Political Philosophy*, Vol. 22, No. 2, pp. 231-257.

Sumption, M. and K. Hooper (2013), *The Golden Visa: "Selling Citizenship" to Investors*, Migration Policy Institute, Washington, D.C.

Notes

[1] Beblavý et al. (2014, pp. 3, 32-33).

[2] European Commission (2011).

[3] For a critical assessment on the EU Blue Card Directive for highly qualified third-country workers, see Eisele (2013).

[4] European Commission (2005, pp. 5 and 7); the Policy Plan stated that "the vast majority of Member States need these workers [highly skilled workers], because of shortfalls in the labour market pool of highly qualified workers".

[5] European Commission (2010); the Europe 2020 Strategy identifies "Youth on the move" as a flagship initiative which has the "aim to enhance the performance and international attractiveness of Europe's higher education institutions and raise the overall quality of all levels of education and training in the EU, combining both excellence and equity, by promoting student mobility and trainees' mobility, and improve the employment situation of young people".

[6] European Commission (2007b, p. 3).

[7] European Commission (2014, p. 3).

[8] European Council (2014).

[9] Carrera and Guild (2014).

[10] Council of the European Union (2010).

[11] European Commission (2001, 2006, 2007a).

[12] Carrera et al. (2011).

[13] Directive 2011/98/EU of the European Parliament and of the Council of 13 December 2011 on a single application procedure for a single permit for third-country nationals to reside and work in the territory of a member state and on a common set of rights for third-country workers legally residing in a member state.

[14] Council Directive 2009/50/EC of 25 May 2009 on the conditions of entry and residence of third-country nationals for the purposes of highly qualified employment.

[15] Directive 2014/36/EU of the European Parliament and of the Council of 26 February 2014 on the conditions of entry and stay of third-country nationals for the purpose of employment as seasonal workers.

[16] Directive 2014/66/EU of the European Parliament and of the Council of 15 May 2014 on the conditions of entry and residence of third-country nationals in the framework of an intra-corporate transfer.

[17] European Commission (2013a).

[18] Carrera et al. (2011).

[19] European Economic and Social Committee (2004, point 2.1.4.).

[20] Cholewinski (2014).

[21] Guild (2011).

[22] Groenendijk (2014).

[23] Eisele (2013).

[24] Ibid.

[25] Acosta Arcarazo (2014).

[26] See Eisele (2014).

[27] Ravenstein (1885, 1889).

[28] See Hun Kim and Ma (2011, pp. 36-37).

[29] Ibid.; Lee (1966).

[30] See Massey et al. (1993).

[31] Massey et al. (1998).

[32] De Somer (2012, p. 8).

[33] EU Charter of Fundamental Rights of the European Union, Official Journal C 83, 30 March 2010, p. 389.

[34] Ruhs (2014).

[35] Ruhs and Martin (2008); Castles (2006).

[36] Ryan (2014).

[37] On the debates on alleged social welfare tourism, see Guild et al. (2013).

[38] Cholewinski (2014).

[39] Acosta Arcarazo (2014).

[40] Groenendijk (2014).

[41] Ibid.

[42] On the role of social investment strategies, see Working Paper No. 5 of the NEUJOBS research project, which explores the interplay of the post-industrial change and welfare state transformation in Europe in the 21st century.

[43] See Castles (2004); Cornelius et al. (1994); Bigo and Guild (2005); Guild and Mantu (2011); Czaika and de Haas (2013).

[44] Castles (2004).

[45] Ibid.

[46] Kahanec (2014).

[47] Ibid.

[48] Fullerton (2014).

[49] Fullerton (2014).

[50] Gabriel refers here to Alboim and Cohl (2012); see also Gabriel (2011).

[51] Desiderio (2014).

[52] Kahanec (2014).

[53] For an analysis on the concept of 'low-skillness', which is blurred and fuzzy on the EU and member state levels as well, see Kureková et al. (2013).

[54] Popova (2014).

[55] Kahanec (2014).

[56] Gabriel (2014).

[57] On the 'cataloguing' of foreign workers into various categories, see De Somer (2012, p. 4)

[58] Carrera (2014); Shachar and Hirschl (2014); Sumption and Hooper (2013).

[59] *U.S. Border Security, Economic Opportunity, and Immigration Modernization Act 2013*, bill number S. 744, 113th Congress (2013-2014).

[60] On the EU perspectives on the 'attractiveness' of the US labour immigration system, see Eisele (2014).

[61] Ibid.

[62] Peers (2014).

[63] Ibid.

[64] Carrera et al. (2011, p. 7).

[65] Desiderio (2014).

[66] European Commission (2013b, p. 5).

9. Policy puzzles with the employment of Roma

*Vera Messing**

Roma are the largest non-migrant ethnic minority group in Europe and an extremely vulnerable one. Their population is estimated to be between 9 and 12 million (roughly equal to the population of Belgium) and in comparison with the rest of the continent, it is a young population with a higher-than-average share of working-age individuals.[1] In contrast with other ethnic minority groups, they have no historical homeland and live spread across most European countries, but they are particularly concentrated in Romania, Bulgaria, Hungary, Spain, Serbia and Slovakia, which are home to over half of Europe's Roma.[2]

In some European countries, the widespread exclusion of Roma from the primary labour market adds considerably to the challenge of meeting the Europe 2020 target of an employment rate of 75% for those aged 20-65. The estimated economic and fiscal costs of the exclusion of Roma from the formal labour market are staggering, ranging from €231 million in Serbia to €887 million in Romania.[3] Furthermore, Roma are a young population with relatively high fertility rates, and therefore can and should be regarded as an important resource in ageing European societies. However, in spite of numerous ways and funds to support the Roma population in European societies, their labour market situation has not improved significantly. Most of the programmes are not efficient and do not actually reach out to vulnerable Roma. In this chapter, therefore, we examine the most important factors behind the poor employment situation for Roma and potentials for active labour market policies (ALMPs) to influence

* Vera Messing: Research Fellow at the Center for Policy Studies, Central European University, Budapest.

opportunities for unemployed Roma in five European countries: Bulgaria, Hungary, Romania, Slovakia and Spain.

Figure 9.1 Roma population in Europe

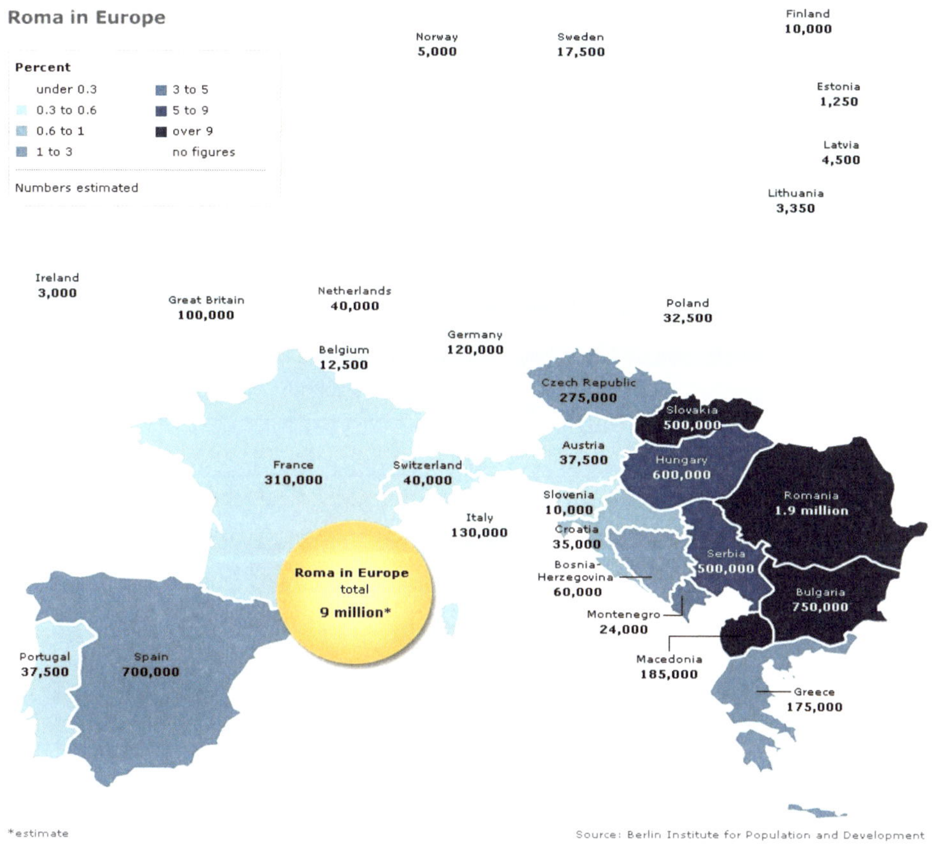

9.1 Roma face widespread exclusion from the primary labour market

The analysis of the position of Roma in the labour market is complicated by a lack of ethnic data, as well as competing definitions of who the Roma people are. What we refer to by 'Roma' or 'Gypsies' is not a politically, socially or culturally homogenous group. 'Roma/Gypsy' may be understood rather as an umbrella term denominating population groups with very different ethnic identities, languages, traditions, history or level of inclusion, even within the same country and definitely across Europe.

Many people identify Roma based on visible signs of poverty and exclusion, irrespective of whether or not the individual himself or herself identifies with the Roma people, and therefore some authors[4] argue that the concept of Roma/Gypsy is more a construction reflecting the perceptions of the majority society than an actual ethnic community. It is also important to note that in contrast to public perceptions, the majority of Roma are indigenous minorities, meaning that they have been citizens and lived for centuries in their respective countries, and - with a few exceptions - they are settled and are by no means nomadic in today's Europe. The common feature of Roma is that they experience a high level of social exclusion, prejudice and discrimination in all European countries.

Figure 9.2 Employment of Roma versus non-Roma living in their vicinity

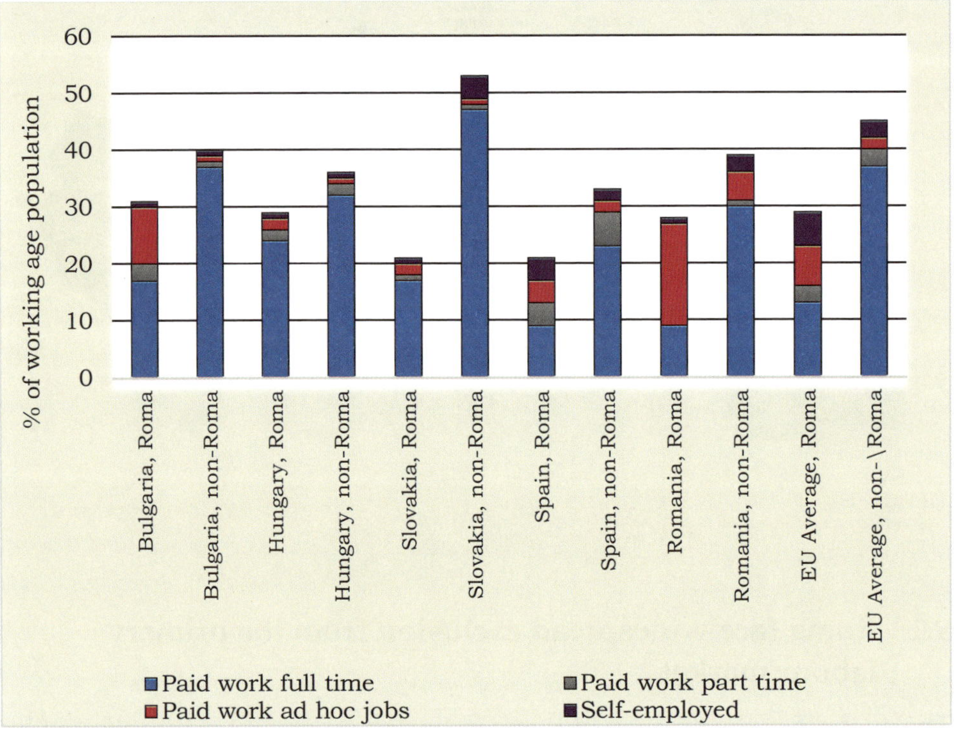

Note: This figure summarises employment of Roma as measured by the FRA Roma survey in 2011, which investigated Roma living in spatial concentration. Even though the survey is not representative of all Roma in Europe and employment is measured by indicators that are not comparable with EUROSTAT indicators collected in the course of the Labour Force Survey, to date this is the only comparative source of information at a European level. The survey covered also non-Roma living in the vicinity of Roma and found that the employment gap between the two groups is significant.

Source: FRA (2011).

A pilot survey conducted by the European Union Agency for Fundamental Rights (FRA) and the United Nations Development Programme (UNDP) covered Roma who fall under the broad definition of the Council of Europe (including, for example, Roma, Gipsies, *Gitanos*, *Sinti*, Travellers, *Kalé* and *Gens du voyage*), independent of their citizenship or whether their lifestyle was sedentary, semi-sedentary or mobile.[5] According to the data, Roma citizens have employment rates well below the average of other citizens and non-Roma living in their vicinity. The maximum observed value was recorded in Bulgaria, where 30% of working-age Roma are in employment. The data point not only to the low level of employment among Roma,[6] but also to the unfavourable employment structure for Roma in many countries. It is notable that - especially in Bulgaria, Spain and Romania - less than half of the total 'employment rate' consists of stable, full-time employment providing a calculable and due income. Roma are more typically involved in unstable and unsafe employment arrangements, such as part-time jobs, ad hoc jobs or self-employment, the latter frequently being a cover for an unemployed situation. In this context, it is crucial to understand what interventions are accessible and helpful to this population group.

9.2 Low-skillness has different employment consequences in different countries

Several intersecting causes trigger low employment indicators, the effects of which amplify each other. Labour market disadvantage is primarily a result of the dramatically low level of education of Roma in comparison to the rest of the population forming a majority in the respective countries. The UNDP Regional Roma Survey found that self-declared illiteracy is extremely high among Roma in Bulgaria and Romania (13% and 25% of adults, respectively) and, despite some improvement, it remains significant even among young Roma adults. This is not the case in Hungary and Slovakia, however, where illiteracy is negligible and restricted mainly to the older, non-working age cohorts. The lack of essential skills - such as reading, maths and basic computer and communication skills - that are required in the labour market is an important explanatory variable for the low employment rates.[7]

The most important causes for low employment of Roma is their generally low educational levels, together with widespread racial discrimination.

The picture does not improve much when formal education is considered. Romania presents the worst situation, where a third of adult Roma have no formal educational qualifications and only a third have lower secondary or higher education. In Hungary and Slovakia, the situation is significantly better: most Roma complete lower secondary school. However, an upper secondary school qualification (ISCED 3), which can be regarded as a threshold for stable formal employment, is rare even in these two countries. The ethnic gap is immense at this stage: in contrast to 10-19% of Roma, 57-91% of the total population of the respective countries has completed upper secondary education.[8] Although there have been substantial improvements in educational attainment, meaning that younger generations have higher educational levels than older-age groups, a lack of education in Romania and Bulgaria remains a severe problem even for the youngest age groups.

Figure 9.3 Educational levels of adult Roma in four central and eastern European countries

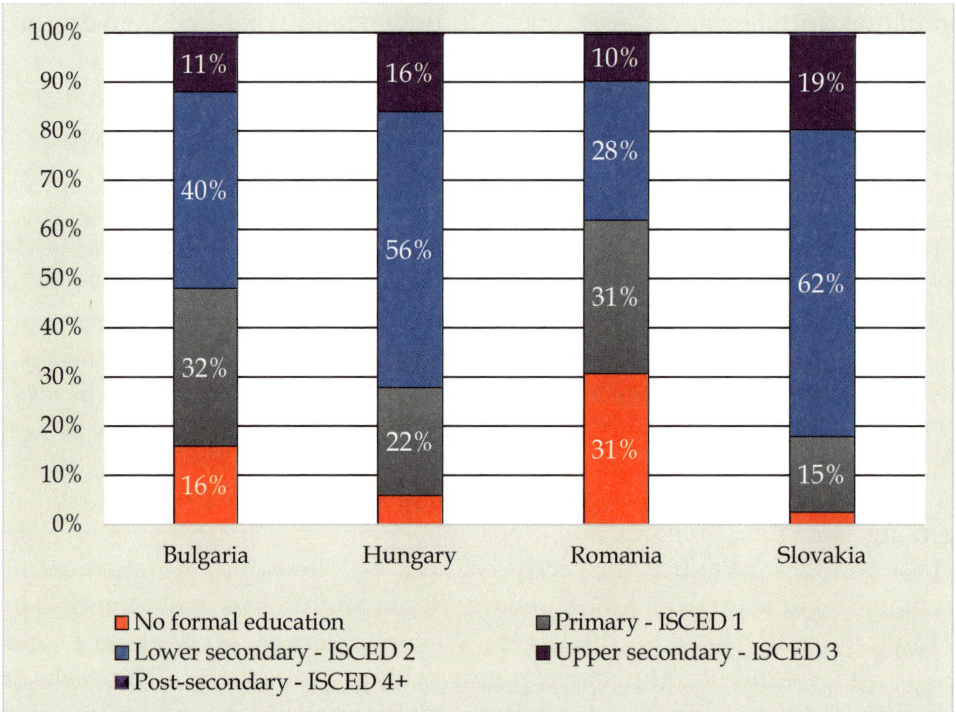

Note: The UNDP/WB/EC survey (FRA and UNDP, 2012) did not include Spain, while data derived from the FRA survey, which is comparative across the EU member states, did not include educational qualifications transferable to ISCED codes.

Source: UNDP/WB/EC Regional Roma Survey 2011.

Low-skillness has different consequences in different countries and sectors of activity.[9] In Slovakia and Hungary, a low level of education has a more powerful effect on employment opportunities than in Spain, Romania or Bulgaria.[10] This discrepancy can be partly explained by differences in the structures of the national economies of the respective countries, more specifically the presence of economic sectors/branches that can absorb the low-educated Roma workforce. In Romania, Bulgaria and Spain, the construction, tourism and agriculture sectors - which employ a considerable share of low-educated workers - make up an important share of the national economies, even though the crisis since 2008 has had a significant negative effect. The Spanish economic boom of the 1990s and 2000s provided plenty of jobs for vulnerable groups, including migrants and Roma. In contrast, in central and eastern European countries, and especially in Slovakia and Hungary, the current situation is determined by the transitional shock of the early 1990s, during which the economies experienced a sharp drop in demand for low-skilled and unskilled work. This change in the economic structure also has important geographical implications: certain regions, and precisely those where a considerable share of Roma live (east and south-east Slovakia, north-east and south-west Hungary), suffered disproportionately due to the decline of heavy industry after 1989. Lasting economic depression and long-term unemployment are extremely widespread in these areas.

Labour market programmes are not equipped to tackle the issue of low-skillness, in general. It is important to understand that economic structures of the post-transition economies continue to determine the demand for qualifications of the labour force to which school systems have not adapted. Therefore, the lack of highly educated workforce and the oversupply of low-skilled workforce cannot be tackled within the framework of labour market policies, but should primarily be addressed through the system of public education. Labour market programmes are equipped to make only minor adjustments and corrections in terms of training in specific areas. Nevertheless, we have identified a few instances in which countries have attempted to deal with the inadequate educational levels of unemployed Roma. For example, in Spain and Hungary, employment offices (EOs) offered training courses tailored to the needs of the local economy.[11] However, the overwhelming experience was that due to inadequate design, poor targeting techniques, a lack of financial support to beneficiaries and discrimination in the selection procedure, meaningful training remained inaccessible for most Roma in Bulgaria, Romania and Slovakia.

Regulatory factors may also contribute to low chances of employment as they inform the investment decisions of multinational companies, which are important employers of the low-skilled workforce. The high cost of officially employing workers is a crucial factor in this respect. Analysing current country-specific regulations on taxes, social contributions and minimum wages, the cost of labour was calculated and sizeable differences were found across the five countries.[12] The cost of employment seems to be an important factor determining the proportion of Roma that had the opportunity to enter the labour market. In Slovakia and Spain, where the cost of employing a person at the minimum wage is higher by a factor of between two and five compared with Romania and Bulgaria, a significantly lower proportion of Roma are formally employed. Hungary is an exception to this rule to some extent: relatively high employment costs are coupled with relatively high employment rates of Roma, but this is due to the fact that beneficiaries of job creation programmes[13] financed by the state are registered as formal employees in the labour statistics. However, public work programmes are not an inherent segment of the primary labour market and do not appear as employment in the statistics for other countries (e.g. Slovakia).

In the framework of ALMP, wage subsidies have the potential to increase formal employment of the low-skilled (and low-productivity) workforce by easing burdens of employment (social security contributions and taxes) for a certain period of time. Such measures were available in most countries but because Roma were not named as a target group and of the fact that numerous conditions were attached to such subsidies (administrative burdens and commitments to provide an employment contract beyond the period of the subsidy), employers were dissuaded from making use of such schemes and Roma typically did not benefit from this measure.

9.3 Discrimination and informal work are distinctive features of the Roma labour market

A very important factor feeding into the low employment rate of Roma is the extensive racial discrimination that Roma/Gypsy people face in central and south-east Europe. Roma are discriminated against during the selection procedure itself.[14] Our empirical fieldwork research also confirmed that ethnic discrimination is not necessarily hidden; in Romania and Bulgaria, job advertisements even indicate explicitly that Roma should not apply, while in Slovakia and Hungary more concealed forms of discrimination are prevalent, such as applicants with Roma names or racial signs being refused without further explanation. Racial discrimination is not exclusive to business employers; state employers and even stakeholders in the labour market, such as employment offices and job centres, may also act in a discriminatory way.

Although relevant legal safeguards against racial discrimination as well as an institutional framework for addressing complaints of discrimination existed in all of the countries, awareness of discrimination as well as the enforcement of anti-discrimination regulation remained weak in the field of employment. A potential way to counteract the consequences of racial discrimination is to target certain labour market programmes specifically at Roma. However, such approaches are rare, usually local in scope and project-based and therefore irregular and unstable. Spain is an exception in this respect: EU funds dedicated to social inclusion are distributed by four NGOs, one of which (the Fundació Secretariado Gitano, or FSG) is a pro-Roma organisation. This arrangement allows Roma to have a significant voice not only in the distribution of large funds dedicated to inclusion, but also in programme design and monitoring. A further consequence of this structure is that in contrast to the project-based financing prevalent in central and eastern European countries, funds dedicated to the inclusion of Roma are stable and calculable over the long run.

Discrimination, combined with high costs of employment and the fact that the recession hit the classic employment sectors of Roma disproportionately hard, results in the extensive exclusion of Roma from official employment, pushing them towards informal segments of the labour market. A number of qualitative in-depth studies[15] and surveys have emphasised that employment of Roma deviates considerably from typical employment in that i) it is usually irregular, ii) it includes activities that are not considered as employment (collecting and trading with goods, waste recycling), iii) it is unstable, and iv) is outside the scope of the formal and sometimes even the legal labour market. Qualitative, in-depth investigations, as well as the EU-wide FRA Roma survey and the UNDP/WB/EC survey[16] covering southern, central and eastern European countries, reinforce the notion that there is significant informal, unreported and sometimes unpaid work hidden behind the recorded low employment rates.

There is significant informal, unreported and sometimes unpaid work hidden behind the low employment rates recorded among Roma.

Here we need to refer to factors that, contrary to public perception, do not enhance the low employment rates of Roma. According to public opinion, the reason for the high unemployment of Roma is their lack of willingness to work. There is no empirical proof for such beliefs; on the contrary, the latest UNDP/WB/EC and FRA surveys reveal the opposite: Roma have an overwhelming preference for safe and regular jobs as opposed to unsafe and irregular jobs. Between 75% and 93% preferred having a secure but modestly paid job to an unsecure job with high income. Another common misconception about the causes of high unemployment is that Roma tend to exploit the welfare systems. An analysis of the financial incentives of staying employed as opposed to turning to the welfare system disproved the feasibility of such a strategy.[17]

9.4 Targeting programmes is an important dilemma of policy design

A crucial dilemma for experts as well as for practitioners is how best to organise active labour market policies (ALMPs). The predominant mode of targeting ALMPs is mainstreaming, which involves identifying characteristics of vulnerability and addressing them, irrespective of the ethnicity of the recipient. The most significant argument in favour of mainstreaming is that it avoids the risk of ethnicising Roma. Policies that define target groups according to factors that cause vulnerability - such as those with low education, in economically disadvantaged regions or marginalised communities, or of a certain age - would have the potential to reach Roma, given that they are overrepresented in these vulnerable groups. In contrast, promoters of ethnically targeted programmes argue that racial discrimination is the most important source of the lack of labour market opportunities, and disregarding this factor necessarily leads to Roma being overlooked by ALMPs.

A crucial guiding document for Roma integration in Europe is the EU Framework for National Roma Integration Strategies (NRIS), which was elaborated under the imperative of EU in 2011. The document was a pioneering step because it represented an explicit political commitment to improve the situation of Roma. This framework document advocated for an ethnically targeted approach, stating that it is "crucial to [...] ensure that national, regional and local integration policies focus on Roma in a clear and specific way".[18] Implicitly, the document aims to assure the channelling of targeted solutions through mainstream institutions; namely, to ensure that Roma are explicitly named as a potential 'at-risk' or 'vulnerable' target population for mainstream measures. This is referred to in EU documents as the principle of "explicit but not exclusive targeting". Although most national social inclusion strategies and action plans follow this idea by naming Roma among the social groups with multiple vulnerabilities, our research found hardly any signs of implementation of this principle in labour market policies in the four central and eastern European countries.

The most recent EU document on Roma integration, the effects of which have yet to be seen, is the European Council's recommendation on effective Roma integration measures:

> With a view to promoting the full equality of Roma in practice, take effective policy measures to ensure their equal treatment and the respect of their fundamental rights [...] This goal could be achieved either by means of mainstream measures or by means of targeted measures, including specific measures to prevent or compensate for disadvantages, or by a combination of both, paying special attention to the gender dimension.[19]

This document does not provide useful guidelines with regard to the most pressing dilemma of policy design, namely, how to reach out to vulnerable Roma and monitor the impact of policies on this segment of the population. Nevertheless, it gives equal weight to ethnically targeted and mainstream interventions.

Formulating an employment programme for the Roma population entails considerable political risk in the countries of central and eastern Europe, where prejudice and negative attitudes towards Roma are widespread, not only within the population but also among politicians and employees of public institutions. Governments are therefore reluctant to explicitly target Roma. In addition, as a result of a lack of data from monitoring activities on the ethnic background of programme beneficiaries, ethnic targeting remains weak. It is no wonder that with the exception of the Spanish ACCEDER programme,[20] ethnically targeted policy interventions are sporadic, local and powerless. We therefore move on from examining just 'Roma employment programmes' to identifying labour market interventions and measures that have the potential to intervene in the low employment rates of the Roma population.

9.5 Mainstream schemes: Job creation, regional development programmes and labour market services

Active labour market policies are often considered an effective tool for promoting labour market inclusion and tackling long-term unemployment, especially in times of economic crisis. For this reason, we first look at government expenditure by type of action in the five countries analysed so far. With the exception of Spain, the level of ALMP spending is well below the EU average in all countries (very close to zero in Bulgaria and Romania), despite the fact that long-term unemployment rates exceed the EU average significantly in four out of the five countries.[21]

*Figure 9.4 ALMP expenditure by type of action and by member state, 2012 (% of total ALMP expenditure)**

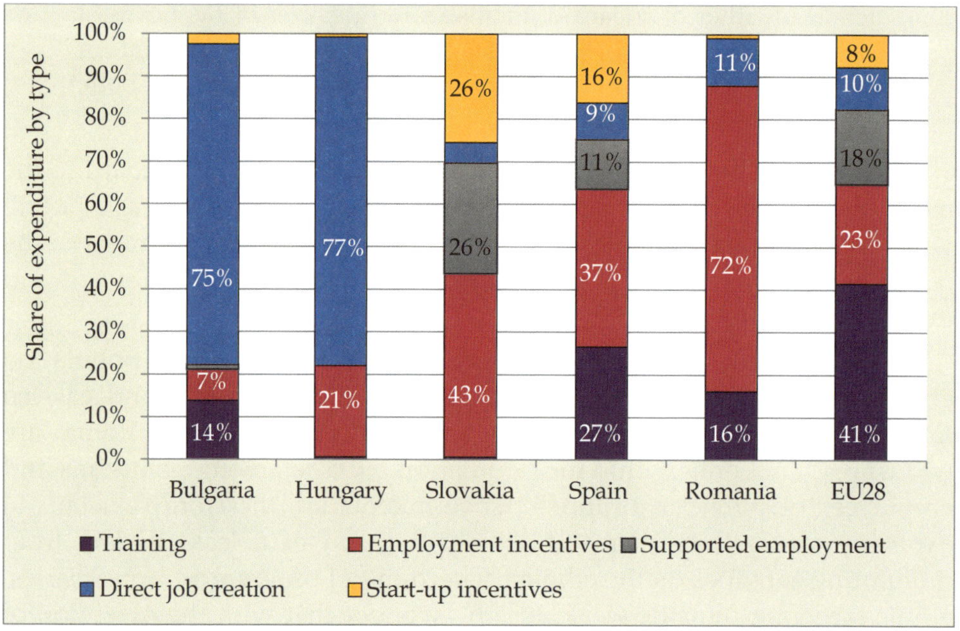

* For Spain, the data refer to year 2011.

Source: Eurostat database.

However, it is not only the level of spending on ALMPs but the combination of the various measures that matters. According to Figure 9.4, some countries apply a true mix of ALMP measures (Spain and Slovakia), while others display a dominant preference for one measure and dedicate most of their funds to this (Hungary and Bulgaria).

Direct job creation programmes in the form of public work programmes (PWPs) and public employment programmes (PEPs)[22] were the most widely available measures to unemployed Roma in Hungary,[23] Bulgaria and Slovakia,[24] while their implementation was significant but not overwhelming in Spain.[25] The scope and content of direct job creation varied significantly among the four countries, with Hungary standing out in terms of the share of the ALMP budget spent on direct job creation (more than two-thirds). However, the positive impact of direct job creation programmes on labour market inclusion was often mitigated by the very design of these programmes. Public work and public employment programmes are either a combination of labour market and social welfare policy measures (e.g. participation in public work is tied to the receipt of social welfare allowances, as in Hungary), or can be the exclusive terrain of social policy (as in Slovakia). Our fieldwork investigation[26] identified important weaknesses in direct job creation schemes that worked to the detriment of their efficiency and resulted in counter-effective outcomes in some cases. The most significant problems with job creation programmes can be summarised as follows:

Roma employees at employment offices improve the implementation of ALMP for Roma at the local level.

- In Hungary, Slovakia and Bulgaria, public work schemes trap beneficiaries (especially marginalised Roma) in the cycle of welfare support and PWPs/PEPs. These programmes proved to be extremely inefficient in supporting the return of the unemployed to the primary labour market because they did not offer any additional labour market services - such as training, orientation, job search or consultation - and no limitations were set concerning the number of occasions an individual could benefit from the schemes. Also, in most of the cases - in Hungary, Slovakia and Bulgaria - direct job creation programmes offered mundane, superfluous activities. Such programmes in fact became a form of mandatory work imposed on the welfare-dependent and long-term unemployed and failed to improve employment opportunities for their beneficiaries. That no outcome indicators related to labour market inclusion were formulated by the programmes reflects the fact that these programmes were not really meant to support labour market inclusion.

- Job creation following the logic of workfare enhanced local hierarchies and structures that result in the exposure and powerlessness of Roma and unemployed in other vulnerable groups. This was the case in Hungary, Slovakia and Bulgaria, where participation in public employment was tied to entitlement to social welfare benefits.
- In Hungary, where the scope (the number of beneficiaries) of the PEPs was too large and the range of potential beneficiaries was defined in a non-restrictive way, the programme distorted the local labour market equilibrium. Even the highly skilled temporary unemployed were addressed by job creation and as a result, public institutions replaced some of their regular workers with PEP beneficiaries.

In sum, PEPs/PWPs offered short-term solutions that did not address the causes of long-term unemployment. Job creation programmes might be an effective form of intervention in severely marginalised regions, for the most vulnerable population groups and for a restricted period of time, but only when implemented in a carefully designed manner and with a wide range of additional services offered to beneficiaries. It is important to understand that PEPs could become popular despite their poor performance because they entail significant political gains. They offer short-term employment for those with serious difficulties in the open labour market and are therefore supported both by programme participants and the local middle classes, who see them as a tool to activate the 'indolent' poor and Roma. In addition, the political elite regards them as a means of improving labour statistics, an important indicator of governmental performance in crisis-hit economies.

Public work does not address the causes of long-term unemployment.

A few programmes - typically EU-funded development programmes in Hungary and Slovakia - address the issue of regional inequalities and the explicit marginalisation of Roma. In Slovakia, marginalised Roma communities are targeted explicitly by including them as a horizontal priority in the country's development programmes. In Hungary, the most underdeveloped micro-regions with a large share of Roma receive substantial support for complex development of their economies, human resources and infrastructure. In Catalonia, geographical targeting is applied by the *Llei de Barris* (Neighbourhood Law) programme, which addresses certain impoverished urban zones. Such geographical targeting is theoretically an appropriate way to reach out to a significant share of vulnerable Roma without ethnicising poverty and long-term unemployment. However, these programmes are complex in nature, meaning that they focus on intersecting spheres of disadvantage (such as infrastructure, housing, education and community development) and have a less explicit focus on employment. Our field research, as well as evaluation studies of the respective programmes, show that geographically targeted complex development programmes failed to reach the most disadvantaged in the course of their implementation. Lack of meaningful inclusion of Roma NGOs in the design and implementation at the local level was one of the major reasons why these programmes were likely to disregard the actual needs of the marginalised Roma communities.[27]

An important prerequisite for improving the labour market inclusion of Roma is that employment offices (EOs) – the state agent assigned the mission to support the unemployed in their efforts to reintegrate into the labour market – provide high-quality, tailored services to clients in vulnerable situations. Yet, we found significant variation in this respect. In all of the central and eastern European countries, EOs were seen by unemployed Roma as purely administrative units that manage registration of unemployed status without providing meaningful support. Moreover, unemployed Roma described frequent experiences of open discrimination and humiliation by EO staff in Romania and Bulgaria.[28] Therefore, Roma, and especially those living in marginalised areas, are often reluctant to turn to the EOs, whose staff are unsupportive and whose services do not meet their needs. To improve the implementation of ALMPs at the local level, EOs in Bulgaria, Hungary and Spain employed mediators of Roma background, who turned out to be less prejudiced and discriminatory towards Roma clients and had better communication capacities and knowledge of the community.[29] Consequently, Roma clients displayed greater trust towards them and the office. In Slovakia, social workers provided personalised counselling to unemployed Roma.[30]

Geographical distance constituted an additional barrier. In all of the countries (except Spain), Roma residents of small rural settlements had difficulties in accessing the EO situated in the town serving as the centre of their micro-region. Either travel expenses were not covered (Romania and Bulgaria) or their reimbursement was delayed (Hungary), causing difficulty for the economically deprived rural Roma people to access this service. A suitable solution for bridging geographical distances was found in one Hungarian settlement, where the EO operated a mobile office with regular office hours in each settlement within its service area.

9.6 Policy implications: Monitoring, targeting and anti-discrimination

A crucial obstacle to understanding the impact of labour market support and services on unemployed Roma is the lack of employment data disaggregated by ethnicity. Collecting information and monitoring outcomes with regard to the participation of Roma in ALMPs is a key prerequisite of programme targeting and design, and the EU could play a pioneering role in this effort. The legal framework in individual countries makes it difficult to collect information on the ethnic background of ALMP beneficiaries. Nevertheless, depending on the regulatory environment, there are several options for obtaining the most important information.

Employment data disaggregated by ethnicity are crucial for the design of successful policies.

First, self-declaration of beneficiaries' ethnic background (including an option for multiple ethnic identification) could become a part of anonymised monitoring of ALMP impact in those countries where the collection of data on ethnicity is not banned. Such data would allow for an analysis at the programme, region or population group levels, or a combination of these. As such programmes are predominantly financed by EU funds, the EU is in a position to urge national governments to collect anonymised data on ALMP beneficiaries' ethnic background in a sensitive manner, respecting the right to self-identification and multiple identities.

Another data source with the potential to inform policy-makers is Roma surveys (either conducted by the EU Fundamental Rights Agency or by national governments), which should ask about participation in various types of ALMPs.

Finally, harmonisation of data collection is a truly supranational mission, so EU institutions could play an important role in encouraging national statistical bodies to collect information about self-declared ethnic background of respondents in large-scale EU-wide comparative surveys, such as the Labour Force Survey or Statistics on Income and Living Conditions (EU-SILC). Such data collection should take into account the sensitivity and complexity of ethnic identities and offer the possibility of multiple identification. This arrangement would produce reliable data on the presence of the Roma population in ALMPs as well as some outcome indicators at an aggregate level.

The targeting of programmes is a genuine challenge for policy-makers: in addition to finding ways to identify the populations most in need of support, they must take into account political forces and public attitudes, as well as the challenges of implementation posed by the individual targeting techniques. Our research highlighted that exclusive ethnic targeting of employment programmes is rarely a feasible and efficient way to reach out to Roma, especially in countries where discrimination and anti-Roma prejudice is widespread and strong. In addition, ethnically targeted programmes have no instruments to ensure that their beneficiaries are Roma. On the other hand, with the exception of those programmes that have little or no impact on employment opportunities (such as public work schemes), mainstream programmes usually do not reach out to Roma either. However, targeting programmes according to a careful ***combination of the factors*** behind vulnerability (low education, age, health situation, living in marginalised regions, having small children) together with the adoption of the EU principle of "explicit but not exclusive targeting of Roma" may enable a significant number of Roma to be reached. Thus, mainstream programmes can and should identify an ethnic target about the share of Roma among beneficiaries at an aggregate level. The formulation of such targets raises the awareness of EO workers and creates an important incentive to reach out to unemployed Roma.

Improvements in the ***delivery of services by employment offices*** to marginalised Roma communities would automatically support their employment opportunities. Presently, employment offices tend to focus their efforts on administrative duties, such as registering the unemployed or publishing announcements, and fail to provide genuine support to the unemployed. Service delivery could be improved via various approaches in parallel. Where prejudiced and negative attitudes of EO servants present a substantial problem (Bulgaria and Romania), implementing awareness-raising and sensitivity training for EO servants is essential. Surveying client satisfaction in EOs, including experiences of discrimination, could also inform the development of EO services. To achieve greater outreach to and understanding of marginalised Roma communities, it is desirable to employ staff from the Roma community in EOs. However, Roma staff members should not be seen as exclusively responsible for treating Roma clients, as such a practice would 'ethnicise' both Roma mediators and Roma clients. The problem of geographical accessibility of EO services for Roma living in marginalised areas could be resolved with a change of logic: the services should go to the clients instead of the currently prevalent principle that 'clients should travel to the office'. In this spirit, the development of a system of mobile employment offices providing services in smaller, marginalised settlements at established dates and times could be a beneficial step.

Different active labour market programmes have different potential to reach out to and support vulnerable populations, and marginalised Roma in particular. The basic principle of designing ALMPs should give preference to market-compatible ways of intervention, offering incentives for employers rather than creating a secondary labour market or administratively punishing the unemployed (as is the case in several central and eastern European countries). Presently, direct job creation (public work and public employment programmes) is a key programme type in most of the countries reaching marginalised unemployed Roma. However, these programmes have failed to facilitate sustainable employment. Direct job-creation programmes for the most marginalised and vulnerable segments of the labour market may only be appropriate if they meet a number of conditions, the most important of which are the following:

- They offer meaningful activities that add value and, ideally, are operated in the form of job try-outs.
- They are part of a complex intervention including more of the following elements: tailored training, personalised mentoring and efficient job-match services.
- They are offered only to the unemployed in the most vulnerable situations and only for a limited period of time.
- Their design ensures that beneficiaries are not trapped inside the vicious circle of public work-social benefit.

Training cannot reconcile the immense ethnic gap in educational attainment, but it can make adjustments and corrections in areas where the disequilibrium in the labour market appears to be local. Still, the research has identified certain steps aimed at improving the impact of training programmes for unemployed Roma.

- The content and qualifications provided by training programmes should be regularly adjusted to the needs of the local labour market.
- Training programmes should be as practical as possible, and organised in cooperation with local firms.

- As opposed to the prevalent 'one-size-fits-all' approach of many training programmes, courses should be more personalised and adapted to the needs and capacities of unemployed individuals.

Anti-discrimination and affirmative action is a neglected approach; in central and eastern European countries the enforcement of the principle of non-discrimination is rare. Although there is an extensive academic and policy debate about the pros and cons of affirmative action, we argue for the positive impact of some measures such as i) employing Roma in public offices in charge of designing and implementing ALMPs, ii) giving preference to Roma applicants for jobs in public offices, and ii) promoting active participation of Roma NGOs in the design and monitoring of ALMPs targeting the disadvantaged long-term unemployed. The EU, as a supranational entity formed on the basis of shared values of non-discrimination and promoting human rights, could play a pioneering role in encouraging national governments, as employers of state institutions and service providers, to not only adopt but to actively implement anti-discrimination and affirmative action on their own terrain.

Bibliography

Bereményi, Á. (2013), "Case studies report on the implementation of labour market policies for Roma at local level: Spain", in V. Messing (ed.), "From benefits to brooms", NEUJOBS Working Paper No. D19.3, NEUJOBS Project (www.neujobs.eu).

Borovicova, K., B. Fabo, M. Kanahec and V. Messing (2013), "Overview of the labour market situation of low-educated and Roma population and regulations affecting their employment", NEUJOBS State of the Art Report, NEUJOBS Project (www.neujobs.eu).

Brüggemann, C. (2012), "Roma Education in Comparative Perspective. Analysis of the UNDP/World Bank/EC Regional Roma Survey 2011", Roma Inclusion Working Papers, United Nations Development Programme, Bratislava.

Csepeli, Gy and Simon (2004), "Construction of Roma Identity in Eastern and Central Europe: Perception and Self-identification", *Journal of Ethnic and Migration Studies*, Vol. 30, No. 1, pp. 129-150.

de Laat, J. (2010), "Economic Costs of Roma Exclusion", Europe and Central Asia Human Development Department, World Bank, Washington, D.C.

European Commission (2011), "An EU Framework for National Roma Integration Strategies up to 2020", Communication from the Commission to the European Parliament, the Council, the European Economic and Social Committee and the Committee of the Regions, Brussels.

FRA (2009), *EU-MIDIS. European Union minorities and discrimination survey. EU MIDIS Data in Focus Report 1: The Roma*, European Union Agency for Fundamental Rights, Vienna.

_____ (2013), *Roma Pilot Survey. Technical Report: methodology, sampling and fieldwork*, European Union Agency for Fundamental Rights, Vienna.

_____ (2014), "Poverty and employment: The situation of Roma in 11 EU Member States", European Union Agency for Fundamental Rights, Vienna.

FRA and UNDP (2012), *The situation of Roma in 11 Member States. Survey results at glance*, European Union Agency for Fundamental Rights, Vienna.

Köllő, J. and Á. Scharle (2011), "The impact of the expansion of public work programs on long-term unemployment", in K. Fazekas and G. Kézdi (eds), *The Hungarian Labour Market 2012*, Budapest: MTA KTI.

Kureková, L. and J. Konsteková (2013), "Case studies report on the implementation of labour market policies for Roma at local level: Slovakia", in V. Messing (ed.), "From benefits to brooms", NEUJOBS Working Paper No. D19.3, NEUJOBS Project (www.neujobs.eu).

Kureková, L., C. Haita and M. Beblavý (2012), "Being and Becoming Low-skilled: A Comprehensive Approach to Studying Low-skillness", NEUJOBS Working Paper No. 4.3.1, NEUJOBS Project (www.neujobs.eu).

McGarry, A. and A. Tremlett (2013), "Challenges facing researchers on Roma minorities in contemporary Europe: Notes towards a research program", ECMI Working Papers No. 62, European Center for Minority Issues, Flensburg, Germany.

Messing, V. (2013a), "Case studies report on the implementation of labour market policies for Roma at local level: Hungary", in V. Messing (ed.), "From benefits to brooms", NEUJOBS Working Paper No. D19.3, NEUJOBS Project (www.neujobs.eu).

_____ (2013b), "Active Labour Market Programs with a Potential Impact on Roma Employment in Five Countries of the EU", NEUJOBS Working Paper No. 19.2 (with contributions from Á. Bereményi, L. Kurekova, J. Konstekova, A. Pamporov and F. Pop), NEUJOBS Project (www.neujobs.eu).

_____ (2014), "Methodological puzzles with surveying 'Roma'/'Gypsy' populations", *Ethnicities*, Vol. 14, No. 6, pp. 811-829.

Messing, V., A. Bereményi, L. M. Kureková, J. Konsteková, A. Pamporov and F. Pop (2013), "From Benefits to Brooms, Case Studies Report on the Implementation of Active Labour Market Policies for Roma at Local Level", NEUJOBS Working Paper No. 19.3, NEUJOBS Project (www.neujobs.eu).

O'Higgins, N. (2013), "Roma and non-Roma in the labour market in Central and South Eastern Europe", Roma Inclusion Working Papers, UNDP, March.

OSF MtM (2011), "Köves út végén. A területi egyenlőtlenségek csökkentése és a romák helyzetének javítása – jelentés az LHH Program első szakaszának eredményeiről" (Decreasing regional inequalities and improve situation of Roma. A report on the results of the first phase of the Most Disadvantaged Micro-regions programme), Budapest.

OSI (2005) "Current Attitudes toward the Roma in Central Europe: A Report of Research with non-Roma and Roma Respondents".

Pamporov, A. (2013), "Case studies report on the implementation of labour market policies for Roma at local level: Bulgaria", in V. Messing (ed.), "From benefits to brooms", NEUJOBS Working Paper No. D19.3, NEUJOBS Project (www.neujobs.eu).

Pop, F. (2013), "Case studies report on the implementation of labour market policies for Roma at local level: Romania", in V. Messing (ed.), "From benefits to brooms", NEUJOBS Working Paper No. D19.3, NEUJOBS Project (www.neujobs.eu).

Richardson, J. and A. Ryder (2012), *Gypsies and Travellers. Empowerment and inclusion in British Society*, Bristol: The Policy Press.

Salner, A. and C. Kostal (2013), "Lessons from Slovakia's Comprehensive Approach", Slovak Governance Institute, Bratislava.

Sprocha, S. (2011), "Population forecast of the Roma population in Slovakia to 2030", in *Slovak Statistics and Demography 2011(4).*

Szalai, J. and C. Schiff (2014), *Post-colonial, Migrant and Roma Youth in Education across Europe. Being 'Visibly Different'*, Basingstoke: Palgrave.

van Baar, H. (2012), "Socioeconomic mobility and neoliberal governmentality in post-socialist Europe: Activation and the dehumanization of the Roma", *Journal of Ethnic and Migration Studies*, Vol. 38, No. 8, pp. 1289-1304.

[1] FRA Pilot Survey 2011

[2] http://hub.coe.int/web/coe-portal/roma

[3] de Laat (2010).

[4] McGarry and Tremlett (2013); Richardson and Ryder (2012); Csepeli and Simon (2004).

[5] FRA (2013).

[6] It needs to be pointed out that depending on 1) the definition of who is regarded as 'Roma', 2) the method of survey sampling, 3) operationalising employment and unemployment indicators, and 4) the timeframe of the unemployed status, various surveys have published very different employment indicators (Messing, 2014).

[7] Brüggemann (2012).

[8] EUROSTAT- Labour Force Survey (2011).

[9] Kureková et al. (2012).

[10] Borovicova et al. (2013).

[11] Bereményy (2013).

[12] Borovicova et al. (2013).

[13] Job creation programmes labelled "public work programmes" reach out to approximately a quarter of the unemployed in Hungary.

[14] FRA (2009).

[15] Salner and Kostal (2013); Pop (2013); Köllő and Scharle (2013).

[16] FRA (2014); FRA and UNDP (2012).

[17] For exact calculations, see Borovicova et al. (2013).

[18] European Commission (2011).

[19] Council Recommendation of 9 December 2013 on effective Roma integration measures in the member states (2013/C 378/01).

[20] ACCEDER was called to existence through the joint financing of the ERDF and ESF under the Spanish Multiregional Operational Programme (OP) 'Fight against Discrimination', being the only ESF in Spain focusing openly on the Roma population. The programme is massive: an FSG report claims that in the period of 2000-12 it has attended 70,414 people, maintaining an approximately 70% share of Roma clients; signed 47,868 work-contracts; organized 1.928 training courses; assisted 143 start-up businesses; and concluded agreements with more than 200 companies about potential internship schemes for ACCEDER users.

[21] EUROSTAT (2012).

[22] 'Public employment programmes' or 'public employment' refer to public work schemes through which the central governments (or local governments, public employment services or other actors) create publicly financed temporary jobs for unemployed. In Hungary and Spain, such employment results in employment contracts, while in Slovakia the payment is registered as a top-up to social welfare benefit and remains a part of social welfare subsidies.

[23] Public employment schemes.

[24] Anti-flood measures.

[25] Employment plans.

[26] Messing et al. (2013).

[27] Salner and Kostal (2013); OSF MtM (2011).

[28] Pop (2013); Pamporov (2013).

[29] Messing (2013b).

[30] Kureková and Konstekova (2013).

10. SOCIAL SERVICES AS AN OPTION FOR SUSTAINABLE EMPLOYMENT GROWTH

*TOMÁŠ SIROVÁTKA AND BENT GREVE**

Many welfare states in Europe continue to register high levels of unemployment, in particular long-term unemployment among young people. The ongoing crisis raises the question of how to ensure that there will be jobs in the future so that Europe can move towards 2020 with growing participation rates and lower levels of unemployment. Employment in post-crisis Europe is further affected by the continuous restructuring of production and of societies, and the rising competition from low-income countries that compete on the basis of low wages. There is therefore a need to create not only jobs in traditional agriculture and industrial production but also services jobs, which cannot be outsourced.

The services sector encompasses a broad and diverse range of jobs. This chapter focuses on a specific services sub-sector: health and social work (HSW).[1] This sub-sector is an integral part of welfare states. Although its primary goal is to support societal development, at the same time it creates employment opportunities for both unskilled and highly skilled labour. Health and social services is therefore an area in which the welfare state has the possibility to create jobs as part of a social investment strategy. Social services can provide new jobs while at the same time it might raise the level of welfare provided by many welfare states.

This chapter addresses a number of questions relating to both the past trends and the future of employment in the health and social services sector. We look at the drivers of demand and supply that influence

* Bent Greve: Department of Society and Globalisation, University of Roskilde, Denmark; Tomáš Sirovátka: Institute of Public Policy and Social Work, Masaryk University, Czech Republic.

employment in the sector and consider possible future developments. Special attention is given to the financing of the welfare state and the governance of employment growth in social services, and particular attention is also paid to the prospects for employment of those most at risk in the labour market (e.g. the unskilled).

10.1 Differences in employment in social services across the EU countries are huge

The remarkable growth of social services in Europe began slowly after World War II, in connection with increases in female labour market participation, the ageing of the population and the growth of the public sector. The role of social services in contemporary societies has increased due to the societal, economic and demographic changes since the 1970s. The increasing emphasis on social services is further seen as a general contemporary trend in welfare state architecture.[2] Employment in social services can serve as an indicator of development. When using expenditure on social services (such as 'in kind social protection expenditure') to measure their development, a difficulty arises in that many services are supported through cash benefits used to purchase a specific service, and these specific cash benefits are difficult to distinguish in the data. Similarly, only public expenditure on social services is available to be measured, while private expenditure is not.

The increasing expenditure on social services is a general trend in contemporary welfare states, better measured by increases in employment in social services than simply public expenditure on social services.

Box 10.1 Limitations of the data on employment in health and social services

- Eurostat does not usually publish data on employment in health services and social services separately (due to possible reliability problems resulting from the sample size in many EU member countries).
- The demarcation between health care and social care is often blurred, especially in long-term care. There is a similar problem with the distinction in the education sector.
- The distinction between home and institutional care is often blurred, especially in countries that provide cash care allowances.
- It is often hard to obtain data on informal arrangements; nevertheless, informal care options may be available. In the long-term care sector in particular, there may be more informal than formal workers.

After the year 2000, employment in the HSW sector in many EU countries grew much faster than in many other sectors of the economy: it was the third-fastest-growing sector in the EU economy between 2000 and 2007.[3] Employment in HSW is less cyclical than employment in the rest of the economy, as it is largely financed by public funds.[4] In 2010, the employment rate in health and social services accounted for 6% of the total population of productive age. Over the last ten years, employment in the sector has increased on average by 0.7 percentage points per year (see Table 10.1). The variation across EU countries is stark, ranging from 2.7% in Romania to 14% in Denmark.

Social services expanded, yet the variation across EU countries is huge, with the highest employment in social services in Scandinavia and the Netherlands, and the lowest in the southern and eastern European countries.

Four groups of countries can be distinguished. The first cluster, which is quite distant from the other clusters, consists of four countries where the employment rate in health and social services is between 10.6% and 14.0% (Sweden, Finland, the Netherlands and Denmark). This is followed by a group of countries where the employment rate is between 8.4% and 9.1% (Belgium, France, Germany and the UK). In the third cluster, the employment rate in the sector is slightly above average for this sector across Europe, at between 6.1% and 7.7% (Luxembourg, Austria and Ireland). In the large fourth group - a southern, central and eastern cluster - the employment rate in social services ranges between 2.7% (Romania) and 4.8% (Portugal). The change in employment from 2000 to 2010 also varies within each cluster. In the first cluster, there was very strong growth in employment in the Netherlands (+3.4 percentage points), but a decrease in Sweden (-2.7 percentage points). Growth was quite strong in the second and third clusters, particularly in Ireland (+2.5 percentage points) and Germany (+2.1 percentage points). In the fourth (southern, central and eastern) cluster, only moderate growth mostly of below 1% prevailed, while Slovakia, Hungary, Bulgaria, Lithuania and Poland stagnated.

Table 10.1 Employment rates in health and social services, 2000-2010

	2000	2005	2010	*Change 2000-2010*
Denmark	13.3	13.2	14.0	*0.7*
Netherlands	9.9	11.3	12.3	*3.4*
Finland	9.4	10.5	11.2	*1.8*
Sweden	13.3	12.0	10.6	*-2.7*
UK	7.8	8.8	9.1	*1.3*
France	6.5	7.8	8.4	*1.9*
Germany	6.5	7.4	8.6	*2.1*
Belgium	7.2	7.5	8.4	*1.2*
Ireland	5.2	6.6	7.7	*2.5*
Austria	5.4	6.3	7.0	*1.6*
Luxembourg	5.1	6.2	6.1	*1.0*
Portugal	3.7	4.5	4.8	*0.9*
Malta	4.0	4.1	4.6	*0.6*
Czech Republic	3.9	4.4	4.5	*0.6*
Spain	3.0	3.8	4.3	*1.3*
Italy	3.3	4.0	4.1	*0.8*
Slovakia	4.0	3.9	4.0	*0*
Slovenia	3.3	3.6	3.9	*0.6*
Lithuania	3.9	4.2	3.9	*0*
Hungary	3.6	3.8	3.7	*0.1*
Poland	3.6	3.1	3.5	*-0.1*
Estonia	2.9	3.6	3.5	*0.6*
Greece	2.6	3.0	3.3	*0.7*
Cyprus	2.5	3.0	3.0	*0.5*
Bulgaria	3.0	3.0	3.1	*0.1*
Latvia	2.8	3.4	2.9	*0.1*
Romania	2.1	2.3	2.7	*0.6*
Average	5.3	5.8	6.0	*0.7*

Note: Sectors N (Q) by NACE: health and social services.

Source: Eurostat (2012) and own computations, adapted from Sirovátka and Greve (2014).

The picture is similar when the share of employment in health and social services (including employment services) is analysed. There is a cluster of countries where this share is between 15% and 20% of total employment (Denmark, Finland, Sweden and the Netherlands), and a second cluster where it is between 10% and 14% (Belgium, Germany, France, the UK, Austria, and Ireland). The third cluster, where the share of employment in health and social services is between 7% and 10%, is comprised of Luxembourg, Czech Republic, Spain, Malta and Portugal, while the remaining countries exhibit lower shares of employment in the sector (see Table 10.2).

Table 10.2 Employment in health services, social and employment services as a share of total employment, 2010 (%)

NACE rev. 2	Human health activities (Q86)	Residential care activities (Q87)	Social work without accommodation (Q88)	Employment services (N78)	Social services only	Total HSW
Denmark	7.1	4.6	7.5	0.7	12.8	19.9
Netherlands	7.2	4.8	4.4	1	10.2	17.4
Sweden	6.9	4.9	3.6	1.4	9.9	16.8
Finland	7.3	3.3	5	0.3	8.6	15.9
UK	7.2	2.5	3.4	0.8	6.7	13:9
France	6.9	2.2	4	0.5	6.7	13.6
Germany	7.2	2.7	2.3	0.9	5.9	13.1
Ireland	8.4	1.2	3.2	0.3	4.7	13.1
Austria	6.6	1.6	1.5	0.4	3.5	10.1
Luxembourg	4.8	1.9	2.7	:	4.6:	9.4
Malta	5.4	2.3	:	:	2.3::	7.7
Spain	4.9	1.4	1.1	0.2	2.7	7.6
Italy	5.3	1.1	0.9	0.2	2.2	7.5
Portugal	4.2	1.7	1.4	:	3.1:	7.3
Czech Republic	5.1	1.2	0.7	(0.1)	2	7.1
Hungary	4.3	1.5	0.9	0.2	2.6	6.9
Lithuania	5.7	0.7	:	:	0.7::	6.4
Poland	4.5	0.6	0.8	(0.1)	1.5	6.0
Slovakia	4.5	1.2	1.1	(0.2)	2.5	6.0
Slovenia	4.2	1.3	(0.4)	:	1.7:	5.9
Greece	4.8	0.3	0.5	:	0.8:	5.6
Bulgaria	3.7	0.5	1	:	1.5:	5.2
Latvia	3.6	0.7	(0.6)	:	1.3:	4.7
Cyprus	3.4	0.5	0.4	:	0.9:	4.3
Romania	3.6	0.4	0.5	:	0.9:	4.5
Estonia	4.7	:	:	:	:	:

Source: Own calculations using Eurostat Labour Force Survey (LFS) (data on the specific types of service are not available); adapted from Sirovátka and Greve (2014).

The variation in the share of employment in health services across EU countries is relatively limited. However, there are differences when looking at the share of total employment accounted for by social services: in Denmark it equals 12.8%; in Finland, Sweden and the Netherlands it lies between 8% and 11%; in Belgium, Germany, France and the UK, it is between 5% and 8%; in Luxembourg and Ireland it is close to 5%; while in the remaining countries it is below 4% (and below 2% in many post-communist and southern European countries).

The identified clusters overlap somewhat with Esping-Andersen's welfare state typology: there appears to be a social-democratic cluster, a continental/liberal cluster, a Mediterranean cluster and an eastern European cluster.[5] Employment in health and social services is lowest in eastern European countries with low GDP, and therefore seems to be driven by both the institutional setting and budget.

10.2 Social services is a female-dominated sector in which the workforce is ageing rapidly

In 2009, 78.2% of employees in the HSW sector were women. The female employment rate in the sector is growing mainly in countries with a previously lower female employment rate, while in countries with a previously higher female employment rate it has decreased slightly. Of the new jobs in the sector during the decade after 2000, 81% were taken by women.[6] Eurostat LFS data from 2010 confirm this finding for all the sub-sectors under consideration, with the exception of employment services. In health services, the share of women in total employment ranges from 62.9% and 63.5% (in Italy and Greece, respectively) to 85.6% and 86.7% (Finland and Latvia); in residential (social) care it ranges from 75.9% (Germany) to 90.1% (Portugal); and in social work/services without accommodation it ranges from 74.7% (Germany) to 94.4% (Greece). In most countries, over 80% of workers in residential care facilities and social work without accommodation are women.[7]

There are several reasons for this domination by women. First, jobs in social services are 'easy entry jobs' for most women, even those who are low skilled, since there are many jobs in the sector that require limited skills or experience. Second, employment in social care began to grow at a time when many women were entering the labour market. Finally, services display lower productivity levels and growth rates than other industries.

This lower productivity is reflected in lower wages, which may make the jobs attractive primarily to second earners in a family.

There is already some evidence that the workforce in HSW is ageing: the share of people aged over 50 working in the HSW sector in the EU increased from approximately 20% to 28% between 2000 and 2009.[8] However, the extent to which ageing will lead to labour supply shortages in the future is not entirely clear. This is due to the possible impact of migration and a possible increase of the supply of labour in case demand for labour goes up, with the option to move from inactivity to employment, including staying longer in the labour market, and for some to increase the number of hours they work.

10.3 There are job prospects in social services for both highly skilled and low-skilled workers

Another question is whether the growth of employment in social services will continue and how much the low-skilled groups, which are most affected by unemployment risks, will profit from this. The evidence from the EU countries where social services are relatively more developed shows that growing employment in health and social services brings not only jobs for professionals in health and social care, but also many jobs cleaning and performing other tasks in home help or help within institutions in care services. What matters is the public support for these services, the purchasing power of the clients and effective regulations.

The comparison of the educational level of workers in the HSW sector broken down by age group shows that in the group of countries where employment in social services is high (e.g. Denmark, Sweden and the Netherlands), the share of low-skilled 'help service jobs' is also relatively high, especially for those aged over 50 and below 30 (typically above 20%, and up to 30% in Denmark for those over 50, and around 15-23% for the group aged under 50). In the second group, represented by Belgium and the UK, where employment in social services is above average, and also in Spain and Italy where it is below average, the share of low-skilled 'help service jobs' is above 20% for the group aged over 50, and about 10% for the group aged under 30. In Finland, Germany and Austria (where employment in social services is high or above average), the share is between 10% and 15% for all age groups except the group below 30 in Germany, where it is 23% (see Table 10.3).

Table 10.3 Education levels of workers in the HSW sector by age, 2000 (%)

	Age	Education High	Medium	Low
Denmark	15-29	26.1	51.1	22.8
	30-49	50.4	34.7	14.9
	50+	40.1	29.9	29.9
Sweden	15-29	29.1	55.6	15.4
	30-49	46.7	44	9.3
	50+	42	33.5	24.5
France	15-29	39.2	48	12.8
	30-49	38.1	43.3	18.6
	50+	36.2	34.3	29.6
Netherlands	15-29	32.6	51.5	15.8
	30-49	38.9	48	13.1
	50+	37.8	40.8	21.4
Germany	15-29	20.3	56.1	23.6
	30-49	37.3	53.7	9
	50+	39.1	49.1	11.8
Italy	15-29	51.9	39	9.1
	30-49	41.9	41.5	16.6
	50+	44.8	31	24.2
Belgium	15-29	50.5	38.7	10.8
	30-49	51.6	35.5	12.9
	50+	50.6	27.6	21.8
Spain	15-29	70.7	22.1	7.2
	30-49	60.3	25.7	14
	50+	51	24.2	24.9
United Kingdom	15-29	43.1	46.1	10.8
	30-49	52.8	36	11.1
	50+	45.5	34.7	19.8
Austria	15-29	17.3	66.7	16
	30-49	25.3	64.2	10.5
	50+	32.1	53.6	14.3
Finland	15-29	35.6	50.8	13.6
	30-49	54.9	41.8	3.3
	50+	41.5	47.6	10.9
Czech Republic	15-29	34.8	63	2.2
	30-49	25.1	71.7	3.2
	50+	23.6	67	9.4

Note: Rows add up to 100%.
Source: Labour Force Survey; own calculations; adapted from Sirovátka and Greve (2014).

The general conclusion is that in countries where the share of social services in the whole health and social services sector is high, job opportunities for low-skilled employees are also high, although this depends on the ability to support the service sector either through public or private resources.

On the other hand, in countries such as the Czech Republic where employment in health social services is quite low, the share of unskilled workers in social services employment is only 9% for those aged over 50 and 2% for those aged under 30. This finding may indicate current problems, but also indicates a huge potential for future job generation for unskilled workers in the social services sector in countries like the Czech Republic – the conditions for this being sound public finances, adequate financing of services from both public and private sources, effective regulation of service providers (i.e. quality standards) and access to services.

10.4 Employment growth in social services will be driven by growing demand for these services

There is a broad range of drivers and factors that stimulate the development of social services and employment in social services. On the demand side, the growth of employment in social services will be driven primarily by 'general drivers' of social services growth. Changing roles for women and their growing labour market participation and employment are leading to increasing demand for social and community services, mainly care services.[9] There is also a more general trend for services to dominate industrial production due to the demand shift towards services sectors.[10] This means that countries where the economy is performing well and where the purchasing power of the population is high should generate higher demand for social services due to public as well as private purchasing of such services.

Social services provide jobs both for high- and low-skilled workers, even among the younger generation.

The impact of rising overall purchasing power may vary across countries, depending on income inequalities. The Keynesian assumption of the volatility of demand due to increasing income inequalities provides an argument for the introduction of inbuilt stabilisers such as income redistribution, among other things, in order to stimulate demand for services.

Population ageing is also an important driver of employment growth in social services, due to rising demand for elderly care, long-term care and healthcare.[11] Not only is an increase in the volume of services needed with the increase in the numbers of elderly people in need of care, but also "[due to the] level of dependence and the poly-pathologies of the elderly, long-term care services are increasingly called upon to provide more professional and often more medical services to a broader and more differentiated segment of the population".[12]

Finally, the emerging new social risks are increasingly putting pressure on the provision of various social services: the challenges of work-family reconciliation, especially for single parents (demand for care services); challenges emerging from the dynamics of the post-industrial labour markets such as out-dated skills (demand for employment services and lifelong learning); and challenges of poverty and social exclusion (demand for social assistance services, social housing, social work services and emergency services).

10.5 The impact of drivers of supply is less clear

There are both potentially negative as well as positive drivers of labour supply in social services. A hypothetically 'negative' supply factor is represented by Baumol's disease;[13] the problem being that productivity growth in the service sector is slower than in manufacturing. The traditional interpretation is that if wages in services are tightly coupled to wages in manufacturing, employment expansion in private services will be slowed down.

There are three possible responses to the cost-disease problem. The first, allowing labour costs to adjust, may result in many services disappearing due to low earnings and lack of labour supply. Another possible approach (typical of Nordic and continental countries) is to adjust earnings in the services sector to the level of earnings in the overall economy. Due to high labour costs, personal services would then grow very sluggishly, if at all (resulting in jobless growth). The third solution is to subsidise services via government production or subsidies to consumers (through something like special tax benefits).[14]

Thus, the productivity lag could foster employment growth in the sector if services were to be produced by government, or consumers were to be subsidised when purchasing the services. This is why the impact of the crisis on the public budgets for social services can have strong negative implications for employment in social services if the purchasing power of the population does not enable public provision of the services to be counterbalanced.

Then there is a range of positive factors stimulating labour supply. First, the theory of the political business cycle explains that political elites are interested in positive election results and strive to avoid electoral punishment. The downsizing of the public sector can result in a loss of votes, especially if welfare programmes are involved. Some studies posit that globalisation leads to an increase in welfare services in response to public demand stemming from their fears of economic changes.[15] Furthermore, there are pressure groups with an interest in promoting employment in the public sector. Vested interests matter a lot: service providers tend to form coalitions with service consumers. Since social services are labour-intensive and also consist of highly skilled and influential professional groups (such as civil servants, doctors and teachers), their interests are very likely to play a role.[16]

Second, the public sector serves as a buffer against the risk of economic instability, the expectation being that the public sector is relatively large when other employment possibilities are scarce or that public employment grows as a response to growing unemployment.[17] Since governments follow anti-cyclical public employment policy in order to reap electoral benefits, rising unemployment should have a positive effect on public employment growth; rising public budget deficits cause a reduction in the growth of public employment, whereas rising GDP per capita should have the opposite effect.[18] For example, in a situation of rising budget deficits, the rising cost of public employment might lead to a reduction of public social services employment in the future. Overall, it seems that according to the theory of the political business cycle, support for the supply of social services depends on several circumstances.

If voters evaluate officials on their recent performance, politicians can be expected to shift the use of the political business cycle mechanism towards policy domains that are easier for them to manipulate, such as public employment, which is more 'street visible'.[19]

Finally, path dependency is an important factor. In the period of welfare state expansion, social services have developed well in some countries. This is because the expansion of social services was easier in the period of welfare state expansion than in the phase of welfare state retrenchment, when new programmes are hard to finance and require an expansion of the resource base and/or a reallocation of resources away from established programmes.[20]

Moreover, according to the 'timing hypothesis' which claims that the advancement of policies responding to new social risks (typically this is a substantial part of public/social services such as education, active labour market policies or childcare) is difficult for those countries that are confronting these risks later, or in the face of emerging challenges from population ageing and economic austerity affecting welfare programmes.[21] When considering the path dependency hypothesis and the timing hypothesis together, it is highly likely that the development of social services will be difficult in times of crisis and post-crisis periods, especially for those countries where these services are still underdeveloped, with the difficulty being greater if public finance debt is high. This is the case for the countries in southern Europe and post-communist central and eastern European countries.

To sum up, there are convincing theoretical as well as empirical arguments for employment growth in social services in the future, as evidenced by the employment growth between 2000 and 2010. The financial and fiscal crises did little to alter the continuous growth of employment in social services that has lasted since 2000. When using data that capture employment figures year-by-year for the EU27, the evidence shows that there was an increase in employment in social services each year from 2008 to 2010 with little variation.

10.6 Growth in social services is supported by several key factors

An empirical examination of the factors influencing the employment rate in social services among EU countries in the period 2000-10 relies on the Pearson correlation coefficient of the employment rate in social services with the variables listed in Box 10.2. This singular measure was chosen because the complexity of the relationships among these variables could make attempts to distinguish the dependent and independent variables misleading. The variables listed in Box 10.2 were therefore used to shed light on the differences in employment rates in social services across EU countries.

> *The complex mix of demand and supply drivers provides strong arguments for the expectations of the growth in social services.*

Box 10.2 Factors influencing employment in social services

- Financing of the welfare state (government revenues, tax on labour, social protection expenditure, social protection expenditure in kind)
- Demographics (population ageing - old age dependency, fertility rate)
- Political-economic cycle captured by proxy variables that directly influence the supply and demand for social services (GDP growth, public deficit)
- Employment patterns (employment rates, unemployment rates - total, male, female)

An analysis of three time points between 2000 and 2010 reveals persistent country differences during the period. This indicates that the range of factors that influence employment in social services is stable over time. A high level of employment in social services is associated with a higher level of government revenues, higher expenditure on social protection (both total and in-kind), a higher level of employment (total, male and female), a lower level of unemployment (total, male and female) and perhaps higher fertility rates. In 2000 and 2005, it was also associated with a lower level of public finance deficit, but in 2010 this relationship no longer existed. Similarly, while in 2005 stronger economic growth was associated with lower employment rates in social services, in 2010 the opposite was true.

These findings indicate that fiscal policies have been the most important factor: sufficient financing has been associated with higher employment in social services. Second, sound public finances, indicated by a low public deficit, has also had relevance both for sufficient financing and for the growth of employment in social services. There was a positive correlation between GDP growth and employment in social services in 2010; the causal relationship can, of course, work in both directions. Finally, a negative correlation between employment in social services and the public deficit was indicated in 2000 and 2005. A public deficit obviously reduces the possibilities for the government to support employment in social services.

Table 10.4 Correlation coefficients between employment rates in social services and selected variables in the EU in 2010

	Employment rate in social services (N or Q) correlated with:		
	Strong > 0.66	**Moderate > 0.33**	**Weak, insignificant**
Correlation coefficients PE in 2010	Social protection expenditure in kind (.853)***	Employment rate women (.677)***	Public deficit
	Total government revenues from taxes and soc. Security contributions (.782)***	Employment rate men (.574)***	Unemployment rate men
	Social protection expenditure total (.780)***	Unemployment rate women (- .482)**	Old-age dependency
	Fertility rate (.747)***	Unemployment rate total (- .412)**	
	Employment rate total (.741)***	GDP growth (.383)**	
	Tax on labour (.690)***		

Notes: Employment in the public sector and social services: NACE: N (Q) Health and social work; ** significant at the 0.05 level; *** significant at the 0.01 level.

Overall, strong drivers of employment growth in social services have been confirmed. First, growing female employment combined with policies to reconcile family and work result in increases in social services employment. The development of social services creates new job opportunities for women and at the same time enables them to balance their work and family lives, thus facilitating participation in the labour market. Second, politics matters: a deliberate strategy to foster public-sector employment with an emphasis on social services in times of economic slowdown has been identified. This is underpinned by pressure groups (employees in the public sector) and a strong legitimacy of social services among the public (social services address life-cycle risks affecting all classes/groups). Third, financing of social services plays a crucial role, and public financing still represents the major part of this. For this reason, the level of public revenues, the levels of public expenditure on social services and specific 'services-related benefits' and, finally, sound public finances, indicated by the level of public-finance deficit, play a role. However, at the same time, private finance is becoming increasingly relevant.

The ageing of society, as indicated by the old-age dependency ratio, did not prove to be significantly correlated with social service employment. Welfare state models and family models may imply alternative or informal caring options when public social services are insufficient, for example in post-communist countries or in southern Europe, with the negative consequence of a lower female employment rate. Nevertheless, the impacts of ageing on the demand for social services will be more pervasive in the future due to the expected rapid changes in demographic structures.

In the context of the crisis, however, it is difficult to envisage increased public investment in social services, in particular in countries where this expenditure used to be low and that now are facing increasing public deficits. The key problem, identified mainly in those EU member states (such as southern or post-communist countries) that have not yet developed their social services to levels comparable with other EU countries, is that many are currently facing public-finance deficits due to the crisis and are expecting increases in expenditure on pensions (cash) due to population ageing.

10.7 The fiscal constraints could be alleviated by greater redistribution

Welfare states have been under pressure for several years, with cuts in spending on welfare in many European countries. This section discusses two important issues related to current and future employment in social services.[22] The first is whether and how it is possible to achieve sustainable financing of welfare states. The second is whether there might be certain instruments available that can have a significant influence on the development and creation of jobs in social services.

The ageing of society will become a strong driver for the development of employment in social services in the future.

Recent years have seen a reduction in public sector spending, but also an increase in statutory tax rates and VAT. Fifteen countries in the EU increased VAT in 2012 or in the first half of 2013, and 23 countries have increased either the statutory tax rate or tax base. At the same time, corporate income tax rates or tax bases have been reduced in many EU countries.[23] Taxes as a percentage of GDP have hovered around 40%, on average, across all EU countries in recent years. A decline in the level of GDP therefore reduces the options for financing social services. This, combined with the fact that many countries have experienced pressure on their financial sectors and a need to support them in the wake of the financial crisis, has resulted in less room for financing social services. Taxes on labour are the most important form of tax in the EU. Despite large differences between EU countries due to historical reasons and traditions, there have been some trends towards convergence.

There has been a further general trend of broadening the tax base in many countries over the last few years. This has been done in various ways in the EU member states, and has made it possible to combine lowering tax rates (especially for companies) with maintaining a relatively constant level of revenue as a percentage of GDP. Indeed, "taxing consumption and property appears to have significantly less adverse effects on GDP than taxing income".[24] A taxation strategy in this direction would therefore be effective in creating economic growth and thus possibly more jobs, as would a strategy with a focus on how to tax immobile factors (such as houses and land) more than mobile factors (such as capital). Moving taxation in this direction would also ensure better sustainability of public sector income, although it would not remove the ups and downs resulting from the business economic cycle. Still, there is a problem in that not all countries report tax expenditures regularly and systematically, with obvious implications for the volume of revenue collected and the complexity of the tax system.[25] One area where, despite the attention it has received, there have not been real changes is environmental taxation, which has remained more or less constant over this period.

The ongoing international discussions to ensure a higher level of tax compliance and to reduce tax havens[26] can also be argued to form part of a strategy that will help ensure more stable public sector income, and at the same time may make it possible to increase overall public sector revenues without having to change tax rates. Thus, a movement towards better tax compliance, including international cooperation on fighting tax evasion, will make it possible to establish a better and more sustainable way of financing welfare states.

A higher level of public sector income is only one, albeit important, necessary condition for having the financial means to support the development of jobs in social services. There are, in principle, two different routes that can be taken to increase employment in social services by the welfare state.

One route is increasing the level of employment in social services within the public sector (for example, increasing spending on day-care for children, care for the elderly or healthcare). If there are overall increases in revenues and the limits regarding public sector deficits, then this would, depending on political preferences, be a possible option for increasing the level of employment in the field as a whole.

The other route is using incentives to try to encourage private households and companies to engage more people in social services. This might be done in two different ways. The first is by giving tax rebates, which is contradictory to the broadening of the tax base and implies the use of more tax expenditures.[27] However, an argument for doing it this way is that certain types of services in private households that are part of the hidden economy - such as care and cleaning - could be moved to the open economy, while at the same time the use of social services would be increased. Naturally, the size, structure and level of support need to be carefully monitored to avoid paying large amounts for activities that are already being done.

The other way would be to pay part of the expenditure of private persons in employing people in areas of social services when they document that those employed are registered and have paid VAT, either through a direct economic payment or beforehand by issuing vouchers. This would reduce the cost to the individual buying social services, and thus should in principle increase the demand for social services. Again, there is naturally a risk that society will support people who are already buying this service and also a risk that private providers will increase their prices with the level of public support. So this way would also need to be carefully monitored and evaluated in order to avoid expenditure that will not provide good results for society. Still, the implication is that in order for the welfare state to support the development of social services, a prerequisite is ensuring stable financing of the welfare state.

A combination of individualisation of service accompanied by empowerment of clients, quality standards and targeting both financial support and intensive services are supportive of employment growth in social services.

10.8 Governance of social services may bring employment gains

Employment in social services is influenced by governance of the sector. The process of rearranging the relationships between the state, the market and families in services provision has brought about a trend splitting the functions of regulation, financing and service delivery, as well as the pluralisation of actors. The role of the state as a direct service provider is diminishing, while the market and NGOs are becoming more important.

The processes associated with this phenomenon, seen to some extent in all EU countries, are as follows:

- Marketisation (outsourcing of services delivery to private providers, more competition, an increasing role of private resources in the form of co-payments/fees for services).
- Increasing emphasis on the complementary relationship between formal (professional) and informal (family) services provision.
- Individualisation of services with increasing attention to the needs of clients, choice and empowerment; their choice is greater (through the use of vouchers or through becoming direct purchasers of services) and/or their rights are better guaranteed (rights to services, services quality standards).
- Stronger state regulation (quality standards of services, price limits).

All these elements have an impact on the sustainability and development of social services and on employment in the sector. However, there are remarkable differences among EU countries with respect to these processes, although there are also some common trends.

The evidence indicates that in most countries, mixing public and private sources will be necessary for sustainable public finances. This strategy may bring important employment gains if and when the governance framework provides effective regulation of the use of resources available in the following respects: setting quality and professional standards and systems of the controls; maximising choice for the users of the services; and combining universal accessibility of services with targeted support to users. Nevertheless, in order to fulfil the above tasks, a certain level (threshold) of public financing is necessary.

10.9 More employment in social services in the future

There are possibilities and options for greater employment in social services, given the expected continuing changes in welfare states and given the demographic changes that imply an increasing need for such services. Furthermore, the private sector also seems to be moving towards the services sector and there is an expectation of greater demand for social services, a natural development as societies become richer. People and societies with higher levels of income demand more social services. The political will to support jobs in the area is also important.

An increase in social services will imply greater demand for both highly skilled and unskilled workers in the future. The reason for this is that welfare services comprise different kinds of functions and needs. The development of a variety of jobs in the area of welfare services can be an important feature of a more varied labour market in terms of the qualifications required.

The crisis has not fundamentally changed the general patterns of the demand and supply drivers of employment growth in social services. Nevertheless, some pre-conditions and circumstances have become more important.

First, the business cycle seems to be crucial in determining how countries can successfully grow employment in social services, as it strongly influences the economic opportunities for welfare states. GDP growth, labour productivity growth and low public deficits support growing purchasing power of the population and increasing demand and ability to pay for social services privately, as well as the ability of the welfare state to collect taxes and to support social services. Tax governance and compliance is therefore also important with regard to the ability to ensure financing of public social services.

Second, in countries where the economic realities are less favourable towards financing social services, some specific circumstances may play an increasing role. One important issue might be the ability of policy-makers, and the opportunities available to them, to modernise the welfare state by redirecting expenditure from benefits towards services. This could range from passive spending, with negligible impact on unemployment, to active welfare spending that supports employment and growth (social investments). The other way might be to reduce the relative level of employment in public sector administration, where technological innovations (ITC and others) and governance reforms can make performance more effective and efficient. Finally, this could help legitimise increases in public support for social services.

Third, innovations in welfare technologies can bring increases in employment and improvements in job quality in social services. Seemingly, these technologies replace (unskilled) work in social services such as cleaning and other home help tasks, or health control and aid. On the other hand, they could help to employ professional home care, which would provide more job opportunities even for unskilled workers. At the same time, job quality may be improved in the home care sub-sector, since some routine tasks require less effort while providing more room for an approach focused on personal needs.

In the long term, the first prerequisite for welfare states to continue and perhaps expand employment in the field is therefore sustainable finances, as this will enable the welfare state to have a role in the provision of services, whether public or private. Governance of social services will have an impact on their development and on employment in the sector. An effective combination of public and private resources, the individualisation of the services accompanied by empowerment of the clients and providing rights to services, regulation of quality standards and professional services, support for access to social services and the effective allocation of services with respect to the needs of users are all supportive of growth of employment in social services, as are innovations in welfare technologies.

Social services are needed and can be afforded in the future if EU countries have sustainable finances, i.e. sufficient public financing and effective regulation.

Social services might thus be an option for sustainable growth in welfare and employment in Europe in the years to come, although sustainable finances are important in order to achieve this goal.

Bibliography

Anderson, K.M. and T. Meyer (2006), "New social risks and pension reform in Germany and Sweden", in K. Armingeon and G. Bonoli (eds), *Industrial Welfare States: Adapting post-war social policies to new social risks,* London and New York: Routledge, pp. 171-191.

Baumol, W.J. (1967), "The macroeconomics of unbalanced growth", *American Economic Review,* Vol. 57, pp. 415-426.

Bonoli, G. (2007), "Time Matters. Post-industrialization, New Social Risks and Welfare State Adaptations in Advanced Industrial Democracies", *Comparative Political Studies,* Vol. 40, pp. 495-520.

Bosch, G. and S. Lehndorff (2001), *New Forms of Employment and Working Time in the Service Economy (NESY)*, Final Report, TSER Programme of the European Commission, Wissenschaftzentrum Nordhein-Westfalen, Institut Arbeit und Technik (IAT).

Cusack, T.R., T. Notermans and M. Rein (1989), "Political-Economic Aspects of Public Employment", *European Journal of Political Research,* Vol. 17, pp. 471-500.

Esping-Andersen, G. (1990), *The Three Worlds of Welfare Capitalism,* Princeton, NJ: Princeton University Press.

_____ (1999), *The Social Foundations of Post-industrial Economies,* Oxford: Oxford University Press.

_____ (2008), *The Incomplete Revolution. Adapting to Women's New* Roles, Cambridge, MA: Polity Press.

European Commission (2008), "Biennial Report on Social Services of General Interest", Staff Working Document, European Commission, Brussels.

_____ (2010), "Second Biennial Report on Social Services of General Interest", Commission Staff Working Document SEC (2010) 1284 final, European Commission, Brussels.

_____ (2013), "Taxation trends in the European Union", Brussels.

Eurostat (2012), *Statistical database* (http://epp.eurostat.ec.europa.eu/portal/page/portal/statistics/themes).

Farnsworth, K. (2013), "Occupational Welfare", in B. Greve (ed.), *The Routledge Handbook of the Welfare State,* Oxon: Routledge.

Holman, D. and Ch. McClelland (2011), "Job Quality in Growing and Declining Economic Sectors of the EU", Working Paper 2011.3, University of Manchester.

Huber, E. and J.D. Stephens (2006), "Combating Old and New Social Risks", in K. Armingeon and G. Bonoli (eds), *The politics of post-industrial welfare states: adapting post-war social policies to new social risks*, London: Routledge, pp. 143-168.

Jensen, C. (2008), "Worlds of welfare services and transfers", *Journal of European Social Policy*, Vol. 18, No. 2, pp. 151-162.

_____ (2009), "Determinants of welfare services provision after the Golden Age", *International Journal of Social Welfare*, Vol. 20, pp. 125-134.

Johansson, Å., C. Heady, J. Arnold, B. Brys and L. Vartia (2008), "Taxation and Economic Growth", OECD Economic Department Working Papers, No. 620, OECD, Paris.

OECD (2005), Social expenditure database 1980-2001, Paris.

Pierre, J. (2008), "The welfare state is female: trends in public sector employment in Sweden", in H.-U. Derlien and B.G. Peters (eds), *The State at Work (Volume 1): Public Sector Employment in Ten Western Countries (vol. 1)*, Cheltenham: Edward Elgar, pp. 268-282.

Pierson, P. (1994), *Dismantling the Welfare State? Reagan, Thatcher and the Politics of Retrenchment*, Cambridge: Cambridge University Press.

Pierson, P. (2005), *The New Politics of The Welfare State*, Oxford: Oxford University Press.

Rouban, L. (2008), "The French paradox: A huge but fragmented public service", in H.-U. Derlien and B.G. Peters (eds), *The State at Work (Volume 1): Public Sector Employment in Ten Western Countries*, Cheltenham: Edward Elgar, pp. 222-248.

Sinfield, A. (2013), "Fiscal Welfare", in B. Greve (ed.), *The Routledge Handbook of the Welfare State*, Oxon: Routledge.

Sirovátka, T. and B. Greve (eds) (2014), *Innovation in social services: The Public-Private Mix in Service Provision, Fiscal Policy and Employment*, Aldershot, UK and Burlington, VT: Ashgate.

Taylor-Gooby, P. (ed.) (2004), *New Risks, New Welfare*, Oxford: Oxford University Press.

Tepe, M. (2009), "Public administration employment in 17 OECD nations from 1995 to 2005", Working Papers on the Reconciliation of Work and Welfare in Europe 12/2009, EU project RECWOWE.

Tepe, M. and P. Vanhuysse (2013), "Cops for Hire: The Political Economy of Police Employment across German States", *Journal of Public Policy*, Vol. 33, No. 4, pp. 165-199.

Notes

[1] According to NACE (Statistical classification of economic activities in the European Community) sector Q: human health and social work activities.

[2] Taylor-Gooby (2004, p. 224) argues that "the new social risk policies now being developed do not invariably reflect the characteristics of the existing old social regime".

[3] See Holman and McClelland (2011).

[4] For a discussion on this point, see European Commission (2008a).

[5] Esping-Andersen (1990).

[6] Compare European Commission (2010).

[7] We omit Malta, where it is 64.9%, as an outlier.

[8] European Commission (2010).

[9] Esping-Andersen (1999, p. 60) has argued for the strong association between day-care coverage and the female employment rate, and has also discussed the impact on employment of changing women´s roles (Esping-Andersen, 2008).

[10] Purchasing power is a key driver of this trend. "The service economy is driven by broadening purchasing power throughout the population" and "the disappearance of cheap domestic servants and of the housewife" (Esping-Andersen, 2008, p. 4).

[11] This has been documented by many authors; see Bosch and Lehndorf (2001), European Commission (2010), Jensen (2008; 2009), Esping-Andersen (2008) and Tepe (2009).

[12] See European Commission (2008a).

[13] Baumol (1967)

[14] For a discussion on this point, see Esping-Andersen (2008, pp. 111-114).

[15] Compare Tepe (2009); Rodrik (1998) in Jensen (2009).

[16] For a discussion on this topic, see Pierson (1994).

[17] Compare discussions in Rouban (2008), Pierre (2008) and Tepe (2009).

[18] These assumptions were suggested by Cusack et al. (1989) and confirmed by Tepe (2009).

[19] Tepe and Vanhuysse (2013, p. 5).

[20] These issues have been widely discussed by, among others, Pierson (1994, 2005), Huber and Stephens (2006) and Anderson and Meyer (2006),

[21] Tepe and Vanhuysse (2013), following Bonoli (2007).

[22] This section was inspired by Sirovátka and Greve (2014).

[23] European Commission (2013).

[24] Johansson et al. (2008, p. 42).

[25] European Commission (2013).

[26] See http://europa.eu/rapid/press-release_MEX-13-0905_en.htm.

[27] Farnsworth (2013); Sinfield (2013).

11. EMPLOYMENT TRENDS IN CHILDCARE AND SOCIAL INCLUSION SERVICES

*MICHAELA GSTREIN**

Good quality childcare and social inclusion services are essential factors contributing to inclusive growth, and figure prominently on the EU agenda.[1] Childcare and social inclusion services not only provide new employment opportunities for job seekers[2] and become efficient target areas for social investment (instead of social support) by welfare states, but they also empower citizens and improve people's quality of life.[3] Furthermore, childcare provision is crucial for female labour market participation.[4] The relevance of childcare provision for female labour market inclusion and its importance for social inclusion, societal development as well as smooth social and economic transitions has recently been highlighted in the 'beyond GDP' debate, which broadens the usually growth-focused debate by introducing measures of quality of life,[5] social quality[6] and the effects of income equality.[7]

However, several trends have contributed recently to the decoupling of job quantity and job quality in the childcare and social inclusion services sector. First, the economic crisis often resulted in severe financial cut-backs in public services[8] and a certain reorientation of welfare state policies as a result of budget constraints, sometimes towards subsidised but private care solutions. Second, informal care-related labour migration is putting pressure on wages and working conditions of local services. Third, atypical work is generally on the rise. Finally, it has been shown that

Services impact on people's quality of life and also social inequality. A higher demand for services generates new job opportunities.

* Michaela Gstrein, Senior Researcher, Institute for Advanced Studies, Vienna.

the dominance of female workers in a sector is often related to large and persistent gender gaps in pay.[9]

This chapter therefore examines the impact of these developments on childcare and social inclusion services. The main aim is to shed light on employment patterns, development paths, changes in skills and employment conditions, but also to determine if this sector could offer new employment perspectives, especially for older workers.

11.1 Childcare and social inclusion services high on the EU agenda

The childcare and social services sector has been affected by growing female participation in the labour market and by the Great Recession. Although there are substantial differences in participation rates and the nature of female employment across Europe, women in the EU accounted for the majority of job growth between 2000 and the onset of the crisis. Even then, the female employment rate declined to a lesser extent than that of men in Europe.[10] This appears to be partly an outcome of structural changes in industrial sectors (which mostly concerned men), but also of increases in demand for (and thus employment in) the services sector, which mostly seems to concern women.

The health and social work sector has been growing despite budget cuts.

Despite crisis-related budget cuts in most European countries, the health and social work sector in the EU has been growing over the last ten years. This development has been fuelled not only by innovation, ageing and increasing female labour market participation, but also by increasing expectations of individual, self-determined (but socially supported) life models.

As pointed out in a recent European Commission report on social services of general interest,[11] the health and social work sector - with employment growing faster than in other sectors - has become an important source of job creation in recent years. The same is true for the childcare and social services sector, which is a small but important part of this larger sector.

The Social Investment Package[12] urges European countries to focus more on the provision of various public services, including education-related childcare, long-term care and health. Whereas the document on investing in children[13] stresses the importance of improving access to early childhood education and care in order to enhance the labour market participation of parents with increasingly diverse working patterns (and as a prerequisite for future educational and employment outcomes), the document on investing in health[14] highlights access to quality healthcare as an important element in maintaining a productive workforce and improving the population health status, especially for disadvantaged groups and the less wealthy. The document on long-term care[15] points out that - although it is a responsibility of member states - access for all to financially sustainable, high-quality long-term care is a common objective of EU collaboration in the Social Protection Committee of the European Commission.[16]

11.2 The childcare and social inclusion service sector is influenced by a broad set of factors

The next socio-ecological transition away from fossil fuels will increase the share of work in the care sector[17] - a sector in which, on the one hand, tasks cannot be replaced by machines and, on the other, labour productivity cannot be enhanced much unless a true revolutionary technological change materialises.[18] With the demand for empathy and care work, the challenge might be to increase human labour at lower productivity (and maybe lower income). This view is also reflected in EU reports. While the sectoral focus supplement on health and social services of the EU report on employment and the social situation[19] states that "the share of employment in health and social work (...) has been growing significantly in the last two decades", the European Commission report on social services of general interest finds that wage levels remained below those of the overall economy.[20]

> *Current socio-ecological transitions are increasing the share of work in the care sector – a sector in which productivity cannot grow endlessly.*

The childcare and social inclusion service sector is also influenced by social policies and institutional factors in general. Experts argue that labour market reforms significantly enhanced women's participation.[21] Over the last 20 years, labour market reforms have increased labour force participation of young women by almost 25% and participation of highly educated women by more than 30% across 15 EU member states. However, the labour market reforms are effective only when deregulation is accompanied by sufficient social compensation. Furthermore, Kroos and Gottschall point to the weak professionalisation of caregiving jobs, which generates outsiders and thereby contributes to a trend towards dualisation (i.e. differing working conditions and social status).[22] While 'insiders' in the care sector are characterised by permanent contracts and full-time work, 'outsiders' tend to work part-time or on temporary contracts.

Despite such dualisation, post-modern values regarding the roles of men and women in society, as well as the distribution of time between care and paid work result in a greater institutionalisation of care activities and a growing care sector,[23] in which unfavourable working conditions may also affect retirement plans and result in early exits. While less likely in rich European countries, this seems more common in central and eastern Europe.[24] Thus, monitoring sectoral developments and working conditions becomes an important political issue.

11.3 A strongly female-dominated sector

Who works in the childcare and social inclusion service sector?[25] We show that between 2001 and 2011, more women than men worked in the field, with a trend for growth not only in employment in general, but also in the share of female employees.[26] Despite minor differences between education-related childcare, on the one hand, and social inclusion services and non-educational day care on the other, gender segregation is a general phenomenon of work in this sector, which persists throughout Europe. Women dominate, with 5.6 women for every man employed in the sector in 2011.

In 2011, 5,648 million people found employment in education-related childcare across the EU, while an additional 7,668 million people worked in the field of social inclusion services – together accounting for 6.1% of total European employment.[27] Nevertheless, the size of childcare and social inclusion services within total employment varies throughout Europe. For education-related childcare, it was between 1.4% in Romania and 7.1% in Malta, while for social inclusion services it ranged from 0.4% in Turkey to 12% in Denmark. Women accounted for 88.3% of employees in education-related childcare, and a slightly lower percentage (82.4%) in social inclusion services and non-educational day care. With a total of 11,308 million women and 2,008 million men, the ratio of female to male workers was 85:15.

Childcare and social inclusion services offer jobs for more than 6% of all EU workers, with women accounting for more than 80% of them.

When investigating the age structure over time, it becomes clear that employment in childcare and social inclusion services is generally dominated by young and middle-aged workers (i.e. those between 15 and 49 years of age). Yet, in line with the ageing EU labour force predicted by Dolls et al.,[28] the data show rising numbers of older workers in the sector. On average in Europe in 2011, the share of older employees (i.e. those aged 50 or above) amounted to more than a third (32%) in education-related childcare, and ranged from 20% in Greece to 41% in Italy. For social inclusion services and non-educational day care, the share of older employees varied between 20% (in Austria, Slovenia and Turkey) and 41% (in Latvia). The European average was, at 30%, quite similar to that of education-related childcare. Over the last ten years, the share of older workers in both sub-sectors has increased significantly in most (but not all) countries. Although some of this effect is surely due to ageing of the workforce itself, the strength of this effect in some countries, together with strong increases in female employment, suggest increased older female activity (i.e. new jobs for older women) in this sector.

On average across Europe, a third of workers in the sector are aged 50 or above.

Strong increases in employment of women aged 50 and over (in absolute numbers) from 2007 to 2011 are observed for education-related childcare in Germany, Poland and Italy, while milder increases are observed in Spain, France, Slovakia, Sweden and Hungary. In social inclusion services and non-educational day care, the increase of older female workers is marked in Germany, Spain, France and the Netherlands.

11.4 Increased service demand results in more jobs

Employment trends observed in the last few years (as well as demographic developments and the increasing participation of women in labour markets, with the resulting need for more formal care and social-support arrangements) seem to suggest that the above-described trends will grow stronger. The typical patterns of a work-oriented consumer society, where precious time is spent on a multitude of tasks and the outsourcing of services (from the family to the market) becomes a daily need, also contribute to the expansion of such service sectors.

In contrast to the fast employment growth and job creation in the health and social work sector in general,[29] there seems to be no overall growth trend (either as a share of total employment or in absolute numbers) in education-related childcare (see Figure 11.1). Employment growth in education-related childcare from 2001 to 2007 was modest: the number of people employed increased by only 100,000 for the whole of Europe. However, increases in employment were unevenly distributed across the continent.

Figure 11.1 Number of people employed in education-related childcare, 2001, 2004, 2007 and 2011 (thousands)

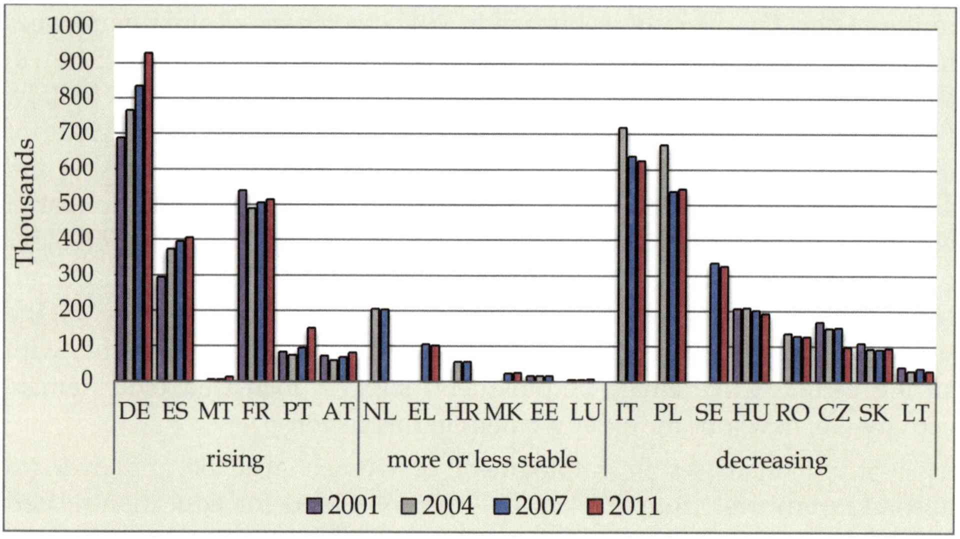

Source: IHS based on Eurostat (2012a).

The number of people employed in inclusion services and non-educational day care increased more strongly (see Figure 11.2). With growth of employment of approximately 600,000 from 2004 to 2007, the childcare and social inclusion services sector has become a substantial provider of jobs in many countries. Yet, the situation is less clear for 2007 to 2011, when approximately 200,000 jobs appear to have been lost again (in particular in France and Germany), probably due to the crisis. The net increase between 2004 and 2011 was thus around 400,000.

Figure 11.2 Number of people employed in social inclusion services and non-educational day-care, 2001, 2004, 2007 and 2011 (thousands)

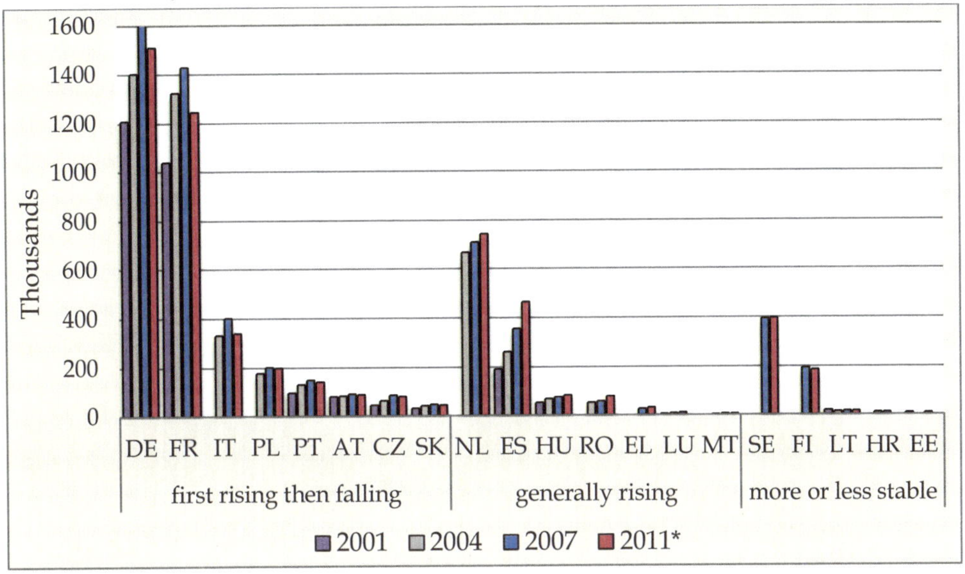

* Data break.

Note: Low reliability for LT (04/07), HR (04), EE (01).

Source: IHS based on Eurostat (2012a).

11.5 Mixed skills dominate social inclusion services

The data analysis shows that those employed in the field of education-related childcare are, as a rule, better educated than the average employee. This results from the fact that educational services tend to require higher educational attainment (such as a certain formal pedagogical or university education) of workers. Many of the jobs are thus for the higher or highly educated.[30]

> *Qualifications in education-related childcare (and schooling) are usually higher than country averages.*

Yet, qualification requirements differ between countries, as do job descriptions and the composition of services offered (and thus skills required). The picture is more diverse in social inclusion services and non-educational day care: there is a mix of qualifications, with different countries exhibiting different splits between higher, medium and lower levels of education (see Figure 11.3). The share of highly qualified workers in the sector is highest in Poland, the UK, Spain and Ireland, and is lowest in

Portugal, the Czech Republic, France and Romania. The largest share of low-skilled workers in social inclusion services and non-educational day care was found in Portugal (and Turkey), followed by Spain and Italy. The Czech Republic exhibited the largest share of medium-skilled workers in this sector. The share of highly skilled was clearly above the country average for social inclusion services and non-educational day care in Poland, Bulgaria and Italy. It was visibly lower in Ireland, Belgium, Finland, Sweden and France.

Figure 11.3 Qualifications of those employed in social inclusion services and non-educational daycare compared to total economy, 2011 (%)

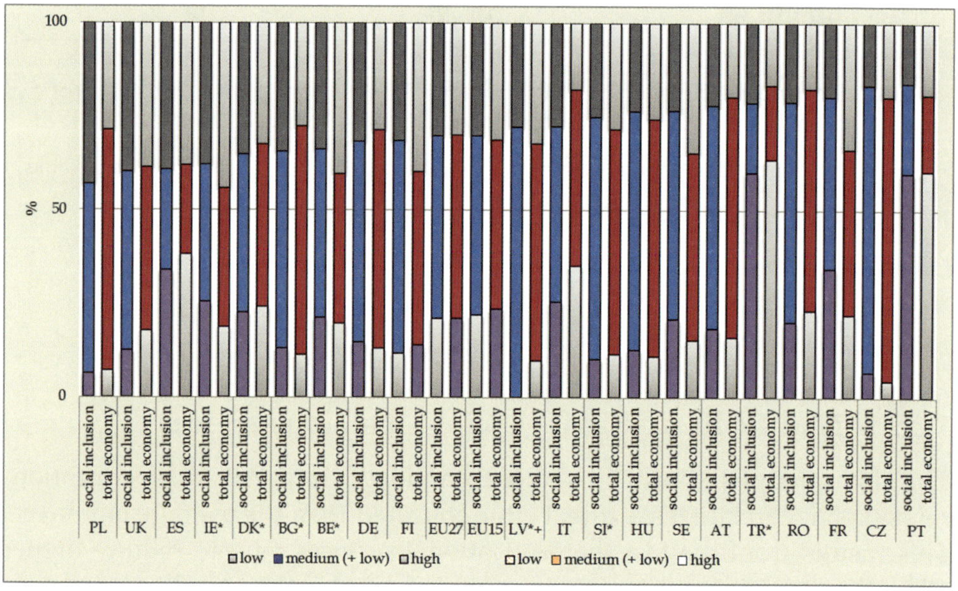

Note: Classification of qualifications: low (ISCED 1+2); medium (ISCED 3+4); high (ISCED 5+6).

Source: IHS based on EUROSTAT, special data order (2011) and online database (2012).

What developments can be detected over time? In line with the predictions of Boitier et al.,[31] we observe generally increasing skill levels in both sectors, resulting in favourable changes in the composition of skills from 2001 to 2011. While this is true for both sectors, in some countries (Germany and Portugal) the share of the highly educated (ISCED 5+6) in education-related childcare declined. In social inclusion services and non-educational day care, the wider variety in the range of skills persists over time, despite overall improvements. Again, only in a few countries (France, the Netherlands and Slovakia) did the share of the highly educated not grow. Accordingly, the initial assumption that new jobs in childcare and social inclusion services might only be of lower quality is not confirmed by the data: overall job growth involved medium and higher skills, but not lower.

11.6 Working conditions vary, but part-time work dominates

Many employees in childcare and social inclusion services work part-time. In general, part-time employment in the sector is above average (where labour market flexibility permits such arrangements). With a large share of those employed being female, the findings point to a strong macro-level correlation between the share of female employees and the share of part-time workers in this sector. This is true for employment in social inclusion services and non-educational day care (Figure 11.4) as well as for employment in education-related childcare.

Yet, the direction of the causality remains unclear. Does the sector require more part-time work - which women are more interested in providing - than other sectors, so that the sector becomes 'female'? Or does the sector attract more women, who often prefer part-time contracts, thereby increasing the share of part-time work in the sector?

Figure 11.4 offers a country comparison of sectoral (s) and national (n) levels of part-time employment in social inclusion services and non-educational day care, while at the same time indicating the share of female workers. While the share of female workers in the sector is similarly high in all countries, the extent of part-time employment varies. The red rings group countries with similar shares of part-time employment in social inclusion services and non-educational day care. The rings around the 10% and 20% lines indicate countries with low or limited labour market flexibility, where part-time work in the sector is (more or less) as low as, or only a little above, the national average across all sectors. The rings around the 40% and 50% lines indicate countries with generally higher labour market flexibility, where part-time work in the sector is more common than the average across all sectors, particularly in social inclusion services.

Figure 11.4 Female employment and part-time work in social inclusion services and non-educational day care, and in the total economy, 2011 (%)

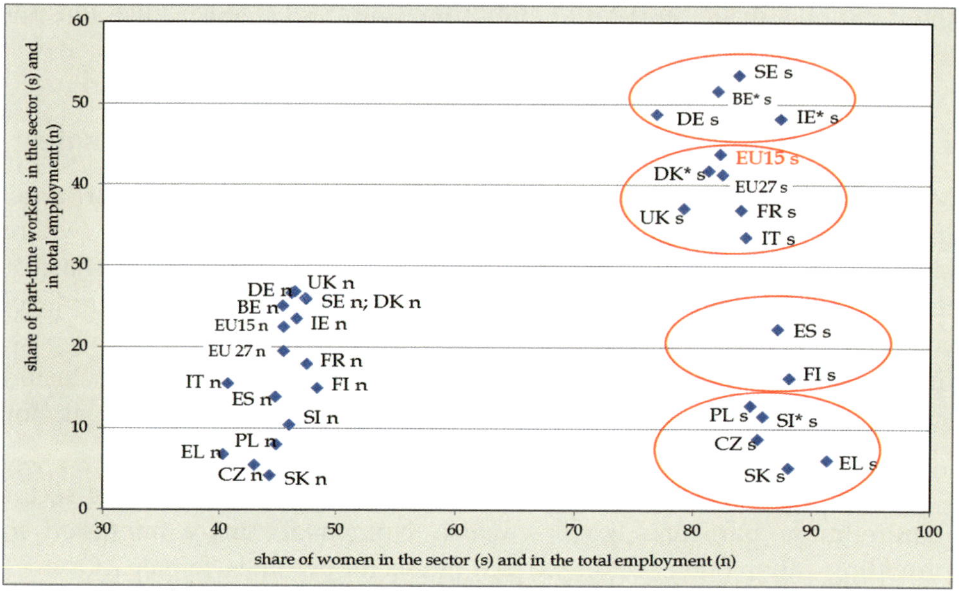

Notes: s = social inclusion services and non-educational day care, n = total economy.

Source: IHS based on EUROSTAT, special data request (2012) and online database (2012).

Despite the large share of part-time workers, fixed-term contracts in the field of education-related childcare are no more frequent than in other sectors of the economy. Interestingly, it is the share of permanent contracts that is generally higher - making it easy for those using education-related childcare services to maintain contact with the same person over longer periods of time. The exceptions are Germany, Italy and Portugal, where the shares of fixed-term employment in the sector are above the national averages.

In social inclusion services and non-educational day care, the incidence of fixed-term contracts is slightly above average (17% in the EU versus a 14% average across sectors), with Spain (33%) and also Finland, Slovenia, Sweden, Greece and Poland (each with approximately 25%) exhibiting much larger shares of fixed-term employees.

11.7 Tailoring policy to country-specific features of the sector

It is clear from the analysis undertaken in the previous sections that countries follow different development paths. Notwithstanding convergence in Europe across many fields, education-related childcare and social inclusion services remain very particular and country-specific. Despite the overall EU trends in employment growth, skill improvements and above-average part-time employment in this sector, we observe different structures in 2011 and different development patterns between 2001 and 2011 across countries in this strongly gendered field of work.

Whether these country-specific deviations are temporary outcomes of the recent economic crisis or are mid-term or even long-term trends will only become clear in the next few years, when welfare policies have adjusted to ageing requirements and (new) budgetary constraints.

Countries follow different development paths depending on their starting position in terms of sectoral size, age structure and welfare-regime orientation. Nevertheless, the overall trend points towards skill increases, an increase of part-time jobs and even greater feminisation of the sector. Therefore, families that use such services should expect a growing share of older but well-educated service providers who are mostly on permanent contracts (and are thus available for a longer period of time). The expansion of the education-related childcare and social services sector will hopefully match needs and allow for the more formal delivery of such services – freeing families up for other important issues of everyday life.

It is important for policy-makers to monitor working conditions, earnings and gender pay-gaps in this changing sector, as well as working on skills upgrading and related educational requirements. With EU discussions about quality of services and availability and access for all, this should also be a primary national target.

Welfare policies also need to be carefully and repeatedly adapted to new emerging needs resulting from both ageing and family outsourcing. Although the actual initiatives might need to consider GDP growth-related budgetary constraints, policy-makers should aim at inclusive social developments and set their policies in order to smooth past and upcoming societal changes related to socio-ecological transformations.

Bibliography

Abbott, P. and C. Wallace (2011), "Social quality: A way to measure the quality of society", *Social Indicators Research*, Vol. 108, No. 1, pp. 153–167.

_____ (2012), "Rising economic prosperity and social quality the case of New Member States of the European Union", *Social Indicators Research*, Vol. 155, No. 1, pp. 419-439.

EPC and Bertelsmann Stiftung (2012), "Creating Second Career Labour Markets. Towards more Employment Opportunities for Older Workers", Bertelsmann Stiftung, Brussels.

Boitier, B., N. Lancesseur and P. Zagamé (2013), "Global Scenarios for Socio-Ecological Transition", NEUJOBS Working Paper No. D.9.2., NEUJOBS Project (www.neujobs.eu).

CEEP (2010), "Public services: supporting the very fabric of European society", European Centre of Employers and Enterprises Providing Public Services (CEEP), Brussels.

Cipollone, A., E. Patacchini and G. Vallanti (2012), "Women Labour Market Performance in Europe: Trends and Shaping Factors", NEUJOBS Working Paper No. D.5.3, NEUJOBS Project (www.neujobs.eu).

Dolls, M., K. Doorley, H. Schneider and E. Sommer (2011), "Structural and behavioural dimensions of Labour Supply in Europe in 2030", NEUJOBS Working Paper No. D10.9, NEUJOBS Project (www.neujobs.eu).

Esping-Andersen, G., D. Gallie, A. Hemerijck and J. Myles (2002), *Why we need a new welfare state*, Oxford: Oxford University Press.

Eurofound (2012), *Third European Quality of Life Survey: Quality of life in Europe – Impacts of the crisis*, Luxembourg: Publications Office of the European Union.

European Commission (2013a), "Investing in health", Commission staff working document, Brussels.

_____ (2013b), "Towards social investment for growth and cohesion – including implementing the European Social Fund 2014–2020", Communication from the Commission to the European Parliament, the Council, the European economic and social committee and the Committee of the regions, COM(2013) 83 final, Brussels.

_____ (2013c), "Investing in children – breaking the cycle of disadvantage", Communication recommendation of 20 February, (2013) 778, Brussels.

_____ (2013d), "Long-term care in ageing societies – Challenges and policy options", Commission staff working document, Brussels.

_____ (2010), "Commission Staff Working Document. Second Biennial Report on social services of general interest", SEC(2010) 1284 final, Brussels.

_____ (2012), "EU employment and social situation, Quarterly overview", Special supplement on health and social services, Brussels, December.

Eurostat (2012a), Special order of Labour Force Survey (LFS), Eurostat, Luxembourg.

_____ (2012b), Online database, Total general government expenditure and employment.

Fischer-Kowalski, M., D. Wiedenhofer, U. Weisz, I. Pallua, N. Possaner, A. Behrens, G. Serio, M. Alessi, E. Weis and W. Haas (2012), "Socio-ecological transitions: definition, dynamics and related global scenarios", NEUJOBS report, NEUJOBS Project (www.neujobs.eu).

Gstrein, M. and L. Mateeva (2013), "Childcare and Social Inclusion Services in the EU – An Employment Analysis", NEUJOBS Working Paper 13/1, NEUJOBS Project (www.neujobs.eu).

Gstrein, M., L. Mateeva, P. Rodiga-Laßnig, P. Abbott and C. Wallace (2013), "Quality of Life in Europe: Quality of Society and Public Services", Eurofound.

Hagerty, M., R. Cummins, A.L. Ferriss, K. Land, A.C. Michalos, M. Peterson, A. Sharpe, J. Sirgy and J. Vogel (2001), "Quality of life indexes for national policy: review and agenda for research", *Social Indicators Research*, Vol. 55, pp. 1-96.

Hausmann, R., L.D. Tyson and S. Zahidi (2009), "The Global Gender Gap Report", Geneva: World Economic Forum.

Inglehart, R. and P. Norris (2003), *Rising Tide: Gender Equality and Cultural Change around the World*, Cambridge: Cambridge University Press.

Kinsella, K. (2000), "Demographic Dimensions of Global Aging", *Journal of Family Issues*, Vol. 21, No. 5, pp. 541-558.

_____ (2001), "Urban and Rural Dimensions of Global Population Aging: An Overview", *Journal of Rural Health*, Vol. 17, No. 4, pp. 314-322.

Layard, R. (2005), *Happiness: Lessons from a New Science*, Harmondsworth: Penguin.

Layte, R. (2011), "The association between income inequality and mental health: Testing status anxiety, social capital, and neo-materialist explanations", *European Sociological Review*, Vol. 28, No. 4, pp. 498-511.

Layte, R., B. Maitre and C.T. Whelan (2010), *Living conditions, social exclusion and mental well-being*, Luxembourg: Publications Office of the European Union.

Maesen, L.J.G. and A.C. Walker (eds) (2012), *Social Quality: From theory to indicators*, Basingstoke: Palgrave Macmillan.

Maselli, I. (2012), "The Evolving Supply and Demand of Skills in the Labour Market", *Intereconomics*, Vol. 47, No. 1, January/February.

Nelson, M. (2012), "State of the art: reconciling work and welfare in Europe", NEUJOBS State of the Art Report No.5/D5.1, NEUJOBS Project (www.neujobs.eu).

Riedel, M. and H. Hofer (2013), "Determinants of the transition from work into retirement", NEUJOBS Working Paper No. 17.1, NEUJOBS Project (www.neujobs.eu).

Wilkinson, R.G. and K.E. Pickett (2010), *The Spirit Level: Why More Equal Societies Almost Always Do Better*, London: Penguin.

[1] See, for example, CEEP (2010) and European Commission (2010a, b).

[2] European Commission (2012b, d); EPC and Bertelsmann Stiftung (2012).

[3] European Commission (2013b; 2013f).

[4] Cipollone et al. (2012).

[5] See, for example, Hagerty et al. (2001); Layard (2005); Eurofound (2012); Gstrein et al. (2013).

[6] cf. Abbott and Wallace (2011, 2012); Maesen and Walker (2012).

[7] cf. Layte et al. (2010); Wilkinson and Pickett (2010); Layte (2011).

[8] cf. Eurostat (2012b).

[9] European Commission (2013a; 2012c; 2009a; 2009b, 2009c); Hausmann et al. (2009)

[10] Daly (2000), cited in Esping-Andersen et al. (2002); Eurostat (2012b).

[11] European Commission (2010).

[12] European Commission (2013b).

[13] European Commission (2013c).

[14] European Commission (2013a).

[15] European Commission (2013d).

[16] Established by TEU, Art. 60, the Social Protection Committee (SPC) is an advisory policy body for Employment and Social Affairs Ministers in the Employment and Social Affairs Council (EPSCO).

[17] Kinsella (2000, 2001).

[18] Fischer-Kowalski et al. (2012); Maselli (2012).

[19] European Commission (2012, pp. 55, 57).

[20] European Commission (2010).

[21] Cipollone et al. (2012).

[22] Kroos and Gottschall (2011), cited by Nelson (2012).

[23] Inglehart and Norris (2003).

[24] Riedel and Hofer (2013).

[25] Employment in education-related childcare includes employment in kindergartens, pre-primary schools and primary schools. Employment in social inclusion services and non-educational day-care includes the relevant parts of social work, which consists of (a) residential care provided for people with mental health problems, the elderly and disabled people; and (b) care without accommodation (i.e. not stationary), comprising day-care for children (crèches, services of child-minders, babysitters and day nurseries for pupils, including disabled children) and social counselling, welfare, referral and similar services

(including day-care) for the elderly and disabled, as well as other social work including in relation to low-income people and the unemployed.

[26] For more details about the data and the methodology, see Gstrein and Mateeva (2013).

[27] Gstrein and Mateeva (2013).

[28] Dolls et al. (2011).

[29] European Commission (2012).

[30] Gstrein and Mateeva (2013)

[31] Boitier et al. (2013).

12. Low-skilled migration: Immigrant workers in European domestic care

Attila Bartha, Olena Fedyuk and Violetta Zentai[*]

Over the last 15 years, since the entry into force of the Amsterdam Treaty, migration policy in the European Union has principally focused on security-related issues of migration, such as border management, visa policy and readmission agreements. In the field of legal migration, the EU directives have, next to creating a right to family reunification and long-term resident status, concentrated on the entry and residence of specific groups, including students, researchers, seasonal workers and highly skilled.[1] EU labour immigration policy is thus characterised by a selective and sectoral approach in the admission of immigrants, and a growing number of countries have been adopting points-based systems. In several EU member countries, however, the unprecedented increase of immigrant labour has occurred in low-skilled occupations. The domestic care sector has attracted a particularly high share of migrants and, in some countries, massive immigration of low-skilled[2] female workers has continued since the onset of the global financial crisis.[3]

---

[*] Attila Bartha: Center for Policy Studies, Central European University and Center for Social Sciences, Hungarian Academy of Sciences, Budapest; Olena Fedyuk: Center for Policy Studies, Central European University and Center for Social Sciences, Hungarian Academy of Sciences, Budapest and University of Strathclyde, Glasgow; Violetta Zentai: Center for Policy Studies, Central European University, Budapest.

These trends[4] raise a number of policy-related questions in the areas of migration, care and employment. Why have certain countries proved to be particularly attractive to immigrant care workers? How are the different European welfare and care regimes, and state and market policy mixes, shaping the inflow of low-skilled migrants into the care sector? What are the impacts of this migration of predominantly low-skilled women on care systems, female employment opportunities and gender equality in the receiving and sending countries? How is the position of the new EU member states that have been among the main sending countries within the European transnational care chain changing? What are the working conditions in the domestic care sector and what kind of policies could ensure that the sector provides decent employment opportunities for both migrant and non-migrant workers along the lines of the socio-ecological transition (SET)?[5]

Welfare regimes, transnational care chains, national state/market care policy mixes and family policies are shaping low-skilled migration into the care sector.

12.1 Migrants are increasingly overrepresented in domestic care employment

Domestic care has been one of the most dynamic sectors for employment in Europe in recent times. Estimations on the basis of EU Labour Force Survey (LFS) data indicate that the number of domestic care workers increased by about 40% in the EU15 member states[6] between 2000 and 2010,[7] and the majority of domestic care workers in the EU are migrant women.[8] Moreover, of the three major sectors where migrants are strongly overrepresented, only 'private households with employed persons' have expanded in terms of employment since the onset of the recent crisis (the two other industries where migrants are significantly overrepresented - hotels and restaurants, and especially construction - suffered significant employment losses after 2007). Altogether, in European OECD member countries, 424,000 new jobs were taken by foreign-born workers in care work-related sectors between 2008 and 2012: employment of immigrants increased by 20.2% in 'activities of households as employers of domestic personnel' and by 44.5% in residential care activities (see Figure 12.1).[9]

Domestic care is a fast-expanding sector in employment terms and a key sector for migrant employment.

Figure 12.1 Three industries with the largest positive and negative changes in foreign-born employment in European OECD countries, 2008-12 (thousands)

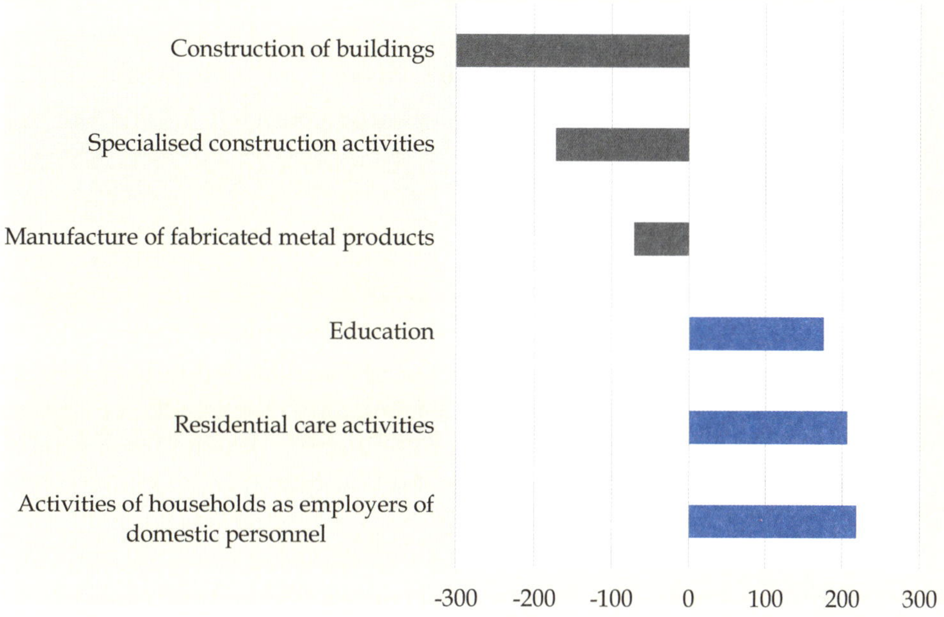

Source: OECD (2013).

Concerning future prospects, the NEMESIS model[10] forecasts a significant increase in care demand to 2025 in Europe: by 15-22% in the tough scenario and 28-39% in the friendly scenario. The care workforce supply will not be able to meet this growing care demand without significant migrant labour inflows, as the supply of domestic care labourers is expected to increase by less than 10% in the tough scenario and by 12-28% in the friendly scenario.[11] Unless major policy changes are made in the field, policy-makers will have to count on a further substantial increase of migrant care workers over the next decades.

12.2 Migrant domestic workers meet European care demand through transnational care chains

The important role of migrant domestic workers has long been recognised in meeting European needs for care.[12] Yet, due to a lack of reliable comparative data and a large component of informal employment of migrant care workers, analysts have been cautious about including the assessment of migrant flows when discussing care policies. From a policy perspective, the key mechanisms can be interpreted as the intersections of migration, employment and national welfare and care regimes.[13] The approach of transnational care chains explores the connection between care work, migration and social and gender inequalities in a global perspective.[14] Care is commodified and mainly female care workers are imported from less developed to more developed parts of the world.

Care chains imply that paid forms of care (whether domestic work or care for children, the elderly or the sick) have become an important source of employment for women in many developing and eastern European countries. Joining the labour force, however, requires a substitute for migrating women's role in their own families. Accordingly, intra-EU migration within European care chains encompasses the exodus of eastern European women from their homes to provide care in the homes of others, and also the impacts of this female migration outflow on care systems and families in central and eastern Europe.

Transnational care chains in Europe involve the migration of eastern European women to provide care in western European homes.

The role of migrants in care provision is fairly uneven across Europe. Why are some countries particularly attractive for immigrant domestic care workers? Several factors matter in this respect, foremost of which are the specific features of national welfare and care regimes: institutional provision of care (e.g. kindergartens, social workers and retirement homes), policies on work-life balance and monetary subsidies for care provision (e.g. welfare payments or tax relief). Moreover, by imposing certain migration regimes or occupational quotas for domestic workers, states can create indirect incentives for a rising market of private care workers of immigrant origin. Concerning the inclusion of immigrant populations, at least two dimensions matter: legal, formal access to citizenship; and the multicultural policy framework shaping the socio-political inclusion of immigrant populations.[15]

It should be noted that migration policy regime typologies and assessments usually have a western receiving-country bias. The attention to new currents of labour migration from central and eastern Europe (CEE) to Nordic, western and southern European countries overshadows migration chains in which CEE countries function both as sending and receiving entities of low-skilled care workers and are thus themselves in the process of building migration policy regimes. In addition, in the predominantly sending eastern European countries, the massive outflow of female care workers aggravates welfare, care and family policy tensions, particularly because of the low level of fertility and the general withdrawal of publicly provided welfare and care services over the last two decades.

12.3 The demand for migrant care workers is typically a demand for jobs with substandard conditions

Two major factors feed the expansion of the care sector in EU countries, and both are related to population ageing in European societies. Low fertility rates have implied an increasing policy focus on childcare services, while the trend of population ageing itself has generated growing demand for elderly care provisions. Moreover, there is an additional factor of a fiscal nature supporting the demand for domestic care workers: the spread of cash-for-care schemes as part of the welfare reform agenda enhances the commodification of care through the direct provision of financial resources to users, and opens up opportunities for the incorporation of paid domestic and care work.[16]

> *Population ageing and the spread of cash-for-care schemes feed the demand for domestic care workers...*

But why are native populations strongly underrepresented among domestic care workers? Indeed, the demand for migrant care workers is a specific form of demand: typically, a need for migrant women who are willing to take jobs with substandard wages and employment conditions that are unacceptable to the native workers.[17] The wage levels of immigrant care workers indicate that they are overrepresented at the lower end of the pay scale of this sector. Paradoxically, stronger immigration controls indirectly support the ability of employers to 'underpay' migrant care workers. Because pull factors of migration dominate in western European care labour markets, stricter border control cannot effectively discourage the arrival of immigrants.[18] And without permission to work, immigrants with irregular status become particularly vulnerable to abuse of working conditions.[19] Employers thus often rely on immigrants who are ready to provide care services in a more flexible, informal and insecure working environment.[20] These substandard working conditions, while attracting a particularly vulnerable segment of immigrants, indirectly close the domestic care sector employment opportunities for native low-skilled workers.

> *... but with sub-standard wages and employment conditions.*

12.4 The liberal and southern welfare regimes are particularly attractive for immigrant care workers

The presence of migrant domestic care workers is fairly uneven across European countries, and Italy and Spain are the two major target countries for CEE migrants in this field. But why are the Mediterranean countries more attractive for low-skilled immigrant care workers than their more developed north-western European counterparts? Most explanations of the care-migration nexus depart from Esping-Andersen's typology of welfare regimes,[21] which distinguished three major types of welfare in Western Europe: the liberal, the conservative and the social-democratic welfare regimes. Following later empirical research, two additions to the original typology of Esping-Andersen seem relevant in order to embrace a larger European perspective: the Mediterranean or southern European regime type,[22] and the post-socialist or central and eastern European[23] regime type. Table 12.1 summarises the care-specific characteristics of European welfare regimes[24] using the main features of care systems: the level of financial generosity, the dominant institution of care and the role of formal versus informal types of care provision. It also presents the migration patterns of care workers in the particular welfare regimes.

The lower the level of generosity in public financing of care, the higher the importance of non-state care-providing institutions (i.e. the market and family), and the stronger role of informality in care provisions in particular may well predict the immigration potential in different welfare regimes. Thus in the Nordic countries, where good quality care is publicly provided, the demand for immigrant care workers is rather limited. The western European Bismarckian countries follow a similar pattern, although the importance of informal relations and the stronger role of family in care results in a less straightforward picture.[25] In the liberal regime, however, less generous financing of care and a stronger role of the market logically implies a higher level of demand for less expensive migrant care services. And in the Mediterranean countries - where public provision of welfare services is more limited, care is traditionally provided by family members and informality plays a dominant role in socio-economic transactions - the specific demand for immigrant care is striking.[26]

Limited public provision of care and a stronger role of informality attracts many immigrants to liberal and especially Southern welfare regimes

Table 12.1 Main features of care in European welfare regimes and migration impacts

Welfare regimes*	Financial generosity of care	Dominant institution of care	Formal vs. informal dimension of care	Migration position in care chains
Social-democratic (Nordic)	High	State	Formal	Receiving, moderately intensive
Conservative (Bismarckian, Christian-democratic)	High	State/mixed	Partly informal	Receiving, moderately intensive
Liberal (Anglo-Saxon)	Medium/low	Market	Partly informal	Receiving
Southern (Mediterranean)	Low/medium	Family	Mainly informal	Receiving, intensive
Post-socialist (central and eastern European new member states)	Low/medium	Family/ state	Mainly informal	Sending within the EU, but receiving in global care chains

* In the EU28, the social-democratic regime is represented by Denmark, Finland and Sweden; the conservative Bismarckian regime by Austria, Belgium, France, Germany, Luxembourg and the Netherlands; the liberal regime by Ireland and the UK; the southern regime by Cyprus, Greece, Italy, Malta, Portugal and Spain; and the post-socialist countries by Bulgaria, Croatia, Czech Republic, Estonia, Hungary, Latvia, Lithuania, Poland, Romania, Slovakia and Slovenia.

Source: Own elaboration based on typologies of Esping-Andersen (1990), Sapir (2006), Williams and Gavanas (2008), Kraus et al. (2010), Hemerijck (2013) and Korpi et al. (2013).

The group of post-socialist countries is more heterogeneous than the other four welfare regime types. Although some of the CEE EU member states follow rather Bismarckian conservative patterns concerning the main features of care, most show a marked similarity with the Mediterranean countries of the EU. This implies that in the future, assuming that wage differentials between western and eastern European countries gradually fall, we can expect that typical CEE countries will provide less migrant care workers to western Europe, and at the same time will also attract an

Familialist care policy patterns support informal care use in several Mediterranean and post-socialist countries.

increasing number of immigrants for domestic care tasks. Thus, post-socialist states will likely become important destinations within the global care chain, importing care workers from the global south and especially from the Eastern Partnership (EaP) countries.[27] This process is indeed ongoing: a share of the migration of Ukrainian domestic care workers has recently been redirected to Poland.[28]

This surprising similarity in care policy features between Mediterranean and central and eastern European countries mainly derives from the re-familialisation policy tendencies in the latter group of countries: over the last 25 years, the post-socialist countries have followed - either explicitly or implicitly - a familialist care policy pattern.[29] As a result, while formal early childcare use (below the age of three) was high in CEE countries compared to western Europe during the state socialist period, today formal care use in early childhood is lowest in the post-socialist countries (see Figure 12.2).

Figure 12.2 Full-time equivalent (FTE) formal and informal care for all children below the age of three, EU27

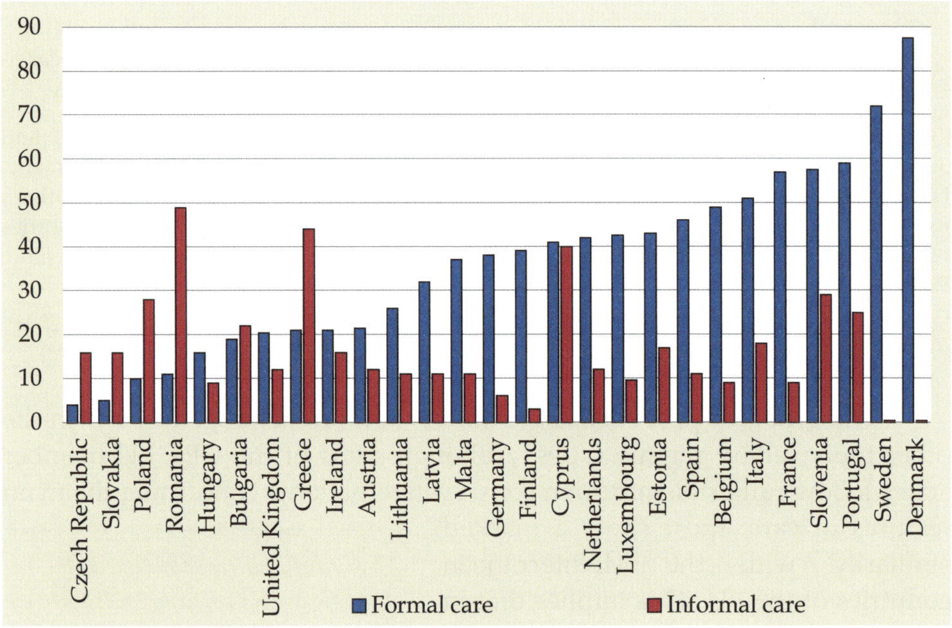

Data source: EU-SILC 2009, calculated by Van Lancker (2013).

The underdevelopment of formal institutional care implies that if parental care is not available (or not desirable) to households, then informal care becomes the dominant option. This provides an indirect incentive for recruitment of migrant domestic care workers in post-socialist member states. At the same time, the traditionally familialist Mediterranean childcare policy shifted in the opposite direction, and public care provision in the early childhood period significantly improved in southern Europe.

Although we know of some cases of childcare and elderly care policy development following different paths,[30] at the country level the two care policy fields typically show similar patterns concerning generosity of public financing and the role of formal versus informal care provisions. Concerning preferences for informal provision of elderly care, at the welfare regime level, Figure 12.3 indicates that informal care is unambiguously the preferred option in post-socialist countries, while formal care is preferred in north-western Europe.

Figure 12.3 Preference for informal provision of elderly care in EU member states, 2007 (%)

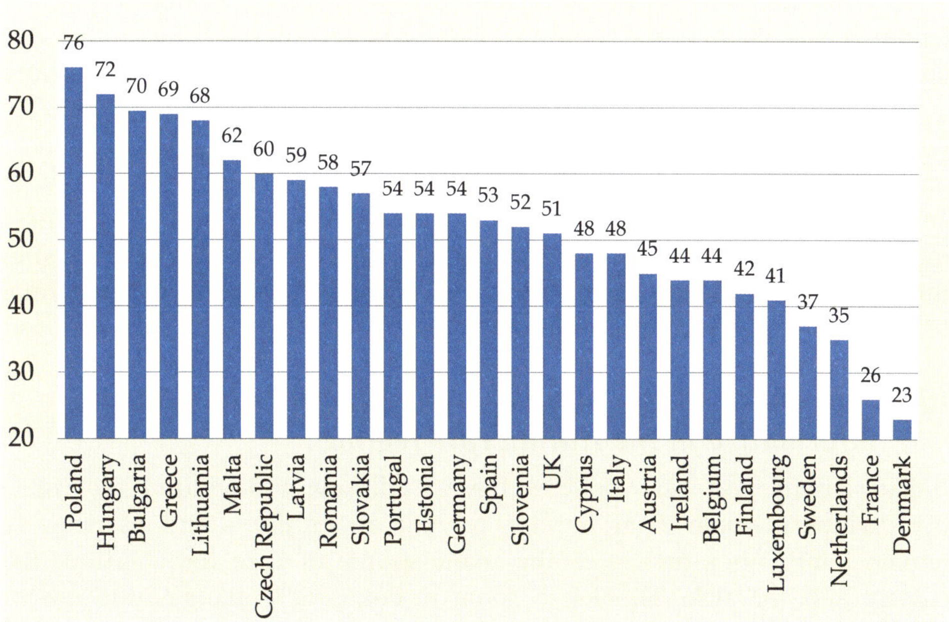

Source: Eurobarometer survey on health and long-term care (European Commission, 2007).

The following three country cases illustrate the care-migration policy nexus: the liberal regime is represented by the UK, the southern regime by Italy and the post-socialist countries by Poland.[31]

i) Migrants on the market: Publicly funded and privately provided care in the UK

Affordability of care provision in the UK is means-tested and sustained through a wide range of monetary allowances, cash provisions, direct payments, tax reductions and insurance schemes. This allows the purchase of informal home care for children, the elderly and those in need of other forms of long-term care. The financing is decentralised through a mix of government grants to local councils, local taxation in the form of the council tax and individuals' own resources. Care services in this system are publicly funded but privately provided; the care-providers' sector features both national and multinational chains as well as smaller agencies and businesses. An emphasis on monetary payments instead of institutional care makes non-parental informal care as important as formal care and significantly reduces state expenditure on care.

This care model gave rise to a particular form of opening for migrant labour in the sector - the 'migrant in the market' model.[32] Most migrants are employed by private care providers, elderly care and childcare agencies, or through au pair programmes, and their share has been steadily increasing in the UK care sector. Migrants are more likely to find agency-based employment in elderly care, while in childcare they are less likely to enter jobs in nurseries and day care centres, tending to find employment instead as private childminders or nannies. This care market often pushes migrants who are ready to provide care services into very flexible, informal or even abusive working conditions.[33]

ii) Migrant in the family: The legacies of familialism and informality in the Italian care regime

Italian labour and care policies have traditionally favoured the 'male breadwinner/female carer' model, relying on family - and particularly female family members - as the main source of care for children, the elderly and the sick. Thanks to some recent policy changes, the use of formal childcare is now high for children above the age of three, and in comparison with Europe as a whole, it is not low for children under three either. The expansion of institutional childcare is linked to increasing labour participation of Italian women and the absence of men from caring responsibilities.

Due to the rapidly ageing population and low fertility rates, a particular place in Italian care demand is occupied by geriatric care. The availability of an inexpensive migrant labour force and state cash support has made it possible for families, even those from lower social strata, to employ home carers. For the last 15 years, care for the elderly living at home has been increasingly provided by immigrants, generating a new carer profile of the *badante*: a migrant woman typically working irregularly in the grey care market.[34] It is estimated that by the end of the 2000s, foreign workers constituted 70-90% of all workers in the Italian domestic care sector.[35]

On the part of the migrants, providing illegal work in the privacy of Italian homes makes them more competitive with other migrants and reduces their own efforts and expenditure on the lengthy and complicated process of regularisation. On the part of Italian households as employers, recruiting an illegal immigrant can cost as little as half the cost of a native domestic care worker, while the negotiation of work conditions and tasks is much easier with a migrant who fears being caught. Considering the high demand in Italian domestic care, migrant workers often become 'invisible' through engaging in live-in informal contracts; they live in their employer's house, have only one free day per week, and sometimes do not leave the house for weeks at a time. This form of work is preferred by first-time and irregular migrants, as it minimises their risk of running into the police and the need to arrange other aspects of their lives, such as accommodation or food. However, it leads to severe cases of exploitation, when their work spills into any hour of the day and night, and their food, freedom of movement, sleeping patterns and daily routines are closely controlled by their employers.

iii) Poland: Repositioning in the global care chain – the return of familialism and employment of a migrant domestic worker as a status symbol

The transformation of the Polish labour market in the last two decades has favoured sectors in which women were overrepresented, which has boosted female participation in the labour market. The country has experienced, however, a return of familialism - supported by the Polish state and the Catholic Church - which has reinstated women's main roles as mother and carer.[36] There are no guarantees for formal care for children under the age of three, making Polish parents and other relatives responsible for some 90% of care for this age cohort. The lack of institutional childcare prompts women to join the lines of the unemployed more often than their male colleagues, and makes their return to the labour market after parental leave more difficult.

Alongside population ageing and the re-emergence of familialism as an ideological guideline for family and care policy, privatisation and the collapse of state-provided institutions of care (particularly homes for the elderly) have also shaped the development of the Polish care system. In addition, the employment of a domestic worker has become a status symbol that also plays an important role in boosting care demand,[37] allowing middle- and upper-middle-class women not only to engage in more lucrative occupations, but also to maintain a certain lifestyle and spend time away from work in more pleasant and personally rewarding endeavours. Thus, structural features of Polish care have become similar to the familialist Italian care regime of the past.

The migration aspects of the Polish care sector should be considered in relation to Poland's repositioning in the global care chain: the country has recently become both an emigration and an immigration country. While migrating Polish women still often use opportunities for informal employment in the domestic sectors of Germany, Belgium, Italy, Spain and Portugal,[38] the improving prospects of material wellbeing (partly from migration-generated income) have significantly increased demand for care and domestic services in Poland itself. Household services comprised 11% of all valid work permits to Poland in 2011, thus constituting the third-largest occupational sector for migrants. The dual migratory status of Poland in the global care chain is clearly demonstrated by the increasing presence of Ukrainian domestic care workers: Ukrainians constitute by far the largest group among all immigrants in Poland, and 21% of them are engaged in domestic work.[39] Indeed, while Poland is at the centre of global care chains, Ukraine is experiencing increasing pressure on its care resources. The massive outflow of Ukrainian women to meet the needs of European care demand leads to their separation from their own families, including children and elderly people who will, in turn, depend on female domestic care within Ukrainian families.[40]

12.5 Decent employment of migrant and native domestic care workers requires strong state regulatory and monitoring capacities and developed gender equality policy

As cash-for-care schemes seem to provide a cheaper and more flexible alternative to formal and institutional care, we can count on the future expansion of these schemes, not only in liberal but also in other welfare regimes. This market-oriented policy, however, can only provide the desired positive aspects (freedom of choice, good quality of care-service provisions and decent employment for care workers) together with decreasing gender inequalities if it ensures quality control, standard basic employment guarantees and a well-established legal institutional context to prevent either ethnic or gender discrimination. Thus, a particular focus on strong human resource policies and good quality employment relationships is crucial to provide decent jobs for (mainly female) care workers, including the large numbers of migrants but also for potential native employees.

The country cases presented above allow us to conclude that migration has been incorporated into national care regimes, giving rise to new care models such as 'migrant in the family' and 'migrant in the market'. The massive inflow of migrant female care workers (typically employed under sub-standard employment conditions and often employed informally) may apparently 'solve' the fiscally sustainable care regime puzzle in the short run. However, the smooth functioning of these market-oriented and migration-induced 'least resistance' policies implicitly assumes strong regulatory and monitoring capacities of states and developed gender-equality policies.[41] Otherwise, they generate new forms of inequalities undermining the success of the socio-ecological transition.[42] Thus, specific policies have to be developed to guarantee not only the quality of privately provided services, but also the employment standards for the care providers themselves. A legal institutional context to prevent discrimination against and unfair treatment of care workers forms part of the fundamental condition of a fair market environment in the field of care.

As pull factors of migration dominate, restrictive immigration policies in themselves will not block irregular migration into the domestic care sector.

Restrictive immigration policies in response to market-driven care demand are unlikely to support sustainable care regimes in receiving countries of care chains. If informality dominates labour transactions in the care sector and the state regulatory and monitoring capacities are weak, while structural pull factors of immigration remain, strict migration regimes in themselves will not block irregular migration into the domestic care sector, but will rather reinforce the vulnerability of migrant care workers.

Market-oriented care policy reforms can be risky in countries with moderate regulatory and monitoring capacities and less-developed gender equality policies.

The issue of immigrant care labour should be addressed in a complex and multi-layered way. The costs and benefits for the sending countries in transnational care chains should also be taken into consideration when the withdrawal of care increases the care burden on households without mothers. Therefore, cross-national welfare and social security provisions should be a priority in establishing legal and fair working conditions for both native and immigrant care workers. The issue clearly calls for the consideration of supranational management of the problem, and in this context the migration policy focus should be complemented by a broader approach of working rights for all (both native and immigrant) workers. Finally, decision-makers should be aware that transformative gender equality policy could modify (i.e. either enhance or countervail) the gender-specific impacts of care policies. Gender equality measures, such as political empowerment of women and enhanced work-life balance, can only drive sustainable care-regime development and general gender equality if they address migrant women in the sector.

Bibliography

Abrantes, M. (2014), "What about the numbers? A quantitative contribution to the study of domestic services in Europe", *International Labour Review*, Vol. 153, No. 2, pp. 223-243.

Bartha, A., O. Fedyuk and V. Zentai (2014), "Gender Equality and Care Choices in the Light of Population Ageing", NEUJOBS Working Paper No. 16.4, January.

Beblavý, M. and M. Veselková (2014), "Future of skills in Europe: Convergence or polarisation?", in M. Beblavý, I. Maselli and M. Veselková (eds), *Let's get to Work! The Future of Labour in Europe Vol. 1*, Centre for European Policy Studies, Brussels, pp. 131-158.

Cangiano, A. and I. Shutes (2010). "Ageing, demand for care and the role of migrant care workers in the UK", *Journal of Population Ageing*, Vol. 3, Nos. 1-2, pp. 39-57.

Carrera, S. and K. Eisele (2015), "Attracting Highly Qualified Immigrants", chapter 8, elsewhere in this volume.

Da Roit, B., B. Le Bihan and A. Österle (2007), "Long-term Care Policies in Italy, Austria and France: Variations in Cash-for-Care Schemes", *Social Policy and Administration*, Vol. 41, No. 6, pp. 653-671.

Duszczyk, M., M. Góra and P. Kaczmarczyk (2013), "Costs and Benefits of Labour Mobility between the EU and the Eastern Partnership Partner Countries: The Case of Poland", IZA Discussion Paper No. 7664, Institute for the Study of Labor, Bonn.

Esping-Andersen, G. (1990), *The Three Worlds of Welfare Capitalism*, Cambridge: Polity.

European Commission (2007), "Health and long-term care in the European Union", Special Eurobarometer 283 (http://ec.europa.eu/public_opinion/archives/ebs/ebs_283_en.pdf)

Fedyuk, O., A. Bartha and V. Zentai (2014), "Migrant Domestic Care Workers: State and Market-based Policy Mix", NEUJOBS Working Paper No. 13.2, February, NEUJOBS Project (www.neujobs.eu).

Ferrera, M. (1996), "The 'Southern' Model of Welfare in Social Europe", *Journal of European Social Policy*, Vol. 6, No. 1, pp. 17–37.

Genet, N., W. Boerma, M. Kroneman, A. Hutchinson and R.B. Saltman (eds) (2013), *Home Care across Europe: Case studies*, European Observatory on Health Systems and Policies, London.

Gstrein M. (2015), "Employment in care services", chapter 11, elsewhere in this volume.

Heinen, J. and M. Wator (2006), "Child Care in Poland before, during, and after the Transition: Still a Women's Business", *Social Politics: International Studies in Gender, State and Society*, Vol. 13, No. 2, pp. 189-216.

Hemerijck, A. (2013), *Changing Welfare States*, Oxford: Oxford University Press.

ILO (1999), "Decent Work", Report of the Director-General, 87th Session of the International Labour Conference, Geneva.

_____ (2010), "Decent work for domestic workers", Report IV(1), International Labour Office, Geneva.

Jegermalm, M., and G. Sundström (2014), "Stereotypes about caregiving and lessons from the Swedish panorama of care", *European Journal of Social Work* (published online).

Kahanec, M., K.F. Zimmermann, L. Kureková and C. Biavaschi (2013), "Labour Migration from EaP Countries to the EU. Assessment of Costs and Benefits and Proposals for Better Labour Market Matching", IZA Research Report No. 56, Institute for the Study of Labor, Bonn and CEU, Budapest.

Kindler, M. (2012), *A Risky Business? Ukrainian Migrant Women in Warsaw's Domestic Work Sector*, Amsterdam: Amsterdam University Press.

Korpi, W., T. Ferrarini and S. Englund (2013), "Women's Opportunities under Different Family Policy Constellations: Gender, Class, and Inequality Tradeoffs in Western Countries Re-examined", *Social Politics: International Studies in Gender, State and Society*, Vol. 20, No. 1, pp. 1-40.

Kraus, M., M. Riedel, E. Mot, P. Willeme, G. Rohrling and T. Czypionka (2010), "A typology of Long-Term Care Systems in Europe", ENEPRI Research Report No. 91.

Kureková, L., M. Beblavý and C. Haita (2012), "Qualifications or soft skills? Studying job advertisements for low-skilled staff in Slovakia", NEUJOBS Working Paper D.4.3, NEUJOBS Project (www.neujobs.eu).

Lutz, H. and E. Palenga-Möllenbeck (2010), "Care work migration in Germany: Semi-compliance and complicity", *Social Policy and Society*, Vol. 9, No. 3, pp. 419-430.

_____ (2012), "Care Workers, Care Drain, and Care Chains: Reflections on Care, Migration, and Citizenship", *Social Politics*, Vol. 19, No. 1, pp. 15-37.

OECD (2013), *International Migration Outlook*, Paris: OECD Publishing.

Orozco, A.P. (2009), "Global perspectives on the social organization of care in times of crisis: Assessing the situation", UN-INSTRAW Working Paper No. 5, Gender, Migration and Development Series.

Pascouau, Y. (2013), "Intra-EU mobility: The 'second building block' of EU labour migration policy", LAB-MIG-GOV Issue Paper No. 74, FIERI Research Institute, Turin.

Ruhs, M. and B. Anderson (eds) (2010), *Who Needs Migrant Workers? Labour Shortages, Immigration and Public Policy*, Oxford: Oxford University Press.

Sapir, A. (2006), "Globalization and the Reform of European Social Models", *Journal of Common Market Studies*, Vol. 44, No. 2, pp. 369-390.

Schulz, E. and J. Geyer (2013), "Societal Change, Care Need and Long-term Care Workforce in Selected European Countries", NEUJOBS Working Paper D12.2, NEUJOBS Project (www.neujobs.eu).

Sen, A. (2013), "Work and rights", *International Labour Review*, Vol. 152, No. S1, pp. 81-92.

Szelewa, D. and M.P. Polakowski (2008), "Who cares? Changing Patterns of Childcare in Central and Eastern Europe", *Journal of European Social Policy*, Vol. 18, No. 2, pp. 115-131.

Tolstokorova, A. (2009), "Who Cares for Carers? Feminization of Labor Migration from Ukraine and its Impact on Social Welfare", *International Issues and Slovak Foreign Policy Affairs*, Vol. 18, No. 1, pp. 62-84.

Tomka, B. (2006), "East Central Europe and the European social policy model: A long-term view", *East European Quarterly*, Vol. 40, No. 2, pp. 135-159.

Triandafyllidou, A. and S. Marchetti (2014), "Europe 2020: Addressing Low Skill Labour Migration at times of Fragile Recovery", RSCAS Policy Papers, 2014/05, European University Institute, San Domenico di Fiesole.

Van Hooren, F.J. (2010), "When Families Need Immigrants: The Exceptional Position of Migrant Domestic Workers and Care

Assistants in Italian Immigration Policy", *Bulletin of Italian Politics*, Vol. 2, No. 2, pp. 21-38.

_____ (2012), "Varieties of migrant care work: Comparing patterns of migrant labour in social care", *Journal of European Social Policy*, Vol. 22, No. 2, pp. 133-147.

Van Hooren, F.J. and U. Becker (2012), "One welfare state, two care regimes: Understanding developments in child and elderly care policies in The Netherlands", *Social Policy and Administration*, Vol. 46, No. 1, pp. 83-107.

Van Lancker, W. (2013), "Putting the child-centred investment strategy to the test: Evidence for the EU27", *European Journal of Social Security*, Vol. 15, No. 1, pp. 4-27.

Veselková, M. and M. Beblavý (2014), "Emerging megatrends and scenarios in the socio-ecological transitions", in M. Beblavý, I. Maselli and M. Veselková (eds), *Let's get to Work! The Future of Labour in Europe, Vol. 1*, Centre for European Policy Studies, Brussels, pp. 14-28.

Veselková, M., N. van der Gaag, B. Boitier, N. Lancesseur and P. Zagamé (2014), "How much work will there be? Where is it going to come from?", in M. Beblavý, I. Maselli and M. Veselková (eds), *Let's get to Work! The Future of Labour in Europe, Vol. 1*, Centre for European Policy Studies, Brussels, pp. 29-55.

Williams, F. (2012), "Converging variations in migrant care work in Europe", *Journal of European Social Policy*, Vol. 22, No. 4, pp. 363–376.

Williams, F. and A. Gavanas (2008), "The Intersection of Childcare Regimes and Migration Regimes: A Three-Country Study", in H. Lutz (ed.), *Migration and Domestic Work: A European Perspective on a Global Theme*, Aldershot: Ashgate, pp. 13-28.

Wright, M. and I. Bloemraad (2012), "Is there a trade-off between multiculturalism and socio-political integration? Policy regimes and immigrant incorporation in comparative perspective", *Perspectives on Politics*, Vol. 10, No. 1, pp. 77-95.

Notes

1 See Pascouau (2013) and Carrera and Eisele (2015).

2 Most studies of the care sector assume that care work consists of low-skilled jobs. Although we do not break with this tradition of wording here, we are aware that the distinctive feature of care jobs are sometimes less related to the skill level than to the low prestige and unpleasant working conditions of these jobs; see Ruhs and Anderson (2010) and Van Hooren (2012). Lutz and Palenga-Möllenbeck (2010, p. 425) underline the high ratio of educated women among migrant care workers in Germany; in addition, they mention various specific skills required of care workers such as empathy, emotional intelligence, patience and high tolerance of frustration. This issue is implicitly explored by Kureková et al. (2012) as well as Beblavý and Veselková (2014, p. 144), who describe "the surprisingly demanding nature of 'low-skilled' jobs".

3 See OECD (2013).

4 On the dynamics of changes in the EU population and labour force, see Veselková et al. (2014).

5 'Decent work' is certainly a normative concept (such as 'decent job' and 'decent employment' as well). However, we believe that it fits into the approach of the socio-ecological transition (SET) well. The concept was elaborated on by Amartya Sen, among others, and an important motive behind it was the refusal to dissociate economics from ethics (Sen, 2013). The issue of decent work has been on the global policy agenda since the ILO initiative of 1999 (see ILO, 1999).

6 EU15 refers to those EU member states that joined the EU before 2004 - namely Austria, Belgium, Denmark, Finland, France, Germany, Greece, Ireland, Italy, Luxembourg, the Netherlands, Portugal, Spain, Sweden and the UK.

7 Abrantes (2014).

8 ILO (2010).

9 OECD (2013, p. 82).

10 In the NEUJOBS project, the NEMESIS model (New Econometric Model of Evaluation by Sectoral Interdependency and Supply), constructed by the ERASME team, is used to quantitatively explore the main socio-economic and environmental challenges for the EU in the framework of the socio-ecological transition (SET) without policy intervention and according to the global context.

11 Schulz and Geyer (2013, p. 40); see also and Gstrein (2015).

12 Particular childcare and elderly care policy measures in individual countries may have different impacts on migrant populations being attracted to these two segments of domestic care. Our study, however, concentrates on the structural and

institutional features of welfare and care regimes, assuming that they are shaping childcare and elderly care policy choices similarly over the long run.

[13] Williams (2012).

[14] Orozco (2009).

[15] Wright and Bloemraad (2012).

[16] Da Roit et al. (2007).

[17] Ruhs and Anderson (2010).

[18] Triandafyllidou and Marchetti (2014).

[19] Cangiano and Shutes (2010).

[20] Van Hooren (2012).

[21] Esping-Andersen (1990).

[22] Ferrera (1996); see also Sapir (2006) and Hemerijck (2013).

[23] Tomka (2006).

[24] In order to avoid confusion, we have included variants of the welfare regime type names in the table.

[25] Recent empirical studies (e.g. Jegermalm and Sundström, 2014) suggest that voluntary informal care can play a significant role even in the Nordic countries, but there it occurs in a way that is complementary to public care provision (and not as a substitution of formal care).

[26] See Williams and Gavanas (2008) and Van Hooren (2010).

[27] Eastern Partnership (EaP) countries are: Armenia, Azerbaijan, Belarus, Georgia, Moldova and Ukraine. The Eastern Partnership initiative was launched by the EU in May 2009, as an enhanced regional cooperation policy developed for eastern European and southern Caucasus states.

[28] Kahanec et al. (2013).

[29] Szelewa and Polakowski (2008).

[30] For instance, for the Netherlands, see Van Hooren and Becker (2012).

[31] For a more detailed discussion of the country cases, see Fedyuk et al. (2014).

[32] Van Hooren (2012).

[33] Williams (2012).

[34] Da Roit et al. (2007, p. 658).

[35] See Van Hooren (2010) and Genet et al. (2013).

[36] Heinen and Wator (2006).

[37] Kindler (2012).

[38] Lutz and Palenga-Möllenbeck (2012).

---

[39] Duszczyk et al. (2013).

[40] Tolstokorova (2009); Lutz and Palenga-Möllenbeck (2012).

[41] Bartha et al. (2014).

[42] Weak monitoring capacities of the state imply that market-based policies in the care sector encourage the discussed specific demand features, thus boosting a secondary, informal and underpaid labour market segment with long working hours and substandard employment conditions. This type of development obviously contradicts the desired sustainability transformation strategy of the SET, where productivity gains are translated into a reduction of working hours; see Veselková and Beblavý (2014).

13. The future of labour in Europe: Key messages for policy-makers

Iain Begg[*]

Many recent analyses have shown that the EU is struggling to escape the grip of the most severe economic crisis in its history. Forecasts for 2015 and 2016 from bodies such as the European Commission and the IMF suggest, at best, anaemic growth with little prospect of making inroads into the high level of unemployment that has become the norm since 2008 in a majority of (although, tellingly, not all) EU member states. New political parties with agendas that are highly critical of their established peers have proliferated, yet comprehensive and credible solutions seem to elude decision-makers, notwithstanding a parallel proliferation of pacts and policy packages. As the renowned Italian thinker Antonio Gramsci put it, "the old is dying and the new cannot be born… in this interregnum a great variety of morbid symptoms appear".

This chapter builds on the findings and policy analyses presented in Chapters 1 to 12 with the aim of drawing out their implications for policy-makers at the EU and national levels. It loosely follows the structure of the book by concentrating, first, on the likely consequences of the evolution of labour demand in key sectors of activity, then turning to the influences on labour supply discussed in Chapters 6 to 8. In each of these sections, key messages for both EU and national policy-makers are summarised. The concluding part of the chapter considers how EU policies and strategic initiatives might be adapted to reflect the long-run policy challenges on both the supply and demand sides of the labour market.

---

* Iain Begg: London School of Economics and Political Science.

13.1 The demand for labour

That the demand for labour in the EU has been insufficient to provide enough jobs is evident from the unemployment data. However, the depth and duration of the recession mask underlying trends in labour demand that, in turn, will affect the longer-term shifts among sectors and types of work that will determine aggregate employment. These include the direct and indirect effects of policy changes such as decarbonisation, with their varied implications for sub-sectors.

What is abundantly clear is that policy choices and the availability of funding will have a pronounced impact on a number of key sectors, and that there will be multiple channels through which policy decisions influence the net creation of new jobs. This section considers jobs in health and long-term care, the demand from older consumers and the outlook for demand for labour derived from energy policies.

Apart from any moral imperatives, the likelihood of a more extensive collective effort to reduce the energy consumption of households will depend on a range of incentives. The rising cost of energy expected as fossil fuels become scarcer would be expected to act as an incentive to curb energy use, although one with distributive consequences associated with fuel poverty.[1] Public investment and/or tax breaks may therefore also be needed to make a significant difference.

A transition away from primary production in agriculture, extractive industries and more traditional industrial jobs has been underway for several decades, with various consequences.[2] It is argued, for example, that the much more limited scope for productivity increases in service activities – often referred to as Baumol's disease – will mean that demand for labour will stagnate if the result is a secular downturn in growth potential. However, the sheer scale and diversity of the service sector jobs across the EU mean that they cannot reasonably be thought of as a single category. Some rely primarily on funding from the public purse, while others depend on either consumer or business demand. Some entail face-to-face delivery, but a sizeable proportion of services can be delivered remotely.

i) Decarbonisation, growth and jobs

As Bert Colijn and Arno Behrens point out in Chapter 2, the net effect of implementation of low-carbon technologies will be the result of a complex process of job destruction and creation. It will also depend crucially on the interactions between technology and energy, and the authors cite evidence for a positive correlation between gains in energy efficiency and technological change. This finding is at least a partial retort to the widespread assumption that European producers may be at a disadvantage from having to bear the costs of decarbonisation. A key policy message from Chapter 1 is that when all the effects are taken into account, the overall impact of decarbonisation on jobs is difficult to estimate unambiguously, but it is also likely to be marginal at most. Increased innovation is, however, a means of tipping the balance towards a positive outcome.

> *Changes in the energy mix will have only a marginal effect on total employment.*

The chapter finds that energy-efficiency gains will be crucial in decoupling economic growth from energy consumption, but also that the scope for achieving targets is considerable. The greatest reductions in carbon emissions will arise in the power sector, but there will need to be provision for increased as well as climate-friendly generating capacity. A consequence is that productivity in electricity generation will fall, accentuating fears about the effect on the competitiveness in global markets of EU exporters. A reduction in energy use per unit of output may, however, offset this risk and policy-makers will have to reflect on how the overall impact of policy (regulation, taxation, incentives for energy-saving innovation) affects these costs. This will be important to counter the impression that rising unit costs of electricity production in itself is damaging.

Because the total employment in energy industries is under 1% of the employed labour force, changes in the energy mix will not have a marked effect on total employment in the economy. The more likely scenario is that relatively low-skilled jobs in mining will be replaced by higher-skill jobs in renewable production. To this extent, policy-makers should recognise that there will be different human-capital demands as a result of decarbonisation.

Key messages for policy-makers: Decarbonisation, growth and jobs

At the EU level

- There are credible and convincing scenarios under which the EU can fulfil its decarbonisation commitments using known technologies.
- The global impact of decarbonisation in Europe risks being undermined by energy-intensive activities relocating to other parts of the world, and this should be taken into account in assessments of structural change.
- The effects of energy policies on jobs should be central to policy analysis and not relegated to a second-order question.

At the national level

- Each country has to find a national pathway for decarbonisation that reconciles the achievement of targets with a strategy for jobs.
- In electricity generation from renewables, there is a need for redundant capacity to reflect the unreliability of sources such as wind and solar. While unavoidably adding to costs, there are likely to be benefits in generating more jobs.
- Measures to enhance energy efficiency have to be implemented alongside a shift to alternatives to fossil fuels to mitigate the rise in unit costs of electricity.

ii) Transport

Since transport accounts for fully one-third of EU energy consumption, how the sector evolves will have a significant impact on overall energy demand. The sector has had a poor record since 1990 in curbing emissions of greenhouse gases (GHG) and therefore must find ways of reducing these emissions rapidly if it is to conform to the latest EU ambitions, as agreed at the October 2014 European Council (see Box 13.1). As Chapter 3 explains, there are two main options. The first is to change the dominant propulsion technology so as to emit less carbon, either by electrification or by a switch to bio-fuels on the premise that these can be carbon neutral. Design changes in vehicles to facilitate greater fuel efficiency would add to this effect, but the likely impact on jobs is hard to accurately predict.

Box 13.1 Long-term energy policy

Some shifts in the EU's long-term energy policy were agreed at the European Council meeting on 24 October 2014. A target of reducing GHG emissions by at least 40% by 2030, compared with the 1990 level, substantially extends the target of 20% set for 2020, but with the difference that it will be a collective EU target rather than one towards which each member state aspires. The sensitivity of the target for some member states is visible in paragraph 2.2 of the Conclusions, which ambiguously states that "all Member States will participate in this effort, balancing considerations of fairness and solidarity". For a different benchmark - change by 2030 relative to 2005 - the range will be from 0% to -40%. There will be a similar approach to renewables and energy efficiency gains, with an aggregate 27% reduction foreseen in both areas, again to be delivered by various national commitments. It is striking that paragraph 3 of the Conclusions states that "targets will not be translated into nationally binding targets", albeit with the counter-point that member states are free to set higher national targets.

There was also agreement on the next stages of the EU emissions trading system (ETS) after 2020, when the cap on emissions will be tightened at a higher annual rate than in the run up to 2020. However, free permits will continue to be issued so as to avoid impairing international competitiveness. In addition, the ETS terms for member states with low GDP will be much more generous. A clear policy message is that threats to economic activity and jobs have been taken into account in energy targets. The agreement nevertheless provides for innovation that may be transformative and thus affect future jobs, and singles out the transport sector as one where special effort is needed.

The alternative is behavioural change aimed at curbing demand for mechanised transport using regulatory and fiscal instruments, while also enhancing collective solutions. Some results are surprising from a policy perspective. For example, the extent of congestion in cities means that cycling is often the fastest intra-urban mode of transport. Comparative data collated by the European Cycling Federation show the huge gap between cycling rates in countries where travel to work is dominated by cycling, such as the Netherlands (a third), Denmark and Hungary (around 20%), and those where fewer than 5% consider it their main mode of travel. This disparity signals the potential for energy savings and for job creation associated with constructing cycling infrastructures.

Figure 13.1 Decarbonisation and jobs in transport

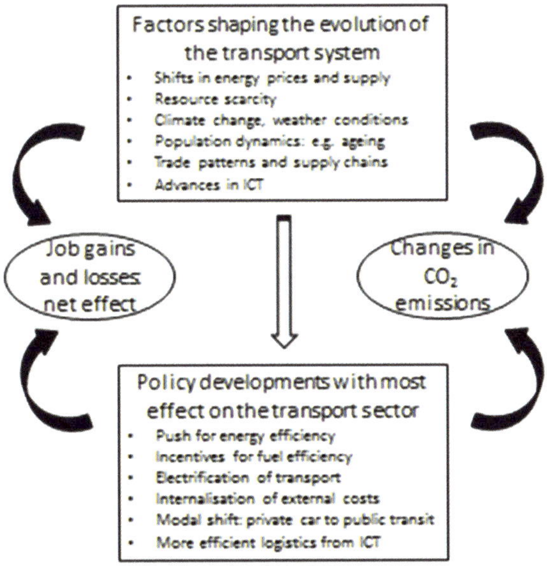

Source: Elaborated from Heyndrickx et al. (2013).

Key messages for policy-makers: Transport

At the EU level

- Transport reform policy involves a number of trade-offs that are not always made explicit when difficult policy choices have to be taken.
  - Increasing jobs, for instance, may be associated with more limited reductions in emissions.
  - Similarly, if there are energy-efficiency gains in transport, any resulting cost savings may induce higher demand, although the net effect would still be expected to be a cut in emissions.
- To the extent that the interplay between regulation and transport (or housing) investment affects the pace of energy-saving investments, a test of the potential for job creation should be introduced in parallel with attaining decarbonisation objectives.
- A switch from manufacturing of transport equipment to services is likely, with ramifications for the types of jobs the sector offers.

At the national level

- Strategies to promote cycling - extensive in some countries and cities, but limited in others - can have the 'win-win' outcome of reducing emissions and improving public health.
  - Both national and municipal tiers of government can contribute to the realisation of these goals through infrastructure investment to provide dedicated road space and cycle parking/storage, and through publicity campaigns.
  - This is an area where multi-level governance can come into its own.

iii) Housing

As one of the largest components of consumer demand, what happens in housing is bound to affect jobs. A transition towards lower energy consumption will have a number of effects on jobs, depending on the combination of subsidies, regulatory and other microeconomic influences, and macroeconomic trends. Optimising the mix of regulatory interventions and price signals will not be easy. While technologies exist that allow houses to come close to having net zero energy demand, they require social and user acceptability to boost their application.[3] Equally, there are challenges around how best to finance the costs of investment in curbing energy in housing, linked to the fact that so much personal-sector wealth is tied up in housing. A policy issue here is whether existing financial mechanisms such as mortgages could be used more imaginatively to release capital.[4]

One of the main means by which housing is expected to lead to net job creation is in renovation of property to reduce energy consumption. As the chapter by Kees Dol et al. makes clear, the resulting jobs will mainly be in construction and related activities. Experts find that, although there are considerable uncertainties, the potential can be measured in hundreds of thousands of new jobs.[5] Although it is projected that there will be net job creation, there is considerable uncertainty about how substantial the effect will be, not least because the parameters used and the assumptions the authors of the projections make are vague. A policy message is nevertheless that there is potential in this sector, some of it contingent on policy choices not yet made. The jobs would be in the production of materials, the installation of energy-saving equipment or insulation, services associated with planning and certification and, possibly, around the financing of investments in renovation. Many of these may draw on existing skills, but there will also be a need for adaptation and upgrading of skills to meet new standards.

Compared with large-scale infrastructure, low-key renovation and greening projects in housing can be undertaken quickly and could therefore offer the prospect of the win-win outcome of reducing unemployment and making progress towards energy targets, all without a heavy burden on public funds. However, specific social and financial impediments to greater renovation need to be addressed, including the reluctance of older homeowners to undertake such investments and the creation of suitable financial instruments.

In the changed post-crisis economic environment, the effects of housing on labour mobility warrant fresh thinking. For many households, housing is a major financial asset, but one that is both illiquid and prone to loss of capital value in a downturn, with asymmetric effects. Regions that prosper will tend to have rising property prices and vice versa, with the result that unemployed owner-occupiers in recession-hit regions will be unable to move easily to regions of buoyant labour demand without suffering a sizeable capital loss. Private rented accommodation may offer some help, but will also be subject to rising prices in prosperous areas.

Key messages for policy-makers: Housing

At the EU level

- Given its high share in consumer demand, housing should be central to an energy-efficiency strategy.
    - Housing targets should be introduced into a revised Europe 2020 strategy.
- A rapid boost to investment could be achieved by an EU-wide scheme, with some co-financing from the EU budget, to improve insulation in housing, with the potential for a triple dividend from higher investment, progress towards energy-efficiency targets and the provision of jobs for construction workers.
    - Innovation in the regulation of mortgage finance could help to mobilise locked-in equity in housing as a means of funding such investments.

At the national level

- From a labour market perspective, assisting very small businesses to contribute to green job creation raises distinctive policy questions. Specific skills in construction and the use of insulation materials will need to be nurtured, including training linked to compliance with regulations.
- Training to facilitate a sufficient supply of the skills required to accelerate energy-saving investments in housing and transport should be enhanced, particularly for small-scale projects.
- From the perspective of labour mobility, the mix in the supply of housing is critical. A sufficient stock of rented accommodation in areas of high-labour demand should be encouraged.
- Information campaigns should be developed, particularly targeted at older homeowners, to explain the benefits in terms of personal comfort and wellbeing, as well as the financial gains of investing in energy-saving renovations.

iv) Health and long-term care services

An inevitable consequence of an ageing population is that an increasing share of demand, and thus jobs, will be associated with servicing the needs of older people. Progressively, EU countries are adapting to the fact that older citizens represent not only a larger share of the population, but also an increasingly affluent group. To the extent that the consumption patterns of older citizens diverge from those of younger cohorts, there will be shifts in demand affecting different sectors. As Chapter 6 shows, one of the sectors most affected by this key demographic trend is health and social care, a sector which in the EU increased in terms of jobs by over 25% during the 2000s and is expected to grow further over the next 10 to 15 years.

The share of health and social services in total employment varies widely, with more than double the EU average of 6% (2010) in Denmark and the Netherlands, but barely half the average in the countries of central, eastern and south-eastern Europe (according to the data presented in Chapter 11). This suggests considerable scope for expansion in this latter group, provided that funding difficulties can be overcome. The high proportion of female workers is striking, reaching 80% in several market segments and occasionally over 90%. It follows that employment in care is also crucial for women, even if the notion of 'women's occupations' is anathema to many in today's EU. The existing workforce in these services is ageing rapidly.

Who provides the services for the elderly is a core policy question. In Denmark, as documented in the chapter by Erika Schulz and Johannes Geyer, one in five employees works in the health and care sectors. Elsewhere, the proportion is much lower (6-7% in Poland, Italy and Slovakia), either because provision is lacking or because more of the burden is assumed by unpaid family members. Much of the difference is the result of the very high provision (and associated employment) of residential care and social work in Denmark, in contrast to its limited availability in Poland and Italy (barely 1% of employment). With welfare reform on the political agenda everywhere, these sorts of disparities both offer competing models for the future and prompt awkward questions about public spending priorities and the regulatory oversight of privately provided services.

In NEUJOBS research on low-wage occupations, Moira Nelson finds that the highest shares of employment in the care sector are in the Nordic countries and the UK, but that the latter also had the highest growth in the two decades up to 2010. Her research suggests that these countries (and the Netherlands) are similar in three respects. First, they are more likely to provide training for low-wage workers. Second, the incidence of poverty (measured relative to the median wage) is highest among low-wage service workers. And third, their proportions of jobs in cleaning are quite closely clustered.[6]

Workers in the sector are typically female, part-time and, perhaps most significantly, older, presaging a potential labour supply shortfall as these older workers exit the labour market. Depending on demand for these services (or, perhaps more accurately, the policy choice on funding the sector), there could therefore be a shortfall of labour supply. The prospect of exit is especially pronounced for professionals, notably physicians, while the expectation is that the rise in demand will be for the relatively more qualified, such as those working in hospitals rather than in community healthcare. The resulting policy dilemma is how to ensure that future demand can be met, and this will require rapid decisions where the training is lengthy, as is the case for medical professionals. The alternative of attracting highly qualified immigrants is contentious for other reasons.

Health and care demand is also subject to a range of uncertainties. New treatments and expectations of rising quality raise expected demand, but there may also be trends associated with a cleaner environment or a shift away from fossil fuels that improve the general health of the population. Shifts in household composition towards more single-person households in the middle of the age distribution and geographical mobility affect the scope for informal care, the bulk of which is undertaken by women. This leads to a tension between informal care and the aspiration to boost female-employment rates, although the long-standing assertion that care commitments deter participation is questioned in the research findings. Of the five countries studied, it only clearly does so in Italy.

Projections of increases in the dependent population expected to require care vary hugely. In two of the cases studied in Chapter 5 (Denmark and Germany), the overall increase is relatively small compared with Italy, Slovakia and Poland, although greater in all cases in the friendly scenario. However, differences in life expectancy and the demographic mix mean that Denmark faces by far the greatest increase in people over the age of 75 requiring care.

A policy message here is that distinctive national approaches will be adopted, offering a diversity of policy experience. However, the analysis also reveals the uncertainty about how the risks associated with different forms of morbidity affect impairment that might necessitate policy intervention. Decisions will, however, be needed on how to deal with the increased incidence of mental illness among older people.

Care workers are projected to increase in four of the five countries studied, but not by enough to keep pace with projected care demand, while in the fifth (Italy) the workforce will decline, accentuating the gap between the workforce and demand. The findings also note that resort to illegal workers is widespread in Italy. The sorts of policy innovations that might bridge these gaps include enhancing informal care, immigrants as carers and improved conditions in the sector to make the activity more attractive. All these are problematic, whether for reasons of cost and uncertainty about future willingness to allocate sufficient funding (especially from the public purse), social acceptability or conflict with other socio-economic objectives. But the arithmetic is such that it will rapidly become a pressing policy issue.

Key messages for policy-makers: Health and long-term care services

At the EU level

- Employment in care services is substantial across the EU, but faces a range of hard political choices.
- It is a sector requiring a range of skills, but some of the lower-skill jobs are likely to prove increasingly unattractive to those now obtaining better qualifications.
- Activating older workers is recognised as essential to maintain a suitable balance between the economically active and inactive segments of the population.

At the national level

- Among the various forms of organisation of care services, what works best in the national institutional context should take into account the impact on jobs.
- New models of caregiving or of provision of residential facilities are needed to reflect the changing age and impairment mix of recipients of care.
- The official retirement age has to be re-examined in the light of increasing life expectancy.

13.2 Labour supply

Under any credible scenario, the EU labour supply will shrink over the coming decades as ageing affects more countries, although the different incidence among member states of this phenomenon is in itself a challenge to EU policy-makers. As NEUJOBS projections have shown, large differences are anticipated in the rate at which these changes occur, with some countries already seeing an impact while for others it will only arise after 2030.[7] An ageing society has two principal solutions to ensuring a sufficient labour supply: activating a higher proportion of the population (including those outside standard working-age groups) or boosting the labour supply with immigrants. Further increases in the employment rate of women and activating other specific groups excluded from the mainstream labour are key policy orientations.

Greater labour market participation and/or immigration could mitigate the negative aspects of workforce ageing.

i) Employment of women

The sustained increase in the number of women working has been one of the most significant societal developments since the 1980s. As explained in Chapter 6 by Iga Magda and Agnieszka Kamińska, it has been encouraged by a steady enhancement of women's educational qualifications, but women continue to face obstacles in the labour market. In view of the looming decline in the size of the working-age population in most EU countries, there is a compelling policy interest in ensuring that barriers to female employment - whatever their origin - are dismantled.

The research summarised in the chapter shows that although women, on average, have higher educational qualifications than men, they find it harder to secure a first job. The main explanation put forward is that it is mothers rather than childless women who have most difficulty in making the transition into (or back into) employment. However, the evidence suggests that women also find it harder generally to make other labour market transitions. These are, manifestly, empirical results derived from highly aggregated analyses and it is important to recognise that in several member states the picture is much more positive. Equally, the low employment rates for women in certain areas point to more specific institutional blockages that need to be overcome.

One is that in most EU member states, relatively more women than men are not in education, employment or training (NEET). This is a phenomenon with a cumulatively adverse impact, because the initial detachment from the labour market can be self-reinforcing if it means that future employers regard the NEET period as a stain on the potential worker's record. The key policy question that arises is whether the number of NEETs overall, and specifically female NEETs, can be significantly reduced by appropriate reconfiguration of labour market institutions and their interactions with the educational system. Magda and Kamińska suggest that one answer is to combine apprenticeships and tertiary education – perhaps along the lines of the German VET system, although a counter-argument is that overly early stratification reduces opportunities later in the working life.

The comparatively low employment rate of mothers of prime working age (25-54) is well below the EU average in much of southern Europe (Portugal is an exception), although also in the UK. As might be expected, the employment rate of mothers is highest in the Nordic countries (and in the Netherlands) and in Slovenia, where the data for 2011 show that it was higher for mothers than for the 25-54 age group as a whole. France, as well as Austria and Belgium, also employ relatively more mothers, suggesting that well-developed and affordable childcare facilities are influential. A policy implication is that it is the detail of the welfare system rather than the over-arching regime that most influences the job opportunities for mothers. A further consideration is the generosity of parental leave, which, while often seen as desirable from a societal perspective, can lead to an erosion of human capital that reduces the employability of women.

Mothers are somewhat less likely to access lifelong learning (LLL), suggesting that work-life balance is a dimension of training provision that requires more effort by policy-makers. Being employed in the first place is associated with obtaining LLL, but those working in agriculture and industry are less likely to be offered LLL. For public employment services, a policy message is that they may need to be more pro-active. In a context of more frequent changes of jobs and more rapid obsolescence of skills, the scope for those who withdraw temporarily from the labour market – especially for maternity – to retain or enhance their skills will increasingly matter. A possible answer would be to widen the scope of lifelong learning provision to include the temporarily inactive, thereby supporting post-maternity transitions back to work.

Affordable childcare facilities and shorter parental leave are associated with greater female labour market participation.

There are big gaps between the duration of working-life, with women in southern Europe working for fewer than 25 years, more than 10 years less than the average for their Nordic counterparts. Fairness in pension entitlements presents many thorny issues. A contributions-based model discriminates against women who withdraw from the labour force, but the opposite implies higher costs for men for the same benefits.

The arithmetic of the length of working life-times matters, as well as the employment rates of different age groups. A policy initiative to increase the number of years women spend in employment would make a substantial difference, and might therefore be an additional basis for targets, complementing those for age cohorts. Given the low rates of employment of older women in many member states and the limited opportunities for reversing this in the short term, a medium- to long-term policy question is how subsequent generations of older women can be retained in the labour market. Once again, the very large disparities in national rates can be a basis for change. A crucial factor is access to, and take-up of, training by older workers.

Another quandary around retirement ages is how to go about equalising male and female statutory ages for pensions and other age-related social benefits. On the one hand, the sustainability of pension systems calls for a gradual edging-up of the pension age, necessarily meaning that the threshold for women has to rise more rapidly. But as the gap between male and female statutory retirement ages narrows, there is a risk that certain age cohorts will be disproportionately punished. It is important, however, to take account of the incidence of benefits other than pensions and of levels of public pensions in relation to other assured sources of income. Systematic collection and diffusion of national experiences can provide insights for those countries still to act.

Magda and Kaminska raise the further point that there are long-run interactions, such as between the inducement provided by generous maternity arrangements (for example, in systems as disparate as those of Hungary and the UK) to remain economically inactive and the scope for accruing pension and other old-age benefits. While their conclusion is, not unreasonably, that there are no easy solutions, it is also incumbent on policy-makers to explore the scope for marginal changes to make a tangible difference to any inequities.

The employability of women has been an enduring priority in EU policy. As Chapter 7 shows, there have been significant shifts in employment rates among different segments of the female workforce: with more women entering tertiary education, younger cohorts have seen a decline in employment rates, whereas older women are now much more likely to be employed than in previous generations. There are both stock and flow explanations for these transitions. Overall, women are better educated and because there is a positive association between education and employment, the outcome is a better employment rate.

There are still huge differences across countries in employment rates of mothers. An obvious explanatory variable is the provision of publicly funded childcare, but there is also a socio-cultural dimension at play. For example, as NEUJOBS national policy reports on Hungary and Germany explain, it has long been the norm for mothers to look after small children at home, and this is reinforced by the incentives in the welfare system.[8] It follows that an over-arching policy goal of increasing the employment rate of mothers has to recognise that there are wider societal factors to take into account.

A possible answer is to explore the scope for different forms of working. Teleworking, flexible hours or part-time working are types of arrangements that can enable mothers (and even, in the relatively small number of member states such as Sweden where parental leave is shared, fathers) to remain connected to the labour market. The attractions are clear. Given that the median worker with young children is increasingly well-educated, extended periods of inactivity not only risk the 'hysteresis' effect of increasing detachment from the labour market and a more demanding transition back to work, but also lead to a societal loss in the form of a reduced return on human-capital investment.

It is the more highly educated women in a number of member states who experience the largest pay gaps relative to men. There appears to be a link between work-life balance policies and the gender pay gap. However, the care model can make a difference: formal provision seems to be better for gender equality than private cash-based arrangements, but there is a trade-off with costs, with formal care costing more. The conditions for care workers may be part of the story in fostering greater gender equality.

Key messages for policy-makers: Employment of women

At the EU level

- In rethinking the flexicurity model, the distinctive needs of older women and working mothers should be identified and appropriate solutions found.
    - The tools of the open method of coordination can be helpful in this regard.
- Although many of the required policy responses are well understood and many helpful policies have indeed been devised, NEUJOBS research suggests that an implementation problem has still to be overcome.
- Job quality and equal pay for women continue to be labour market problems and will require further initiatives.

At the national level

- Increasing the employment rate of women, especially returning mothers, by identifying obstacles and customising support should be accorded urgent priority.
- Given the prospect of extension of working life by changing jobs, the provision of LLL should be extended or strengthened for sectors or groups, including those not currently economically active, in which it is less common.
- The interaction between the statutory retirement age and activation should be re-examined.

ii) Inclusion of Roma

The Roma minority is, according to Chapter 9 by Vera Messing, by far the largest in the EU, at some nine or more million, although given that it comprises groups with different traditions in different member states, it can be misleading to think of Roma as a homogeneous group. What is abundantly clear, however, is that there is widespread discrimination against Roma and that policy efforts to overcome their social exclusion have proved to be ineffective. There are many reasons for this state of affairs. Discrimination manifests itself in poor access to housing, sub-standard educational provision and very low employment rates compared with other groups, with especially low skills.

Messing finds that there is a cumulative disadvantage resulting from the high levels of illiteracy in some countries (although mainly among older-age cohorts in Hungary and Slovakia), a lack of basic numeracy and associated workplace skills, and generally low educational qualifications for those that reach secondary education. Even in Slovakia and Hungary, where Roma educational attainment is higher than in neighbouring Romania and Bulgaria, fewer than one in five achieves a higher secondary qualification, and tertiary education is a rarity. There is overt racial discrimination against Roma in Bulgaria and Romania, even in the way jobs are advertised, while elsewhere it may be more hidden but nonetheless equally potent in excluding candidates from interviews, for example on the basis of names. The NEUJOBS research reveals that even the public sector engages in such discrimination.

Countries offering relatively more low-skilled jobs - particularly in sectors such as agriculture, tourism and construction - employ relatively more Roma, and the decline of manual jobs in industry after 1989 in Slovakia and Hungary was associated with substantial job losses. Even in Hungary, the relatively higher employment rate of Roma is inflated by counting those on public-works programmes.

A policy dilemma emphasised in the chapter by Messing is whether key employment policy instruments, such as active labour market policies, should be specifically targeted at groups such as the Roma, or should instead have their eligibility determined by the main labour market attributes associated with low employment rates, including locality, level of education and age. To the extent that racial (in the case of the Roma) or any other form of discrimination is itself the main impediment to employment, specific targeting can be justified, although there can be risks of a backlash if other relatively deprived groups perceive (rightly or wrongly) that the targeted group is obtaining special treatment. Messing notes that the 2011 EU Framework for National Roma Integration Strategies tries to reconcile the two options by advocating "explicit but not exclusive targeting". Careful evaluation will be needed to see whether this compromise approach achieves the desired results, not least because the indications from the work of Messing and colleagues is that implementation in the four countries they study shows little sign of change.

The functioning of public employment services is another area of concern for policy-makers. The NEUJOBS research in chapter 8 reveals that Roma are deterred from using these services by the attitudes of officials, thereby creating a catch-22 in which the lack of support means the services are not used, adding to the likelihood of Roma being confined to the informal economy. There is some risk of employment traps in a circle of public works and welfare schemes. This is a problem that other countries, including the Scandinavian pioneers of ALMP, have struggled to resolve over the years, but one in which there are lessons in relation to the Roma that can be learned, for example in the ways that Sweden has recently tried to thwart the 'carousel' through which the same individuals go from one public programme to another without truly re-entering the labour market.

Key messages for policy-makers: Inclusion of Roma

At the EU level

- Social inclusion strategies face a profound test of credibility in dealing with the Roma populations and have to be sensitive to the diverse circumstances of this group in different member states.
- In instances where there is documented discrimination against Roma, there is a *prima facie* breach of EU law and norms; naming and shaming should be a first level of response, but the Commission should consider formal proceedings against member states that fail to enforce the relevant legislation, especially in public employment.
- The mutual learning around how to prevent jobs traps should be intensified, so as to draw out implications for the employment of Roma across the EU.

At the national level

- Dealing with the multi-faceted nature of exclusion confronting Roma has to be at the core of the policy response.
- Public policies, including writing-in to contracts for public procurement that any discrimination will lead to penalties or cancellation of the contract, should be used to give a lead to the labour market in preventing discrimination.
- The effectiveness of public employment services in placing excluded groups, notably Roma, should be examined and reforms introduced to counter hidden discrimination or inadequate provision for such groups.
- Involving representatives of excluded groups in different stages of policy-making - from decision-making to implementation - can help make programmes more effective and responsive to needs.

iii) Immigration

Europe is an attractive destination for migrants, but migration leads to tensions that policy-makers in many member states have found hard to resolve. It is also a policy area in which glib populist myths gain political credence, despite the weight of empirical evidence. There is an increasingly fraught debate in many EU member states about migrants, whether from other member states or from third countries, and an often hypocritical reluctance to acknowledge the contribution of migrants to the effective functioning of many sectors of activity. Nor is it just the high-level occupations that are the issue. Many low-skilled jobs would be very hard to fill without migrants, from agriculture through to care services. Moreover, recent EU policy initiatives have sought to put in place a long-term, strategic approach to recruitment of foreign workers at a time when political discourse in several member states has taken a distinctly anti-immigrant turn.

There is a wide spectrum of immigration, from Nobel prize-winning scientists at one end to the impoverished and totally uneducated refugees crossing the Mediterranean in flimsy boats at the other, and it follows that policy responses have to be suitably differentiated. As the chapter by Sergio Carrera, Elspeth Guild and Katharina Eisele recalls, there is a degree of consensus around the need for the EU to attract highly qualified workers, both to fill skills gaps and to provide a spur to competitiveness. It is, therefore, logical that the Europe 2020 strategy should explicitly target attracting the most talented third-country nationals. In this context, immigration is not just about labour supply, but also about the pursuit of the knowledge economy and entrepreneurship. Immigrant workers are, however, also crucial for the care services in many member states, especially in the light of the relatively high age of current care workers discussed above.

Restrictions such as quotas (for example, on the issuance of social security numbers, as recently advocated in the UK) can be in conflict with EU law, but are seen within member states as necessary for a plethora of reasons, including worries about opportunities for those already resident. However, Chapter 8 points out that the criteria adopted are often short-term and politicised, and stresses that migration has to be seen as a much longer-term societal transformation. Restrictions do not, in any case, detract from the attractiveness of a destination and may, almost paradoxically, make favoured destinations more sought-after. These observations have a number of implications for EU policy.

Should there be a points-based system in the EU and, if so, for what attributes should points be awarded? A stock answer is that scarce skills should be the main test. But in the light of NEUJOBS findings about prospective gaps in labour supply for a number of relatively low-skilled occupations, including care, a broader answer may be needed. As discussed by Carrera et al. in their chapter, there is a time dimension to consider. Europe may have a surfeit of low- or unskilled workers at present, but once demographic transitions begin to bite, the position could change quite rapidly. Under-use of immigrant skills is widespread, yet is hard to overcome because of a lack of mutual recognition of qualifications, prompting questions such as what constitutes a 'skill'. Carrera et al. suggest that establishing the meaning of 'medium-skilled' is especially tricky.

It may be that the presumed competition with the US, Canada and other mature economies for the most talented migrants is not an accurate characterisation. If so, it may lead to false policy choices and wrong-headed approaches. The attractiveness of a migrant for the host country may be based on filling an immediate need, but this is not necessarily the same as what attracts the migrant to a destination. Restrictions that suit the host and provide an immediate economic rationale may be contrary to the interests of the individual migrant, not least where the latter has longer-term goals, yet is faced by an asymmetry of power.

The difficulty is not just that of classic 'brain drain', but also one of 'brain squandering'.

The themes covered in Chapter 8 from a legal perspective can be widened to embrace the role of migrants in labour supply in areas that are not primarily connected to competitive advantage or the global search for talent. Compared with a qualified, single, prime-age worker, a family of asylum-seekers manifestly has very different interactions with the fiscal and welfare systems of a host country.

The evidence on the contribution of migrant workers to the provision of care, presented in the chapter by Attila Bartha, Olena Fedyuk and Violetta Zentai, gives an overview of the extent of the dependence on low-skilled migrants, predominantly women. In the EU15, there was a 40% increase in this group between 2000 and 2010. Given the NEUJOBS base scenario projection that care demand will increase by at least 15% and, under certain assumptions, by

Compared with a qualified, single, prime-age worker, a family of asylum-seekers manifestly has very different interactions with the fiscal and welfare systems of a host country.

as much as 40% in the period up to 2025, there are tricky policy issues around how to fill the jobs and how to accommodate the migrants who will inevitably form a significant proportion of the labour supply. However, it is argued by Magda and Kaminska in their chapter that an influx of immigrants to bolster care-sector employment may perpetuate, rather than solve, gender inequality.

Because the role of migrants in care differs greatly among the member states, the thrust of policy is also bound to differ. Many central and eastern European countries are, in effect, providers of the labour supply in western Europe, largely because of financial and other incentives to work in richer member states. Moreover, immigrant care workers, as Bartha et al. emphasise, often take jobs on terms that indigenous workers would not be willing to accept. Young Poles, Latvians or Slovaks who migrate to work in Sweden, the UK or Germany leave gaps in the labour supply in their home countries and, moreover, possess higher qualifications than they need for the work they undertake. To this extent, the human-capital investment of home countries will have lower returns, but the difficulty is not just that of classic 'brain drain', but also one of 'brain squandering'.

Tighter controls on migration risk pushing those in the care segment of the labour market further into the informal economy. There is, therefore, a need for both an EU-level and a national-level policy response. Part-time work in care is much more the norm, in contrast to many other occupations. A policy question is whether this is to be encouraged, amended or resisted. However, there are sizeable differences among the member states.

Interactions between public and private care provision may help to explain some of the less-expected patterns of migration, notably the apparent attractiveness of Spain and Italy, rather than some of the northern member states, for such migrants. Good state provision in the Nordic countries substitutes for private demand, whereas there is a relatively more limited public provision in Mediterranean countries, together with a more receptive approach to informal arrangements. The stronger role of the family may also be a factor. Patterns in CEE countries are more heterogeneous.

Key messages for policy-makers: Immigration

At the EU level

- The EU needs a coherent approach to immigration, capable of overcoming the problems arising from fragmented national policies.
- Clarity is needed on the status of immigrants and how their rights and the restrictions they face are interpreted in different member states.
- Hard law is, however, only one dimension of immigration policy; it has to be complemented by implementation.
- An EU system for the recognition of qualifications of third-country nationals is needed.

At the national level

- Some of the myths that surround immigration need to be confronted head-on if discriminatory and disruptive social consequences are to be avoided.
- More rigorous enforcement of existing rules is called for, especially on discrimination.
- Where the skills and qualifications of migrants are under-used, there is a mutual advantage for the host and the migrants themselves in finding ways to make better use of their human capital.

13.3 Rethinking EU policies: Orientations and governance

With a new European Commission now in office, intent on a fresh approach to growth and jobs, many established norms of policy-making deserve to be challenged. The NEUJOBS project provides a wide-ranging evidence base and, in this volume, highlights several strategically important facets of the evolving EU labour market likely to bear on EU policy choices. In the light of NEUJOBS findings, this concluding section examines the scope for new thinking on some of the principal mechanisms through which the EU level can be influential. In this regard, the Europe 2020 strategy ought to be pivotal, although as the stocktaking paper on Europe 2020 concedes, "the immediacy of the crisis sometimes made it challenging to reconcile short-term urgencies with longer-term needs" (European Commission, 2014, p. 19). The Commission analysis acknowledges that the growth model of previous decades is no longer viable, and the paper emphasises "weaknesses in education and training systems". It also alludes to unemployment and "widening social inequalities" as problems that have not been resolved, while employment and poverty reduction targets have not been met.

As the EU edges out of crisis and thoughts turn to what Alan Blinder et al. have referred to as the "new normal",[9] there is likely to be renewed interest in sustainability as a (or even *the*) defining norm for the socio-economic development of the EU, highlighting the importance of the NEUJOBS transitions. It may be most obvious in relation to resource use and carbon emissions, but it is also highly pertinent in social policy. Quite apart from normative considerations such as equality or inclusion, an ageing Europe cannot ignore the fiscal and macroeconomic imperatives pushing it towards societal changes that will ensure an adequate labour supply and contain the costs of the welfare state. In all these respects, a sustainable Europe will differ from that of the pre-crisis years.

Examination of how well placed EU countries are to achieve successful 'NEUJOBS transitions' reveals highly diverse trends. The evidence also suggests that a country may do well on some transitions, but have shortcomings on others. These differences arise for various reasons, with some countries facing much more rapid population ageing (and, in some cases, a marked decline), or having to contend with unhelpful legacies in skills or in the energy mix. In others, populist reactions to immigration or an inability to find effective ways of integrating excluded groups - Roma being a prime example - have influenced the policy agenda. The tensions that arise and the difficulties in resolving them can best be understood through a political economy lens. Some examples are:

- In energy, the short-term impact of a decarbonisation strategy that, as with Germany's *Energiewende*, substantially raises the unit costs of electricity for industrial as well as domestic consumers, at a time when global competitors are seeing energy costs fall.
- Incompatibilities between established social norms, such as the expectation in Hungary that mothers care for children at home, and the activation of women. A similar effect occurs in Italy, where care for the elderly is expected of female children, also conflicting with activation policies.
- A sense in France that the conjunction of education and social policies is increasingly ill-suited to the employment challenges of the coming decades, but a lack of clear solutions.[10] A specific worry is the large inequalities in educational outcomes in France, which systematically undermine the chances for children from less-favourable backgrounds to obtain jobs.[11]

- Labour mobility in Slovakia being weakened by the nature of tenure in housing markets and deficiencies in infrastructure, aggravating mismatch problems.[12]
- The difficulty of integrating Roma into mainstream society, even when (as discussed in Chapter 9) policies are well intentioned, because of socio-cultural resistance.
- The growing hostility in the UK to EU migrants, despite evidence that they make a sizeable net contribution to public finances and prosperity, which exemplifies the difficulties of resorting to immigration as a solution to labour supply.
- Mortgage commitments, rather than home ownership as such, being the biggest obstacle to labour mobility, although the interaction between the two varies substantially across the EU because of the diverse nature of the systems for housing finance.[13]

These differences complicate policy responses at the EU level and the evidence suggests that, in spite of a plethora of initiatives - including the Europe 2020 strategy, the Compact for Growth and Jobs, Youth Guarantees and many more - their aggregate impact has been disappointing. There has also been a tendency to think that answers can be found in *grands projéts*, typically infrastructure related, but with not enough focus on other drivers of growth and employment.

i) Defining a new approach

The case for a fresh approach is, therefore, becoming more compelling. One way forward has come in the announcement in December 2014 of the European Fund for Strategic Investment, a potentially defining initiative of the new Commission, which took office late in 2014. Its premise is that there has been inadequate investment across the EU, especially since the crisis struck, and hence more investment is necessary to reinvigorate the EU economy and to underpin growth and jobs. For many observers this will be understood as physical and business capital, some of which can be channelled into projects aimed at an energy transition.

An alternative perspective could come from thinking in terms of human capital and its development across a range of policy domains. Social investment, as explained by proponents such as Anton Hemerijck, encompasses three distinct, but interdependent and complementary, welfare policy functions.[14] The first is easing the 'flow' of contemporary labour market and life-course transitions. The second is raising the quality of the 'stock' of human capital and the capabilities of individuals, affording them greater scope to take advantage of opportunities, particularly for employment. A third function is maintaining strong minimum-income universal safety nets as social protection and economic stabilisation 'buffers', a function that may require some redefinition in ageing societies.[15]

Much of the debate on how the EU can adapt takes place under the shadow of heavily constrained public finances, leading to the pessimistic view that little can be done. The easy, if erroneous, policy implication is that extensive changes, in the energy system or in the social field, are unaffordable. While some elements of, for example, a social investment approach are costly in the short term, they have longer-term pay-offs, and some regulatory reforms affecting energy efficiency only have, at worst, indirect costs and may save money. Moreover, as NEUJOBS projections show, there are viable solutions to pensions and other ageing costs.[16] After examining different approaches to retirement ages, they come to the general conclusion that a relatively moderate increase in the official retirement age, for example raising it in line with the increase in life expectancy, can transform the public finances of ageing.

Key messages for policy-makers: Defining a new approach

At the EU level

- Social investment, while acknowledged to have its critics, can become a core policy narrative for the EU as it recasts its policies towards growth and jobs.
- Opportunities for policy learning and sharing of experience in dealing with labour market blockages should be reinforced in EU-mediated processes and policy strategies.
- A successful welfare state is one that, as John Hills explains,[17] offers opportunities for all strata of society, not just those who claim benefits.

At the national level

- Finding a national pathway towards sustainable pensions may be politically difficult, but there are viable examples that can be adapted.
- In reaction to the crisis of recent years, a tough approach to public expenditure has been adopted, but progress on the transitions identified by NEUJOBS can also be made by other forms of policy intervention, calling for a judicious mix of regulatory and budgetary policies.

ii) Social services of general interest

The interactions between labour supply and demand in social services of general interest, especially health and long-term care, highlight some of the long-term policy dilemmas associated with the NEUJOBS transitions. Logically, as the population ages, the demand for care for the elderly will rise, although not necessarily in a linear fashion if advances in preventative healthcare, or new forms of organisation such as those relying on information and communications technology (ICT), reduce the need for direct inter-personal service delivery. As discussed in Chapter 10, there is a range of policy options around both the funding of social services of general interest (SSGI) through the public sector and the possibility of substitution of private provision. There can be little doubt that the demand will remain and that some societal trends, such as increased female economic activity, are closely linked to choices on SSGI.

> *It is the sheer numbers of older people rather than increased care needs on average that make the difference.*

In care services, the jobs for the least skilled tend to be ancillary occupations such as cleaning or similar in-home tasks. Such jobs are less prevalent in poorer countries. All this suggests that there is a 'trilemma' around care jobs of: first, constraints on funding that will squeeze the resources available; second, labour supply in terms of both headcount and mix of qualifications, accentuated by the projections of exit into inactivity of older cohorts in the current workforce; and third, rising demand. Each leg of this trilemma is open to a variety of policy solutions.

The complex political economy of care services is likely to affect the future provision of such jobs. Fiscal policies matter for the scale of service provision, but electoral politics also play a part and are likely to make a difference as populations age, empowering the grey voter as well as the grey consumer. In a period of public finance consolidation, the types of innovations in SSGI that are feasible in the context of welfare-state expansion are harder to agree upon. One consequence may be to accentuate the differences between welfare states. The skills profile of SSGI is quite polarised, but there is evidence that in countries where SSGI are more extensive, it is a sector that generates a high number of jobs for the unskilled. If funding constraints are binding, one policy implication is that a significant source of jobs for the unskilled will be jeopardised.

A difficult challenge is that healthcare costs tend to rise at a faster rate than consumer price inflation, with the result that public budgets face continuing stresses. An ageing population, living longer, is part of the explanation, even if the next cohorts of pensioners are, as a result of better health prevention (the decline of smoking is an illustration), typically healthier than their predecessors. It is the sheer numbers of older people rather than increased care needs on average that make the difference. Health costs have, however, been increased by the upskilling of health professions; a growing proportion of nurses, for example, are expected to have university degrees.[18]

Key messages for policy-makers: Social services of general interest

At the EU level

- A wide-ranging debate should be launched on the role of social services of general interest as a source of jobs and on what the future labour market in this area will be.
- Social services can be a test case for new, more flexible forms of employment attuned to the preferences of workers, not just employers.
- The consequences of cross-border flows of workers in SSGI for the capacity to meet growing demands in lower-income countries and the implications for the stock of human capital need to be monitored.

At the national level

- Although there are unavoidable difficulties in funding SSGI, organisational solutions to the provision of services should be sought and not hidden or rejected for ideological reasons.
- The balance between private and public provision of services should be carefully examined, including assessing the implications for skills and recruitment.
- In countries where social services are relatively under-developed, there is scope for boosting them as a source of jobs, especially for those with low qualifications.

iii) Governance of transitions

A long-run transition will, unavoidably, be disruptive and must be expected to elicit opposition, mainly (although not only) from those adversely affected by changes affecting their standing, wellbeing or prosperity. Only some of the winners and losers will be easily or unambiguously identifiable *ex ante*. At one end of the spectrum, there might be a Polish coal miner losing his job because the brown coal he digs out of the ground is no longer environmentally acceptable; at the other, a single mother could find her disposable income squeezed because a renewable levy has pushed up the cost of electricity that she cannot do without, while a lack of affordable childcare limits her employment opportunities. The remedies in these two cases may be self-evident, but in others they are less so.

Concern about jobs is pervasive in policy-making and is at the heart of the NEUJOBS research, but it is not necessarily the first priority of most of the policy areas examined in this volume. There are several explanations for this. Most policy interventions are organised around sectors; there is an energy policy, a social inclusion policy, a transport policy, a housing policy, a climate change policy, and so on. In each sector there will be primary objectives that constitute the *raison d'être* of the directorate-general, ministry or agency responsible, and the actors involved will be judged principally on how effective they are in achieving these objectives. While there might be credit to be gained from generating jobs *as well*, there would not be if it were a case of *instead*. In these circumstances, jobs are bound to come lower in a hierarchy of policy goals. Given the verdict from the analysis in Chapters 2, 3 and 4 that, under most plausible scenarios, there are opportunities for substantial reductions in emissions to be accompanied by net job creation, the value of a focus on jobs ought to be stressed.

A response to the crisis has been to seek greater flexibility in the labour market, but with different approaches. In Germany and the UK, for example, both hours and wages have been adjusted but on the whole employment headcounts have held up well. Some of the measures, such as the zero-hour contracts (ZHC) in the UK, lead to tensions where multiple goals are pursued.[19] There is especially high use of ZHCs in the hospitality industry, and a fairly high incidence in some public services. The evidence is unclear, however, on whether workers accept ZHCs under duress because of a lack of alternatives, although there are some signs that these contracts apply more to less-qualified workers (although their use in knowledge industries is far from negligible). Elsewhere, job losses have been dramatic, with Italy having seen a sharp recent rise in unemployment, especially pronounced among youth.[20] Among those subject to a bailout and the consequent adjustment programme overseen by the 'Troika' (made up of the IMF, the Commission and the ECB), the most acute labour market effects have been in Greece. It is nevertheless clear that behind the headline data, there have been revealing differences in how labour market institutions in member states have coped. Some of the precepts of the flexicurity model can, arguably, be brought to bear in this context, if suitably updated. Much reduced poverty rates and the concentration of wealth among pensioners pose policy questions around how income is distributed among age cohorts and bear on the sustainability of current pension systems. Starting points differ hugely across the EU, with some member states already having undertaken reforms that keep older people economically active, while in others the employment rates of older workers are markedly lower than for prime-age workers. This diversity is, again, partly a result of institutional differences, but also reflects past policy measures affecting the health, wellbeing and expectations of older people, not least their propensity to be economically active. An underlying question is what sort of work is appealing for older workers; physical work, including several categories of green jobs, may not be.

There is also a broader question of whether the governance system is attuned to offering the right sorts of working conditions or job opportunities. Extending the working-life need not mean either staying in the same job or continuing to work full-time. But unless incentives are reconfigured in the interplay between work and pensions, imaginative options may be hard to sell. Clearly, too, training provision will have to adapt, for example by targeting older workers seeking new types of job.

In developing such ideas for new policy initiatives, strategic choices will need to take account of long pay-off periods transcending customary electoral cycles, as well as sequencing difficulties, including the likelihood that costs are front-loaded while benefits take longer. Attention will also have to be paid to the balance within policy packages. Thus, while welcoming the Commission's Social Investment Package, the European Anti-Poverty Network has expressed its deep worries about viewing social investment as almost exclusively about economic efficiency, with the implication that less attention will be paid to combating poverty and exclusion.[21]

One of the undeniable strengths of the EU is that core elements of the European social model are part of the glue that binds member states together. Social Europe is an idea that, despite many setbacks, will neither go away nor cease to be a component of European integration championed by many stakeholders.[22] Similarly, although there is not much lingering disagreement about either the science of climate change or the need for the EU to act to curb greenhouse gas emissions, it is equally clear that there are widely differing views among policy-makers on what should be done, when and in what sequence. In both cases a crucial, if often unspoken, question is who should pick up the bill, allied to the question of whether action should be taken mainly by national and sub-national policy actors, or whether a more extensive EU role should be contemplated.

A crucial dimension of the political economy of EU policy-making is national preferences, and there are many instances of timid decisions being taken (or, not infrequently, being put off) because finding consensus is just too difficult. For much the same reason, initiatives that might make a significant difference are prone to being watered down. A policy implication is that more effort is required to reconcile such clashes of interests.

Key messages for policy-makers: Governance of transitions

At the EU level

- The common ground in the social models of EU countries continues to be crucial to what the EU stands for and does; while in need of some reinvention, its underlying virtues should be stressed.
- A concerted effort is needed to convince member states to support measures with longer-term pay-offs that also advance the common European interest, even if they are at odds with certain short-term national preferences.
    - Ambiguity about how burdens should be shared should be avoided.

At the national level

- The mix of policy has to be coherent, comprehensive and equitable.
    - An energy policy that seeks to decarbonise yet continues to subsidise fossil fuels is manifestly not coherent.
    - Similarly, an approach that motivates companies to invest in carbon-intensive production abroad rather than adopting alternative technologies does not, ultimately, reduce emissions.
- In an era of fiscal consolidation, policy measures that offer gains in jobs as well as fulfilling other objectives should be given priority.
- Country-specific institutional obstacles to transitions should be identified and dismantled.

iv) A last word...

Many of the specific themes discussed in this volume are already challenging for policy-makers in the EU, and are even harder to deal with when long-term transitions have to be undertaken. At a superficial level, the stark message from Mario Draghi about the demise of the European social model and Angela Merkel's so-called '7:25:50' critique of Europe's commitment to social protection[23] have some resonance, but they overlook the more fundamental point that social risks have to be borne somewhere in a modern capitalist economy. Instead, the question should be whether the means by which European states deal with these risks and the values that underpin them remain attractive. Many of the diverse findings from the NEUJOBS project make clear that socio-ecological transition is not only a long-term challenge, but also one that is being met by significant evolution and policy innovation in all member states.

As Anton Hemerijck, taking issue with some of the more negative assessments, asserts: "both the welfare state and the EU, two major feats of mid-twentieth century institutional engineering, have at critical times been able to reinvent themselves."[24] In the wake of a crisis as severe as that of recent years, an emphatic conclusion of this book is that they not only need to do so again, but will have to do so comprehensively and repeatedly in dealing with long-term socio-ecological challenges.

Bibliography

Begg, I. (2014), "Italy's socio-ecological transition", NEUJOBS National Policy Report No. 1, NEUJOBS Project (www.neujobs.eu).

_____ (2015), "France's socio-ecological transition", NEUJOBS National Policy Report No. 4, NEUJOBS Project (www.neujobs.eu).

Begg, I. and D. Polgar (2015), "Hungary's socio-ecological transition", NEUJOBS National Policy Report No. 5, NEUJOBS Project (www.neujobs.eu).

Begg, I. and F. Müshovel (2015), "Germany's socio-ecological transition", NEUJOBS National Policy Report No. 6, NEUJOBS Project (www.neujobs.eu).

Blinder, A., T.J. Jordan, D. Kohn and F. Mishkin (2013), "Exit Strategies", Geneva Report on the World Economy 15, CEPR, London.

Brinkley, I. (2013), "Flexibility or insecurity? Exploring the rise of zero-hours contracts", The Work Foundation, London.

Charlesworth, A. (2014), "Why is health-care inflation higher than general inflation?", *Journal of Health Services Research and Policy*, Vol. 19, No. 3, pp. 129-30.

Dol, K., J. Doling, M. Elsinga, N. Horsewood, F. Meijer and H. Visscher (2014), "Housing sectors: The demand and supply of labour", NEUJOBS Policy Brief No. 14, NEUJOBS Project (www.neujobs.eu).

EAPN (European Social Policy Network) (2013), "EAPN response to the Social Investment Package. Will it reduce poverty?", EAPN, Brussels.

European Council (2014), "European Council (23 and 24 October 2014) Conclusions", EUCO 169/14, Brussels, 24 October.

European Commission (2014), "Taking stock of the Europe 2020 strategy for smart sustainable and inclusive growth", COM(2014) 130, Brussels, 5 March.

Fischer-Kowalski, M., W. Haas, D. Wiedenhofer, U. Weisz, I. Pallua, N. Posssaner, A. Behrens, G. Serrio, M. Alessi and E. Weis (2012), "Socio-ecological transitions: definitions, dynamics and related global scenarios", NEUJOBS State of the Art Report No. 6, NEUJOBS Project (www.neujobs.eu).

France Stratégie (2014), "Quelle France dans dix ans: les chantiers de la decennie", Paris.

Hemerijck, A. (2012), *Changing Welfare States*, Oxford: Oxford University Press.

Hemerijck, A., V. Dräbing, B. Vis, M. Nelson and M. Soentken (2013), "European welfare states in motion", NEUJOBS Working Paper No. D5.2, NEUJOBS Project (www.neujobs.eu).

Heyndrickx, C., R. Frederix, J. Purwanto and B. van Zeebroeck (2013), "The socio-ecological transition facing the transport sector", NEUJOBS Policy Brief No. D15.4, NEUJOBS Project (www.neujobs.eu).

Hills, J. (2014), *Good Times, Bad Times: the Welfare Myth of Them and Us*, Bristol: Policy Press.

Huisman, C., J. de Beer, R. van der Erf, N. van der Gaag and D. Kupiszewska (2012), "Demographic scenarios 2010-2030", NEUJOBS Working Paper No. D10.1, NEUJOBS Project (www.neujobs.eu).

Lichter, A., S. Siegloch and E. Sommer (2015), "Modelling the evolution of labour supply and labour demand in Europe 2030", NEUJOBS Working Paper No. D10.12, NEUJOBS Project (www.neujobs.eu).

Meijer, F.H. and H. Visscher (2014), "Upgrading energy efficient housing and creating jobs: It works both ways", Delft Working Paper.

Mlecnik, E., T. Schuetze, S.J.T. Jansen, G. De Vries, H.J. Visscher and A. van Hal (2012), "End-user experiences in nearly zero-energy houses", *Energy and Buildings*, Vol. 49, pp. 471-478.

Nelson, M. (2013), "Low-wage service occupations in Europe: An inevitable under-class?", NEUJOBS Working Paper No. D3.7, NEUJOBS Project (www.neujobs.eu).

Tronquoy, P. (ed.) (2012), *La Santé, quell bilan?*, Paris: La Documentation Française.

Veselková, M. (2015), "Slovakia's socio-ecological transition", NEUJOBS National Policy Report No. 3, NEUJOBS Project (www.neujobs.eu).

Wren, A. (ed.) (2013), *The Political Economy of the Service Transition*, Oxford: Oxford University Press.

Zeitlin, J. and B. Vanhercke (2014), "Socializing the European semester: economic governance and social policy coordination in Europe 2020", SIEPS Report No. 2014/7, Swedish Institute for European Policy Studies, Stockholm.

Notes

[1] See the overview in Fischer-Kowalski et al. (2012).

[2] Wren (2013).

[3] Mlecnik et al. (2012).

[4] Dol et al. (2014).

[5] Meijer and Visscher (2014).

[6] Nelson (2013).

[7] Huisman et al. (2013)

[8] See Begg and Polgar (2015) for Hungary and Begg and Müshovel (2015) for Germany.

[9] Blinder et al. (2013).

[10] Begg (2015).

[11] France Stratégie (2014).

[12] Veselková (2015).

[13] Dol et al. (2014).

[14] Hemerijck (2012).

[15] Hemerijck et al. (2013).

[16] Lichter et al. (2015).

[17] Hills (2014).

[18] Tronquoy (2012); Charlesworth (2014).

[19] Brinkley (2013).

[20] Begg (2014).

[21] EAPN (2013).

[22] Zeitlin and Vanhercke (2014).

[23] On several occasions, the German Chancellor has pointed out that if Europe, with 7% of the world's population, 25% of its GDP and 50% of its social spending, is to prosper in competition with emerging countries, it cannot continue to be so generous.

[24] Hemerijck (2012, p. 398).

List of Abbreviations

AFSJ	Area of Freedom, Security and Justice
ALMPs	active labour market policies
CCS	carbon capture and storage
CEE	Central and Eastern Europe
CIM	construction, installation and manufacturing
CSP	concentrated solar power
DST	diversified supply technologies
EaP	Eastern Partnership
EEA	European Economic Area
EESC	European Economic and Social Committee
EO	employment office
ETS	EU Emissions Trading System
EU	European Union
FTE	full-time equivalent
GDP	gross domestic product
GHG	greenhouse gas
GVA	gross value added
HSW	health and social work
ICT	information and communications technology
ILO	International Labour Organization
ISCED	International Standard Classification of Education
ISCO	International Standard Classification of Occupations
LEZ	Low Emissions Zone
LFS	Eurostat Labour Force Survey
LLL	lifelong learning
LTC	long-term care

NEET	Not in Education, Employment, or Training
NGO	non-governmental organisation
NRIS	National Roma Integration Strategies (EU Framework)
O&M	operation and maintenance
PEP	public employment programme
PV	photovoltaics
PWP	public work programme
R&D	research and development
RES	renewable energy sources
RES-E	electricity from renewable energy sources
SET	socio-ecological transition
SHARE	Survey of Health, Ageing and Retirement in Europe
SILC	EU Statistics on Income and Living Conditions
TFP	total factor productivity
UCC	urban consolidation centre
UNDP	United Nations Development Programme
VAT	value-added tax

About the Editors

Miroslav Beblavý is the Coordinator of NEUJOBS and a Senior Research Fellow in the Jobs and Skills unit of the Centre for European Policy Studies (CEPS). He is also a Member of the Slovak Parliament. Between 2002 and 2006, he was the State Secretary of the Ministry of Labour, Social Affairs and Family in Slovakia. His areas of interest include employment and social policy, education policy, fiscal policy, governance and corruption.

Ilaria Maselli is a Research Fellow in the Jobs and Skills unit of CEPS. Her main area of expertise is the analysis of labour markets, in particular in their interaction with education and technological change. She is also a visiting researcher at the Gokhale Institute of Politics and Economics in Pune, India.

Marcela Veselková is a Senior Research Fellow at the Slovak Governance Institute. Within the NEUJOBS project, she conducted research in the area of educational and social policies, skills formation and job quality.

About the Contributors

Attila Bartha, Center for Policy Studies, Central European University and Center for Social Sciences, Hungarian Academy of Sciences, Budapest

Miroslav Beblavý, Senior Research Fellow, CEPS and Member of the Slovak Parliament

Iain Begg, London School of Economics and Political Science

Arno Behrens, Research Fellow and Head of the Energy unit, CEPS

Sergio Carrera, Senior Research Fellow and Head of the Justice and Home Affairs research unit, CEPS

Bert Colijn, Senior Economist at the Conference Board

Kees Dol, Technische Universiteit Delft

John Doling, University of Birmingham

Katharina Eisele, Researcher in the Justice and Home Affairs research unit, CEPS

Marja Elsinga, Technische Universiteit Delft

Olena Fedyuk, Center for Policy Studies, Central European University and Center for Social Sciences, Hungarian Academy of Sciences, Budapest and University of Strathclyde, Glasgow

Marina Fischer-Kowalski, Founder and long-term director of the Institute of Social Ecology, Alpen Adria University, Klagenfurt

Rodric Frederix, Transport & Mobility, Leuven

Johannes Geyer, German Institute for Economic Research (DIW), Berlin

Bent Greve, Department of Society and Globalisation, University of Roskilde, Denmark

Michaela Gstrein, Senior Researcher, Institute for Advanced Studies, Vienna

Elspeth Guild, Jean Monnet Professor ad personam of European Migration Law at the Radboud University Nijmegen, and Queen Mary, University of London; Associate Senior Research Fellow at CEPS and a partner at the London law firm Kingsley Napley

Willi Haas, Senior Researcher and Lecturer, Institute of Social Ecology, Alpen Adria University, Klagenfurt

Christophe Heyndrickx, Transport & Mobility, Leuven

Nicholas Horsewood, University of Birmingham

Silvia Hudáčková, Slovak Governance Institute

Agnieszka Kamińska, Institute for Structural Research, Warsaw

Iga Magda, Vice President of the Board, Institute for Structural Research, Warsaw

Frits Meijer, Technische Universiteit Delft

Vera Messing, Research Fellow, Center for Policy Studies, Central European University, Budapest

Joko Purwanto, Transport & Mobility, Leuven

Marek Radvanský, Institute of Economic Research, Slovak Academy of Sciences

Anna Ruzik-Sierdziñska, CASE - Center for Social and Economic Research and Warsaw School of Economics

Tomáš Sirovátka, Institute of Public Policy and Social Work, Masaryk University, Czech Republic

Erika Schulz, German Institute for Economic Research (DIW), Berlin

Henk Visscher, Technische Universiteit Delft

Dominik Wiedenhofer, Researcher, Institute of Social Ecology, Alpen Adria University, Klagenfurt

Violetta Zentai, Center for Policy Studies, Central European University, Budapest

NEUJOBS PARTNER INSTITUTES

Project Leader: Centre for European Policy Studies (CEPS)
www.ceps.eu

University of Birmingham - College of Social Sciences (BAHM)
www.bham.ac.uk

Center for Social and Economic Research (CASE)
www.case-research.eu

Central European University (CEU CPS)
www.ceu.hu

Delft University of Technology (DU)
www.lr.tudelft.nl

German Institute for Economic Research (DIW)
www.diw.de

Société Européenne d'Economie (SEURECO)
www.erasme-team.eu

Economic and Social Research Institute (ESRI)
www.esri.ie

European Trade Union Institute (ETUI)
www.etui.org

Europrism Research Centre
www.europrism.eu

Institute for Structural Research (IBS)
www.ibs.org.pl

University of Klagenfurt (UNI-KLU)
www.uni-klu.ac.at

Institute for Advanced Studies (IHS)
https://www.ihs.ac.at/

Institute for Human Sciences (IWM)
www.iwm.at

Slovak Governance Institute (SGI)
www.governance.sk

The Conference Board Europe (TCBE)
www.conferenceboard.org

LUISS University (LUISS)
www.luiss.edu

University of Amsterdam - Faculty of Social Sciences (VU)
www.fsw.vu.nl

Netherlands Interdisciplinary Demographic Institute (NIDI)
www.nidi.knaw.nl

Roskilde University (RU)
www.ruc.dk

Leiden University - Department of Economics, Leiden Law School
www.leidenuniv.nl

University of the West of Scotland (UWS)
www.uws.ac.uk

Masaryk University (MU)
www.muni.cz

Institute for the Study of Labour (IZA)
www.iza.org

Institute of Economy Research (SAVBA)
www.ekonom.sav.sk

Transport & Mobility Leuven
www.tmleuven.be

London School of Economics and Political Science (LSE)
www.lse.ac.uk

Observatoire Social Européen (OSE)
www.ose.be

Mannheim University
www.uni-mannheim

Index